THE LEGEND OF JESSIE DARCEY

by TONY RENZONI

Cover images © Anthony Renzoni

www.innovativeinkpublishing.com
Send all inquiries to:
4050 Westmark Drive
Dubuque, IA 52004-1840

Published in the United States of America

CONTENTS

STUDY BUDDIES

Even at a young age, Jessie knew the importance of doing well in school which, in turn, would pay dividends as she got older.

My name is Abby Girardi. I was born and raised in Bridgeport, Connecticut.

When I look back, I am truly amazed at how a nine-year-old would become not only my best friend for life but also a true role model who was a source of so much inspiration for me. The nine-year-old that I am referring to was a gregarious young girl by the name of Jessie Darcey.

When Jessie Darcey and I were in fourth grade at Bridgeport's Webster Elementary School, our teacher—Mrs. O'Brien—assigned to our class a project dealing with the history of Connecticut. Mrs. O'Brien teamed me up with Jessie who I had not known up to that point. I asked Jessie if it would be possible for us to begin working on our assignment at her house which was located one street over from where I lived. Jessie checked with her dad—Mike Darcey—who said it was perfectly fine for me to visit Jessie, for any reason and whenever I would like. This made me happy and relieved.

My older sister Brianna—who I usually refer to as "Bri"— insisted on driving me to Jessie's house each day, against my wishes to simply walk over to her house. You see, the area of town that we lived in at that time was very tough. Gang shootings were rampant, leading to the highest homicide rates in the state and one of the highest in the U.S. Sadly, even the five-minute walk alone to Jessie's house was considered risky, especially for a nine-year-old.

On the very first day that we got together, Jessie and I immediately hit it off and I just knew that we would become good friends. The first thing I noticed was that we were both very outgoing kids with, as my mom would say, "the gift of gab." We both had the same interest in various boys at our school, which sometimes proved to be a major distraction from discussing and researching our assignment. In all honesty, it was more me than Jessie who tried everything possible to stay off track from discussing our school project. Up to that point, I was a rather poor student and, even at that young age, showed no interest in school. I certainly did not receive any support from my mother or older sister. It was Jessie who convinced me not only of the importance of getting an A on this school project but more importantly, to get good grades throughout our school experience. Jessie even promised to be my "study buddy" for tests and assignments throughout our elementary and high school years—provided that I take school seriously and understand the importance of doing well in all my courses. This was so foreign to me but I came around to Jessie's thinking and became determined, like Jessie, to achieve high grades in school. Even at a young age, Jessie knew the importance of doing well in school which, in turn, would pay dividends as she got older. She learned this from her father who convinced her of the value of obtaining a good education.

We both had an interest in sports. Jessie had a strong desire to participate in sports whereas I was content with watching games either in person or on television.

Our tastes in foods were also quite similar. Jessie especially loved pizza, burgers, and ice cream. As for me, any kind of Italian food, cheeseburgers, and ice cream were my favorites. In fact, on weekends, before going over to Jessie's house I would sometimes have my sister Bri drive me first to our local ice cream shop to pick up a pint of one of Jessie's—and my—favorite ice cream flavor such as Rocky Road. Once I got to Jessie's house she would get two spoons. Sitting on the floor in her room, we would dig into the ice cream pint right out of the container, relishing each spoonful. Jessie insisted that this gave us the needed energy to finish our school project. I agreed.

On the days that Mr. Darcey noticed that our studying was lasting longer than expected he would suggest that I stay and have dinner at his house with him, Mrs. Darcey, and Jessie. I seldom would pass up on his offer since Mr. Darcey was a terrific cook. Knowing that Italian foods were my favorite, he would offer to cook an Italian meal, such as spaghetti and meatballs. Such a thoughtful man! There were also times that Jessie and I asked if we could order a pizza from one of the pizza chains to be delivered to the Darcey house. Being two nine-year-old kids, we got such a kick out of pizza being delivered to the door. We were also very curious to see if the delivery boy may have been the brother of one of our classmates. The pizza quality was a bit inferior to the pizza served at a pizza restaurant or, for that matter, the pizza that Mr. Darcey sometimes made for us. But ordering out was something that was fun and made us feel a bit like adults since we were allowed to call the place and to pay the delivery boy at the door.

The one thing we did not have in common was our family environment. I grew up in a very dysfunctional household. My father—John—left when I was only three years old, so I have no recollection of him other than a few photos of an attractive couple kept by my mother—Doris. At times, Brianna would share brief memories of our dad —which were mostly bad memories. I found out from my sister that my father, at times, would become verbally abusive to my mother, especially after a night of heavy drinking. My sister didn't elaborate but would only say that it was best that my father left us, and it was good that I was too young to witness his behavior.

Brianna did tell me that our mom would apologize over and over to her for her husband's outbursts. Without making excuses, my mom tried to explain to Brianna that those angry outbursts were mainly the result of a near-fatal accident that my father was involved in that severely impacted his mental capacity. She told Brianna that she would beg her husband to get help for his drinking and his angry outbursts, only to be told, in no uncertain terms, to mind her own business. Before the accident, as she tried to explain to Brianna, my dad was a good husband and father who did his best to provide for his family. During one tearful discussion, my mom admitted to Brianna that she had no control over her husband when he had these angry outbursts and felt ashamed and helpless. She also confided in Brianna that she was concerned about our safety. She considered calling the police but was afraid that this might escalate things. As painful as it was to see her marriage fall apart, mom admitted to Brianna that she was relieved when he walked out the door. The one encouraging thing was that her husband faithfully mailed her money to be used for household expenses. He had a good, well-paying job in the landscaping business, so he was able to afford mailing her the money, which was very much needed. In my mother's mind, it showed some compassion on her husband's part.

My mom worked two jobs to support the family. But it came at a price for her, and for us. Mom was totally devastated when her husband abandoned her and her two children. She was also becoming extremely tired working so hard at her two low paying, stressful jobs, while at the same time, taking care of her two young children. The result was that my mother turned to alcohol as a way to try to escape her problems. She eventually became an alcoholic. During her moments of sobriety, which were becoming less and less, my mom was a loving, caring mother for both my sister and myself. I do have fond memories of those special moments and lament the fact that she was not able or not willing to get the help that she needed for her alcoholism. Brianna, who is a number of years older than me, tried her best to take care of me and also keep my mother in line. Brianna made sure that my mother was in good enough shape to go to work. In return, she made my mom promise that she would not drink when she was working and also to get help for her condition. We were confident that our mom kept to her side of the bargain by staying sober while working at her two jobs. As hard as it was, she continued to work her two jobs knowing her income was needed to pay the bills. However, we were not as confident that she had the willpower to follow through on receiving proper help for her alcoholism. Brianna did take her to sign up for Alcoholics Anonymous but many times she would make excuses on why she was not able to attend scheduled AA meetings. We both felt that she had every intention to faithfully go to these meetings but lacked the self-discipline to follow through.

During one of my mother's more lucid moments, she shared with Brianna and me a journal that my grandfather kept. By all accounts, he was a strong-willed but loving person. It often made me wonder how different things might have been had my father sought the treatment that my mom begged him to get. But, in reality, that is all water under the bridge. My sister and me both thought it best to keep all of this a secret, not to be shared with anyone.

Unlike her husband, my mom never raised her voice and never tried to upset the household. When she wasn't working, she would withdraw into her room or sit alone in the den for hours. Her periods of depression made it more and more difficult for her to tend to domestic chores or properly care for Brianna and myself. My sister gradually found a need to become the head of the household. Brianna accepted this role, but it was tough on her because at that time she was still in high school and had her schoolwork to concentrate on. In addition, she also found work as a part-time waitress at a restaurant near our house. With the little free time that she had, my sister Bri still wanted to have some semblance of a social life, even if it meant her studies would slip a bit. It helped when she became old enough to get her driver's license which gave her a sense of freedom. I did my best to help out at home, as much as a nine-year-old can be expected to do. Because of all of this, my sister and I vowed to never invite friends over to our house, not knowing the state my mother would be in and knowing that she was in no mood to clean up the house when she was in such a state.

I was embarrassed to discuss our family situation and I didn't want anything to ruin the friendship that Jessie and I had cultivated. This was the reason why I asked to meet at Jessie's house instead of ours.

Jessie, on the other hand, grew up in a loving and nurturing environment. She knew that she could always depend on both her mother and father for their unconditional love and support, no matter the situation. This applied to receiving valuable advice that kids her age needed in order to deal with their everyday "dilemmas", whether they were school related or dealt with everyday life issues. It also applied to receiving support for the sport she had become so passionate about—basketball.

Jessie was so proud of her parents and the loving and supportive way that they raised her. She was especially proud of her father. When she talked about her dad, Jessie's face would light up. Even at age nine, Jessie couldn't say enough good things about her father and once I found out more about Mr. Darcey, I understood why. I got to know about Mr. Darcey's heritage, his accomplishments, and also the struggles he had to overcome. Mr. Darcey used these experiences to instill in Jessie many important basketball skills and, more importantly, many valuable life lessons.

ANTI-SEMITISM

*When Mike was told that it was Tom who drew the swastikas, he nodded his head in agreement,
but said that he had a better way to deal with the situation.*

One of the first things I learned was that Jessie's first name was an homage to Olympic hero Jesse Owens who was a favorite sports star of her dad.

The Darcey's, like my family, lived in Bridgeport's low income housing district which, as I mentioned, had a very high crime rate. But that, in no way, stood in the way of Mike Darcey's goals both in sports and in life.

Mike's dad—Nathan—was a Jewish immigrant. His surname was actually Darshevsky which he anglicized to Darcey after arriving in the U.S. He moved from New York to Bridgeport and set up a successful shoe shop in Bridgeport, having a background in shoe making prior to coming to the United States. Nathan assimilated well into the American culture. Mike remembered that as a young man he would marvel at his dad's work ethic and how he would spend hours each day learning the English language, especially American slang so he could converse better with many of the young people who frequented his shop. Mike's mom (Margaret) worked as a housekeeper in her native Ireland before emigrating to America. Margaret sponsored a young lady by the name of Kathleen Murphy who was the child of a close friend of Margaret's.

Nathan and Margaret met at a festival in Bridgeport. While he had absolutely no sports ability, Nathan managed to win a prize by making three hoops in a row at one of the fair booths. The person who ran the booth was a bit stunned because he knew that the owners purposely made the basketball hoops small so it was difficult to make a shot into the basket. Mike would later joke that he felt that was an omen for him to join the basketball team at school. Nathan immediately gave the large stuffed bear that he won to the shy Margaret. From then on they were inseparable, began dating, and married soon after.

Jessie's dad was a well-known high school basketball player for Bridgeport's Harding High School. Mike was a good shooter but he was more known for his ball handling abilities and for being a true teammate. Classmates and teammates who got to know Mike personally had nothing but kind words to say about him.

Jessie did tell me one unfortunate incident that occurred while her dad was a member of his high school team. It was an incident that Mike conveyed to Jessie which he hoped would teach his daughter a lesson about compassion and forgiveness. Mike told Jessie this story to have her understand that while most people are inherently good, there is a relatively small number of people that harbor evil. Their behavior was destructive in that their goal was to inflict painful words and actions towards others. Unfortunately, Mike became aware of this when he got his first taste of anti-Semitism during his high school senior year.

Recognizing Mike's leadership qualities, the Harding coach named him team captain during his senior year. Coach Nelson's decision was endorsed by all the team players except one—Tom Smith.

Tom had held a grudge against the coach ever since his freshman year. At that time, Tom had a personal run in with the coach. Coach Nelson had taken him aside during one of their practice sessions and told Tom that he needed to hustle more during the game. The coach told him that because of his lack of hustle other players found it easy to dribble by him and easier to position themselves in front of him for rebounds. The coach had meant this as constructive criticism but Tom took it personally. He told Coach Nelson to his face that the coach didn't know what he was talking about and that he was not a good coach. He reminded the coach that he was a star on his basketball team in elementary school. Coach Nelson agreed but noted that he is now in high school and he needed to step up his game to compete at this higher level.

Instead of heeding the coach's advice, Tom held a grudge against the coach throughout his high school years. While sitting on the bench, Tom would constantly complain. He was very vocal in his criticism of the coach and tried in vain to get other players to agree with him. His fellow players got tired of his constant complaining to the point where Tom found himself sitting at the farthest end of the bench, away from his teammates.

He never forgave Coach Nelson for not making him one of the starting five players on the team, feeling that he was as good as anyone else on the squad.

Despite Tom's insistence that he was worthy of a starting position on the team, every other player thought Tom was a below average player and they all agreed with the coach in his decision to not make Tom a starting player. They also felt that Tom lacked the leadership qualities that Mike was blessed with and supported their coach's decision to make Mike the captain of their team. The lack of support for Tom incensed him even further and it became very obvious to his fellow teammates that he was jealous of Mike, especially in Mike's capacity as team captain.

On the other hand, the coach was extremely happy with Mike's performance as team captain and even allowed Mike to be in charge of some of their team scrimmages.

Prior to one of Harding's crucial games against their nemesis Bridgeport High School, Mike noticed some sort of scribbling on his gym bag. When he looked closer, Mike saw that there were swastikas drawn on both sides of his bag. One of Mike's teammates told him privately that he knew who the culprit was. The player told Mike that he saw Tom Smith draw the swastikas on the gym bag while Mike was not in the locker room. He asked Mike if he was going to confront Tom, promising Mike that he would stand by him as a witness to this horrible incident. When Mike was told that it was Tom who drew the swastikas, he nodded his head in agreement, but said that he had a better way to deal with the situation.

With the score tied in the fourth quarter of their game against Bridgeport High, Mike took himself out of the game and, with the coach's consent, signaled to a stunned Tom Smith to take his place on the court. After several minutes, the coach begged Mike to reconsider and reenter the game, but Mike convinced the coach that this was the right move. As expected, Tom did nothing to help the team. In fact, Tom made some critical errors which nearly cost Harding to lose the game. Harding did manage to win, squeezing by with a 68—67 win.

After the game, Tom took Mike aside and asked him why he took himself out of the game and had Tom replace him.

"Tom, I know you were the one who drew the swastikas on my gym bag. Those drawings were very hurtful to me which, apparently, was your intention. But putting you in the game to replace me was my way of showing you the goodness and forgiveness in people."

Tom lowered his head and said in a murmur, "Jeez, what have I done?"

Mike continued, "Tom, I want you to realize that we have more in common than you think. As classmates, teammates, and as fellow human beings, there is no rationale for horrendous acts like that. We should be able to get along despite our nationalities and beliefs. I hope you realize how stupid and hurtful actions like that can be, not only to myself, but to other people of Jewish and other faiths.

"My message to you is to stop this nonsense now before it is too late. I believe you have it in you to do just that. But it's all up to you. I have no plans to share this horrible incident with anyone else, including the coach, assuming that it stops right here. I—"

Tom interrupted saying, "But Mike the game was tied at a crucial moment. In all honesty, I know you are a better player than me." Scratching the side of his forehead, Tom continued, "What I don't understand is why you decided to put me in the game at that moment. We could have lost that game!"

"Tom, for me the game was secondary. I decided to have you replace me so you can see that I was willing to forgive you and forget this unfortunate incident. I also want you to understand that there are more important things in life besides basketball and that there are many good people out there. But it's up to you to make an attempt to understand other people and see the goodness in their hearts. We don't need this kind of hurtful nonsense which only serves to drive us away from each other." Well, I hope you at least consider everything I said." With that, Mike turned away and walked to his locker.

A few days later, Tom Smith took Mike aside in front of the locker room.

"Mike, I want to apologize for what I did. I admit that I was the one who drew those items on your gym bag. I take full responsibility for my actions. Yes, I wanted them to be hurtful to you but I truly regret what I did. You have shown you are a much bigger man than me. If you have it in your heart to forgive me, I give you my word that I will never do anything like this to you or anyone else.

"Thinking about it, I realize my actions were deplorable, but it took someone like you to make me understand. This will not happen again, ever."

With that the two men shook hands and formed a lasting friendship.

JESSIE'S INTRODUCTION TO THE GAME OF BASKETBALL

"I would always have a basketball in my hand ever since I was in fourth grade."

At a family gathering in the spring of 1951, Mike's mom brought along Kathleen Murphy, her friend's daughter from Ireland. Mike and Kathleen were immediately attracted to each other. Mike was instantly captivated by Kathleen, a very attractive young lady with auburn hair and beautiful blue eyes.

They talked for a long time and the conversation gradually turned to sports. Mike asked Kathleen if she was familiar with the game of basketball. Kathleen found that a bit amusing and said that she grew up during a male-dominated time, when girls were banned from many sports activities. However, she was a very fast and agile runner.

Kathleen explained that one of her fun activities growing up was to race her friends up the steep hills in Ireland. They learned to expertly run in between the flock of sheep that inevitably would be herded down the streets where they were running. She proudly told Mike that she learned to run so fast that she would beat the boys all the time in races in the schoolyard. Thinking that Mike would find all of this silly, Kathleen was surprised when he told her he was very impressed and wanted to hear more about her upbringing in Ireland.

Several days after the gathering, Mike worked up the courage to call Kathleen and ask her for a date. Following their first date, they became inseparable. Mike eventually asked Kathleen to marry him and she accepted. The two were madly in love and had a very close, loving relationship.

Despite her lack of knowledge about sports, Kathleen was excited when Jessie, at age nine, told her that she was very interested in learning how to play basketball. Kathleen encouraged Mike to help Jessie out by teaching her the sport she herself was not allowed to play. It was Kathleen's hope that Jessie would have opportunities that she never had. As Kathleen saw things, females had made gains in certain areas but still were not always treated equally. Maybe, thought Kathleen, sports was one way for Jessie to be treated the same as boys her age when it came to sports.

Around the time that Jess and I began to have our study sessions together at her house, Mr. Darcey purchased a new basketball for Jessie. Judging by Jessie's reaction, you would think her father gave her a million dollars!

And so, Mike began to introduce Jessie to the game of basketball. As Jessie later put it, "I would always have a basketball in my hand ever since I was in fourth grade."

At first, he and Jessie would just throw the basketball around as a game, knowing Jessie was only nine years old.

As soon as Mr. Darcey felt that Jessie was comfortable throwing and catching the basketball, he installed a basketball hoop for Jessie in his large driveway. I could see the excitement on Jessie's face once she saw her very own basketball hoop. She immediately grabbed her basketball and began to shoot and dribble around the driveway. Jessie was instantly hooked and begged her father to show her some basketball techniques.

Mr. Darcey agreed to give Jessie lessons, but on one condition. He would teach her how to play basketball but Jessie had to promise him that her studies always would come first and that she would maintain high grades in school. Knowing that I would be around Jessie when she practiced, Mr. Darcey turned to me with a smile.

"And that goes for you too Abby!"

Between our study sessions and watching Jessie practice basketball in her driveway, the Darcey house became my second home. Jessie asked me to join her in her practice sessions with Mr. Darcey but I told Jess I was happy just being on the sideline watching. Actually, Mr. Darcey did find a way to get me involved in Jessie's practices. I was assigned the job of standing in front of Jessie and act like a basketball guard while she was shooting. I really didn't know what I was doing but Mr. Darcey assured me that I was accomplishing their goal.

At that time, our elementary school did not have an organized basketball team for girls. But it was Mr. Darcey's dream that Jessie's love of the game and commitment to the sport would make her competitive with all the other kids once she entered high school.

THE "BUCKET GIRL"

Jessie would always joke that if she became a basketball star I would be the one to get all the credit, referring to me as the "bucket girl"

When Jessie turned eleven years old, Mr. Darcey decided it was time to intensify Jessie's training sessions by teaching Jessie more advanced drills. He was pleased to see that Jessie was maintaining very good grades in school and at the same time had the determination and passion to strive to become a very good basketball player.

What caught Mr. Darcey's eye initially was that Jessie was very fast, quick and agile on the court, even at a young age. He firmly believed she inherited her speed and agility from her mother. With this in mind, he wanted to put Jessie's speed and agility to good use.

Mr. Darcey began to teach Jessie the art of ball handling in basketball. He introduced Jessie to the basketball term "playmaking." As Mr. Darcey put it, "Simply put, playmaking in basketball involves the techniques of good ball handling and passing."

The first thing that Mike did was set up a schedule at home which Jessie gladly adhered to. Mr. Darcey had me set up buckets at strategic places on the ground. Jessie was amused to see that I was the one in charge of moving the buckets around for her. Jess would always joke that if she became a basketball star I would be the one to get all the credit, referring to me as the "bucket girl."

Mr. Darcey also gave me a stop watch. I must have given him a quizzical look because he then explained that my job at some point would be to time some of Jessie's dribbling movements. The idea was to eventually increase the amount of time Jessie would be able to dribble a basketball effectively. For example, knowing that Jessie was right handed, Mike would have Jessie dribble around the buckets I placed on the ground for at least forty-five minutes straight—but using *only* her left hand. At first, Jess found this very difficult. Mr. Darcey assured her that by practicing this exercise each day she will eventually feel just as comfortable dribbling with her left hand as she did with her right hand. But this required patience on her part since it would take her a good deal of time to get it right.

After several months, Mr. Darcey saw that Jess had reached a certain comfort level using her left hand to dribble the basketball. He then asked me to time her dribbling with the stop watch and report the results to him, with Jess always looking over my shoulder. Indeed, there was a marked improvement in the speed and accuracy of her dribbling using both her left and right hands.

Mike taught Jessie other valuable basketball techniques to become a good playmaker. These included: improving her footwork, dribbling the ball close to the ground, having good court vision, dribbling the ball behind her back, passing the ball to someone without looking, and to always be aware of her surroundings and know where her teammates were at all times. He stressed that all of these techniques were not meant for Jessie to be a show off on the basketball court but, if done properly, were meant to deceive the defender, make it difficult to steal the ball, and help her fellow teammates score more points. As an example of how good playmaking can really help the player and the team, Mr. Darcey told us about a professional basketball player that we never heard of by the name of Bobby Steed. He explained that Mr. Steed was one of the best "playmakers" in the history of the National Basketball league. He wanted Jessie to eventually learn the technique of being a great playmaker along with being a good shooter. He went on to say that there may be times when the coach would ask certain players to protect the team's lead by not allowing the opposing team to get the ball. He wanted Jess to be one of those players.

Mike also had Jessie shoot foul shots—one after another—with the goal of making at least 90% of her foul shots. This, too, would take time for her to master. Mr. Darcey explained the importance of good foul shooting.

"Jessie, many basketball games are won or lost by one or two points. The difference between winning and losing a game sometimes rests on the ability of a team's accuracy at the foul line."

Mr. Darcey fully acknowledged that Jessie was still very young and that it would take a good deal of time for her to master all these techniques. But, in his mind, introducing Jessie to these concepts while she was young would pay dividends for her later on, assuming she still wanted to continue playing basketball. I would soon find that Mr. Darcey had nothing to worry about in terms of Jessie's desire to pursue the game of basketball and to give the sport her best efforts.

When we were not involved in school activities, Jessie would run to her driveway and begin practicing her shots and her dribbling. Many times she would do this on her own, on days that neither I nor Mr. Darcey were available.

Mike noticed that Jessie had a gift for shooting baskets at all different areas and was also very comfortable dribbling and passing the basketball. Under Mr. Darcey's watchful eye, Jess learned how to shoot jump shots left-handed. Jessie's father explained the reason why he included shooting left-handed jump shots in their training schedule.

"Jess, this may be a difficult shot for you to learn and I'm not suggesting that you use it all the time. However, if done properly, it can be yet another deceptive move on your part which can work in your favor.

"Knowing you are right handed, a defender's natural reaction would be to try to block your shot on your right side. If you fool the defender by shooting with your left hand, her momentum may cause her to bump into your right shoulder, creating a foul. This would mean you would have the opportunity to score several points at the free throw line.

"When I was in high school I tried this a few times and it worked to my advantage. Even if I didn't make the shot I would have a chance to shoot some foul shots. Of course, I was not comfortable shooting with my left hand so I only tried it a couple of times. But if you can somehow manage to learn how to shoot left-handed it would be yet another option for you in your assortment of shots and trick moves.

"As I mentioned, this may not be something you would be comfortable with or can master, but maybe it's worth a try."

At first, Jess struggled with using her left hand to shoot. She found it uncomfortable and unnatural since she was right handed. However, she gradually found her comfort level and began to master this shot. Her father was a bit amazed at how quickly Jess adapted as he was not sure if she would ever learn to effectively shoot this way.

Mr. Darcey began to see a vast improvement in every facet of Jessie's play, especially in such a very short period of time. With a great deal of self-determination, she adapted very easily to all the basketball fundamentals he emphasized.

It became obvious to Mr. Darcey that Jessie, despite her young age, loved the game of basketball. He would come home from a hard day of work at the local factory and was amazed to find his daughter practicing her shooting and dribbling.

Kathleen loved watching her husband and daughter practice together. This gave Kathleen a sense of pride as she watched her daughter and husband playing a sport they both truly loved.

Jessie's commitment to basketball was unlike anything I had ever witnessed. In a very short time, she was able to master the most difficult drills that Mr. Darcey taught her.

Jessie, indeed, was becoming an all-around basketball player.

Jessie's father also tried very hard to give Jessie some life lessons. One of these lessons was to study hard and to be sure to always stay in the top level of her class. This was especially important once she entered high school. In this way, Mike thought Jessie would not be exposed to some of the kids who were trouble makers and did not take school seriously. Striving to become an excellent student and staying at the top level of the schools she attended was ingrained in Jessie by her dad. It was a lesson that Jessie promised her father that she would always follow through on.

5

JOHNNY D

The Johnny D Band is absolutely horrible!

During our seventh grade at Webster Middle School, our interest in boys intensified.

Jessie liked a boy by the name of Johnny DeMarco. Johnny was a thin, good looking boy with wavy brown hair and a captivating smile. Johnny met Jessie at a school party and he asked Jessie for a "date." I should note that a date in those days usually consisted of a group of kids hanging out together at a party, a movie, or another local function. For this particular date, Johnny asked Jessie to come to a party at his house and for Jessie to hear a band that he recently formed. Naturally, Jessie convinced me to go with her to see Johnny and his band.

Johnny had a false sense of self-confidence which everyone was able to see through, including Jess. What attracted Jess to Johnny was the kindness and generosity that he showed to others but he never owned up to it. I guess it was because it would not fit into the macho image that he tried to project, especially around girls. Several boys our age secretly told us of his generosity but they asked us to keep it quiet. Strangely, Johnny would be embarrassed if we said anything about his kindness, thinking that we would think he was less of a man. But Jess and the rest of us knew he was a good boy and we didn't fall for the bravado image he tried to impress us with. Despite Johnny's shortcomings, he and Jess made a very attractive couple.

Although we were two very outgoing kids, when it came to boys both Jess and I were very shy. Knowing the trepidation she was feeling, I agreed to go with Jessie. My sister Brianna drove us both to the party. Once there, Jessie and I found our way to the snack and soda table.

During our discussion, Jess felt a tap on her shoulder. When she turned around she noticed it was Johnny. After a few awkward moments, Johnny told us that he and his band were about to perform at the party.

Johnny proudly informed us that the name of his band was the "Johnny D Band."

"I thought you should know that I'm the lead singer of the Johnny D band. We've been practicing a lot so I think we're ready to play at different places. I think you will really like our band."

Jess looked at me, playfully lifting her eyebrows, and we did all we could not to laugh when he said this.

Johnny then excused himself as he went to help the group set up their instruments.

During one of their songs, Johnny D tripped over one of the cords on the stage and crashed into Emmett, the band's drummer. The collision caused Emmett's drumsticks to fly across the stage. Both kids were okay and at least it was a distraction from the awful music they were playing. After the they finished their numbers, Jess turned to me to get my opinion of the Johnny D band.

"What do you think?"

"Well…they have a lot of potential."

"Abby, you're such a liar! I can always tell when you lie because your face gets all crazy red. Let's face it, you know as well as I do that the Johnny D Band is absolutely horrible!"

"So, what will you tell Johnny D when he asks how you like his band?"

"Oh, I would just tell him his band has 'a lot of potential'."

With that, we both broke down in laughter.

I met a classmate of ours—Carl—at the party who I liked and we danced a few times after Johnny's band mercifully stopped and normal music began to play. Carl was a shy teenage boy with a crew cut hairdo and a V-neck sweater. He was a perfect gentleman and escorted me back to the snack table where Jess was standing. Before the night was over, Carl asked me out for a date and I accepted. I mentioned this to Jess and we both arranged to make it a double date since Johnny also asked Jess for a date. We decided to go with the boys to a nearby movie theater. The boys were perfect gentlemen. Jess and I felt it was a thoughtful gesture when they both came back to our seats with bags of popcorn and two Milky Way candy bars for both of us without our asking.

Johnny D was in a number of my classes. I began to notice that he was absent for many of his classes. I wasn't sure what the reason was but as the trend continued I figured I better at least inform Jess.

"Jess, I just want to make you aware that Johnny has been missing many of his classes on a regular basis. I'm told he leaves with Emmett right after study period. I'm not sure what that is all about. Maybe there is a good reason, but I wanted you to be aware of this. I wasn't going to say anything to you but I noticed that this trend was continuing. Do you know anything about this?"

"No Abby, I wasn't aware this was happening. Thank you for telling me this. You can be sure that I will be having a nice talk with Johnny. I really like Johnny but this is not something I will tolerate."

The next day, Jess pulled Johnny aside in the hallway before study period.

"Johnny, I'm told that your buddy Emmett has been encouraging you to miss a number of classes. Is that true?"

With a sheepish look on his face Johnny said in a low voice, "Yeh, we've been going to the park to hang around and shoot some hoops. And, Emmett loves to play pinball so sometimes we would hang out at the store and play a few games. I figured it would be okay to have a little fun for a while and when my tests come up I would study really hard."

"Well here's the thing Johnny. I like you a lot but I want to make something very clear. You will stop this nonsense now! You will not miss any of your classes beginning today and you will concentrate on getting good grades. Otherwise you are going down the path of flunking out of school. And, you are not to hang around with Emmett anymore because he is not a good influence on you. I'm telling you this because I care about you and I'm concerned about where this may be heading.

"Getting good grades these next two years is very important if you want to do well in high school. I want you to make this your priority. You have the ability to get good grades but you must take your education seriously. If you continue to miss classes and continue to goof around, that's your choice. But, if you continue this nonsense, I refuse to be your girlfriend or even your friend. Do I make myself clear?"

"Yes, very clear. I guess I didn't realize that cutting classes at times could result in my flunking out, which is the last thing I want. And, I certainly don't want to lose you as a friend!"

Jessie's "tough love" approach with Johnny worked. I noticed that Johnny attended all his classes. He mentioned to Jess that he decided to take her advice and make school his priority. He began studying hard and even told her he received an "A" on his test the day before. Also, he told Jess that he has been avoiding Emmett and now sees what she was saying about Emmett being a bad influence on him.

Jess told me she was happy to hear this and that she was very proud of Johnny.

***

After taking a few years off from school to care for our mother and to concentrate on her full-time job at the restaurant, Brianna did manage to earn her high school degree, graduating with a minimal grade point average. She never bought into the importance of a high school diploma but did so to please our mother. She had no desire to go to her high school graduation, especially since she was older than the other kids, but decided to go when she realized how much it meant to our mom—and me. Jess and I joined my mom in the audience for her graduation exercise.

Brianna's graduation was held outdoors under cloudy skies. We were assured by school officials that rain was not in the forecast. When it began to pour heavily, Brianna turned to me with an "I told you so" look. The graduation wasn't a complete bust since there were tables set up inside the gym with all sorts of goodies, which Jess and I devoured.

***

I made the cheerleading team in seventh grade for our boys' basketball team and Jessie was my biggest supporter, encouraging me all the way. She would make a point of complimenting my cheerleading after each basketball game. This made me feel good since, in my own little way, I was beginning to do well in my own personal "sport." I knew that I would never reach the skill level that Jess had attained, but nonetheless, I was satisfied in what I was accomplishing as a cheerleader. Knowing that her compliments were sincere really boosted my confidence. Jessie once again was the source of inspiration for me to be the best cheerleader on the squad.

6

JESSIE'S RIVAL

Their laughter turned to awe as they witnessed shooting and dribbling that they had never seen before.

When I close my eyes, I can clearly picture the twelve-year-old Jessie.

She stood at five feet, eight inches which was considered tall in those days. She attributed her height to her father and mother who were both tall.

Jessie was a very attractive girl, thin, with long light brown hair and the brightest blue eyes. It was no wonder why so many boys in school were attracted to her. When she played basketball she would put her hair into a ponytail.

One of the things I remember about Jess was the self-assured way she walked. She had very good posture with her head held high, shoulders back, and walked with a steady, purposeful stride.

When the two of us walked towards the outdoor basketball court, Jess would tuck her basketball into her right arm. As we got closer to the court, she would begin dribbling the ball, switching from right hand to left, and sometimes between her legs. Jess would do this almost subconsciously since, at the same time, she would be talking a mile a minute to me. It was obvious to me that walking to any basketball court—inside or out—was walking to her "happy place."

***

Mr. Darcey drove Jess to the local outdoor basketball court in a much safer section of Bridgeport. Of course, Jess would drag me along. Because of the number of adults that showed up at this park, Mr. Darcey felt this was a good place for us, so he and my sister Brianna were not overly concerned about our safety.

It was at this outdoor basketball court that I began to notice the tremendous improvement in Jessie's basketball skills. Mr. Darcey's teaching was beginning to pay off. Jessie always found a way to compete in basketball games with the girls her age. Soon, she also found a way to join in on the boys basketball games as well. Just as Mr. Darcey had hoped, both the girls and the boys who tried to defend her were totally mystified by her brilliant dribbling, sometimes falling down trying to steal the ball from her.

After a few weeks, Jessie thought it was time to put her father's training to the real test. Jess convinced some of the older boys on the court to have her play on their team. At first they appeared to be very skeptical of having this "young girl" play on their team. Finally, they relented and said they would give it a try. Soon, their laughter turned to awe as they witnessed shooting and dribbling that they had never seen before. It was hard for them to believe that all of this was coming from a girl only in seventh grade.

One of the boys Jess played against was a freshman at Wilbur Cross High School in New Haven. His name was Fred Owens and he would occasionally join his friends in Bridgeport to play on their basketball court. Fred asked Jess if she ever heard of Birdie Lincoln, a guard on the Wilbur Cross freshmen basketball team. Jess responded that she had not heard of Birdie.

"Birdie sometimes comes down to Bridgeport to practice with us. She was a star basketball player in her middle school in California. Birdie's family moved to New Haven and now she attends Wilbur Cross. Even in grammar school she had a large following. She was known as "Blazin' Birdie", a nickname she likes and wants to be known as.

"Birdie is a really good basketball player and the coaches all say she may become one of the best high school freshman in the country. Only thing is, Birdie has a real attitude and a lot of kids don't like her, including me. Also, she has a very bad temper at times and many of the high school kids are afraid to hang around with her. So, if she comes down when you're here she may have a problem with how good you are in basketball."

Scratching her head, Jess asked, "Why would she have a problem with that?"

"Because Birdie thinks she's the best, period. She wouldn't want anyone thinking that you're better than she is. I see how good you are and I know you are even better than Birdie. I have to admit that you're the best I've ever seen, male or female.

"But Birdie may not like the fact that you are so much better than her. I'm just telling you this so you won't be surprised with anything she says or does. I do believe Birdie is gonna be mighty jealous when she sees you play."

A bewildered Jess responded, "Thank you for sharing this with me, Fred. I don't understand why she would have a problem with how I play basketball. I just try to do the best I can and try not to worry about what people say. I really try not to compete with anyone in particular. I—

"Well, I know that, and you know that, but Birdie? Well…you'll see."

Two days later, Birdie Lincoln showed up at one of the playground games that the boys had scheduled. Birdie was slightly taller than Jess and walked with a swagger. She had an athletic build and a large tattoo on her right arm, which was a bit uncommon in those days. It was quite obvious that she wanted to draw attention to herself as she walked over to the group of boys, not seeing Jessie standing there.

"Where's this Jessie Darcey that everyone's braggin' 'bout? Tell her 'Blazin' Birdie' is here."

Jess politely put her hand out and said, "Hi Birdie, I'm Jessie Darcey. Glad to meet you." Birdie did not return the handshake.

"Huh! So you're the phenom that the boys here keep talkin' 'bout! You don't look like much of a basketball player to me. Kind of scrawny, if you ask me." Laughing, Birdie asked Jess, "So how old are you Miss Phenom—nine, ten?'"

"Actually I'm twelve years old."

"Twelve years old, give me a break! Fred, are you telling me that this skinny little middle school thing here is the superstar you guys have been talking 'bout? She sure don't look like much to me.

"Ok miss superstar, what's say you and me play a game of "horse" together. Do you know how this basketball game is played or maybe your momma never taught you how it's done."

"I do know how the game is played. Two kids play one-on-one. The person with the ball chooses the shot, sometimes a trick shot. If the person makes the shot, then the other person has to make that same exact shot. If the other person misses, then she gets an "h." The first person who gets "h-o-r-s-e"— by missing those five attempts loses the game. Is that correct?"

"Well, the little smarty-pants got somethin' right! Ok, let's go one-on-one. Are you ready?

"Wait…I thought we were going to play a regular game. And besides, you just got here."

Jess looked over to me and I just shrugged my shoulders not knowing what to say. I never met anyone with such arrogance.

"Oh, so the little phenom is chicken, huh?"

Hearing what Birdie was saying, Fred yelled out, "Jess, take her up on her offer, go for it." Knowing what the outcome may very well be, Fred laughed and shouted out, "It's just a quick game Jess. Then we can play our regular games."

"Ok," said Jess, "just one game of 'horse', okay?."

"One game it is. Now remember, you're playing against 'Blazin Birdie'. They don't call me that for nothin' you know!"

A somewhat bewildered Jess looked over to me again. Her look indicated to me that she really didn't want to compete against Birdie and just wanted to get it over with—win or lose. I tried to think of something to say. I knew Jessie felt a bit awkward since she never competed one-on-one with someone like this Birdie character. But all I could do is shrug my shoulders again.

Birdie motioned to Fred.

"C'mere Fred. Reach in your pocket and see if you have a coin there. If you do, toss it in the air. I call 'heads'."

Fred tossed the coin which landed on the ground.

"Ok, announced Fred, "the coin landed on 'tails'. Jessie gets the first shot."

For her first shot Jess took a jump shot—left-handed—just above the free throw line—*swish*.

The look on Birdie's face was priceless when she saw how easily Jess made that difficult shot

"Wait…", said Birdie, "did you shoot that jumper left-handed?"

"Yes, I did."

Shaking her head Birdie attempted the same left-handed jump shot but the ball didn't even come close to the hoop.

For Jessie's next shot, she had her back to the hoop around the foul line. She then attempted a turn-around shot with just a quick glance of the hoop and made that shot as well. Birdie tried once again to mimic Jess's shot but the ball only hit the backboard.

Fred nudged his friend standing next to him and yelled out, "Way to go Jessie, show her who's boss!"

For her next shot, Jess fired a shot from the side of the court, just inside the outside line. Again, the shot hit nothing but net. And, again, Birdie failed to make that same shot.

The guys on the side of the court were jubilant and shouted encouragement to Jessie. Knowing Jess, I'm sure this caused some embarrassment. But I knew Jess was too competitive to let up on Birdie. Jessie's fourth shot attempt from far beyond the foul line yielded the same results.

Jess made her first four shots—with Birdie missing all four times. Jess knew that if she made the next shot and Birdie failed to make that same shot, then Jess would win their "horse" game and they can play some regular games.

For her fifth attempt, Jess began at the half-court line. She moved quickly to the hoop, dribbling the ball around her back and through her legs five times, and then made a left handed jump shot near the basket. Birdie once again tried to mimic Jess's shot by dribbling between her legs five times. However, on the fifth dribble, the ball hit against her left knee and the ball bounced out of bounds. This made the score "h-o-r-s-e" and Jess won the contest. Jessie completely controlled this competition with Birdie never having a chance to try her own shot.

Since I stood near the two on the court, I could hear Birdie's 'trash talk' throughout the contest. I was proud to see that Jess completely ignored Birdie's comments, which most likely irritated Birdie. When the game was over I did hear Birdie mutter to herself *She was just lucky.*

Fred yelled out, "Birdie, do you now see what we were talking about?"

Birdie did not respond to Fred and did not even look at Jessie. "Well, I just remembered that I have practice to go to. See you in a few days boys." With that, Birdie left shaking her head

All the boys ran over to Jess to congratulate her.

"Thanks guys," said a composed Jess, "But can we now play a couple of games?"

After her games on the court, Jess walked over to me and asked if she correctly handled that contest with Birdie.

"Abby, I felt like maybe I should have missed a shot on purpose, but I guess I'm much too competitive. But I don't consider her a rival like the boys kept saying. I hope I didn't hurt Birdie's feelings. I never wanted to compete with Birdie and her crazy "horse" game!"

"Jess," I responded, "you did exactly what you should have. I know this was a bit awkward for you but maybe by losing so badly, Birdie learned her lesson. Well, let's hope so anyway."

After playing these outdoor games, Jess would always ask how I felt she was progressing.

"Jess, I'm no expert when it comes to basketball but from what I can see you are making tremendous progress on your basketball skills.

"Of course much of your progress is due to my role as the 'bucket girl' during your basketball practices at your house."

Jess smiled and responded, "Well, that goes without saying

MIXED EMOTIONS

As we prepared for graduation which was a few months away, we had mixed emotions about leaving Webster and going off to high school

During eighth grade in Webster Middle School, Jess and I continued to "double date" with various boys we got to know. Jessie was relieved when Johnny D mentioned to her that Emmett would be moving to North Carolina after eighth grade graduation since his father was offered a very good job there. Actually, she was relieved more for Johnny's sake than her own since she knew what a bad influence Emmett was on Johnny.

All of our dates, including Jessie's, were casual dates and neither of us had steady boyfriends. We decided we were still too young and just wanted to have fun—nothing serious.

What *was* serious—for Jessie—was her devotion to the sport of basketball.

Jess and I took full advantage of our eighth grade "status." I guess we felt a bit like big shots and we loved it when kids in seventh grade asked our opinion about certain teachers and other school related matters. We finally reached the zenith level of middle school but knew full well that by the end of the year we would have to start all over again as lowly freshmen in high school.

I continued to be a cheerleader for the Webster boys' basketball team. I must say that I was honored to be named captain of our cheerleading squad. We did very well in the state cheerleading contest, earning the second place award that year. Meanwhile, Jessie continued to elicit praise for her basketball skills from her classmates and other kids in the neighborhood.

***

Jess and I both looked forward to our school's eighth grade semi-formal dance. Brianna went with us as we shopped around for the perfect dresses to wear to our semi-formal. Brianna was amused at how serious we took this dress shopping and would have fun kidding us.

"You know," Brianna noted, "the boys will be so nervous that they won't even notice what kind of dresses you have on. Besides, they will probably just show up without a jacket or tie."

Hearing this, Jess and I looked at each other. A startled Jess whispered to me, "Abby, I never thought about that. What if the boys show up wearing jeans and a crummy t-shirt? We need to talk to them right away!" I agreed.

We finally found two beautiful dresses to wear and we felt we looked pretty good in them. We agreed with Brianna that the boys probably wouldn't pay much attention to what we were wearing, but we didn't care about that.

Jess agreed to go to the semi-formal dance with Johnny D who, much to our relief, disbanded his group. I accepted an invitation to the dance from Carl, the nice boy I met in seventh grade. We made both of the boys promise to wear a jacket and tie, much to their displeasure. Brianna drove the four of us to the school's semi-formal and also agreed to be one of the chaperones. We danced quite a bit, after which Jess confided in me that Johnny D's dancing "skills" were lacking.

"Abby my feet are killing me from Johnny stepping on them when we tried slow dancing. That boy needs to brush up on his dancing 'skills'!"

"Yeh, I noticed that when I was dancing with Carl. Maybe you should enroll Johnny in a couple of sessions at the Arthur Murray Dance Studio." We both laughed at the thought of Johnny D taking formal dance lessons.

It was a very fun night as Jess and I shared special moments with our classmates at the semi-formal.

***

As we prepared for graduation which was a few months away, we had mixed emotions about leaving Webster and going off to high school. In a weird way, it felt like such an adult thing and we both felt a bit of trepidation of what was in store for us in high school. Would Jessie continue her basketball progress and make the high school team? Would we both be able to maintain our good grades throughout high school as we did in our elementary and middle school grades? Would we make new friends in high school?

What really helped us was knowing that we both planned to attend the same high school—Bridgeport High—and we would certainly continue to be best friends no matter what was thrown our way.

***

On one of my visits to see Jessie I was greeted at the door by a very solemn Mr. Darcey. I found this unusual since he always greeted me with a big smile and in a cordial manner. I immediately suspected that something was wrong but didn't say anything. Mr. Darcey motioned that Jessie was up in her room. When I entered Jessie's room I saw that she had been crying. Giving her a hug, I asked Jess what was wrong. "It's my mom. She was just diagnosed with a brain tumor. Abby, I think we may be losing her." I was speechless, knowing what a sweetheart Mrs. Darcey was and how much Jessie loved her. I struggled for comforting words for my best friend.

"Jess, I will keep your mom in my thoughts and prayers that she will recover from this. You know that I'm here for you. Please don't hesitate to call me if you want to talk, no matter what time it is."

"Yes, I know you'll always be there for me," replied Jessie with tears in her eyes.

Mrs. Darcey's condition rapidly grew worse and she passed away within weeks. Unfortunately, she died before she was able to see her daughter graduate from middle school.

For both the wake and the church service, Jessie made sure that I sat next to her, which I felt honored to do. When we returned to her house after the church service, Jessie told me how brave her mom was dealing with the unbearable pain. She told me that she will always have fond memories of the precious times she and her mom spent together. Jessie said that she always cherished the advice that her mom conveyed to her, especially during her final days. Jess shared with me one of her conversations with her mom just before her passing.

"Jessie, life is a gift, so please be mindful of every day. Do well in school but enjoy being with your friends, especially Abby. And please take care of your dad. He is going to need your support once he becomes a single parent.

"Mike tells me that you are very devoted to playing basketball. With your determination I know you will become a basketball star someday. I only wish that I could be around to see that. Please know that you are the love of my life. Stay strong."

Before his wife passed, Mike promised Kathleen that he would do everything in his power to ensure that Jessie, their only child, would get a proper education which would enable her to graduate high school, something that many of the kids in our neighborhood failed to achieve. The hope was that Jessie would be the first member of the Darcey family to attend college. This would enable Jessie to escape the inner city, or "slum" as Mike called it, where crime seemed to get worse with each passing year.

His wife's passing left Mike as a single parent, a job he took very seriously. Mike was determined to be the best father he could be. He was totally committed to raise Jessie in a manner in which she would focus on her studies and, thus, shelter her from neighborhood gangs. He was a loving, devoted father who made a point of spending a great deal of time with Jessie when he wasn't working at the factory.

***

As hard as Mike tried, he could not fully shield Jessie from the intolerance and prejudice shown by some people. He made a point of re-telling his unfortunate experience with his former teammate Tom Smith and how he chose to handle the situation. Mike admitted that Tom's actions were hurtful but he impressed upon Jessie the need for her to not let words or actions like that affect her life.

"Jessie, I know it can sometimes be very difficult, but you need to be the better person in situations like that. No matter what, be above it all.

"If something like that should happen to you, try as best you can to not let it affect you. Hopefully, you will not have to deal with this sort of thing. But if it does come up, try to take the high road and ignore such actions. Believe me, you will feel stronger for it. I promise you.

"I wanted to share that awful experience with you so that you can learn from that incident in the event that you encounter such hateful words or actions."

Living in a predominantly black neighborhood, Jess and I learned early on about racism as it sometimes is applied to people of color. Some of our friends in high school were black and they shared some of the racial experiences they had encountered. Jessie thought of the prejudice that her dad and some of her friends had to deal with. But she never thought she would be the victim of this same prejudice.

***

When our Webster Middle School graduation finally arrived, the event was held inside the gymnasium. As we walked to the line that was forming to receive our school diplomas I noticed that Jessie became very tearful. I knew instantly why that was. Jessie was missing her mom not being able to see her graduate. I gave Jess a quick hug and tried to comfort her as best I could. Looking out to the audience, I was pleased to see my mom and Brianna sitting next to Mr. Darcey. The three of them were all smiles when it was announced that Jess and I graduated at the top of our class. It was something we also were very proud of.

Having graduated from Webster Middle School, our attention turned to high school.

Jessie and I both decided to attend Bridgeport High. She promised to continue to be my "study buddy" throughout high school, which I was relieved to hear. While we knew we would meet and befriend other classmates, our friendship was solid and we would remain best friends. We both were determined to stay in the top classes in high school by studying hard and maintaining excellent grades.

During the summer months that year, Jessie spent a great deal of time on the outdoor basketball courts. She relished playing ball with high school boys and girls and quickly became the best player on the courts.

Knowing how Jessie had progressed so quickly and expertly in basketball, I couldn't wait to see the reaction of the high school coaches when she tried out for the girl's freshman basketball team. I would soon find out.

Jessie and I talked about how we felt as we were about to become freshman at Bridgeport High School. We both admitted feeling a bit nervous but nonetheless excited about what high school had to offer. Not knowing what to expect, Jessie convinced me to look at it as a new adventure rather than something to worry about.

FRESHMAN YEAR AT BRIDGEPORT HIGH SCHOOL

Jessie would make me laugh at the most inopportune times.

Entering high school that first day was filled with wonderment. While the building itself looked rather old, everything else seemed new to both Jessie and myself. New school, new students, new teachers, and new challenges. We both agreed that it was a great relief that we had each other to lean on if or when things got difficult at school.

Jessie and I got to sit next to or near each other for most of our classes, which we liked. We began to size up our teachers to get a sense of how difficult or how easy each class would be.

Jessie would make me laugh at the most inopportune times. We had this math teacher, Miss Grayson, who had very wavy hair. My seat happened to be right in front of the teacher, so I wanted her to see that I was paying close attention to what she was saying. During her presentation, Jessie, who was sitting in back of me, passed me a note. The note said Miss Grayson must have been in a hurry to get to school because her wig was crooked. As I looked up to see what Jessie meant I burst out in laughter, causing Miss Grayson to stop in mid-sentence to issue me a warning that such behavior would not be tolerated in her class.

Jessie, with her sense of humor, would have a nickname for each teacher. For example, Mr. Goode—our English teacher—was nicknamed Mr. "Notso" Goode, and Miss Larsen—our Science teacher—became Miss "Larceny." So silly and juvenile, but funny to both of us.

Surprisingly, our classes didn't pose a problem for either of us. We got off to a good start thanks to our "study buddy" sessions at Jessie's house. Because both of us had a competitive nature, we would challenge each other with a quiz to learn more about each subject. The winner of the quiz would be treated to a chocolate sundae at the local ice cream store. As I think about it now, the study competitions were actually Jessie's idea to make sure I would stay focused on our studies.

Like her father, Jessie did encounter anti-Semitism, although not as blatant as her dad's experience with Tom Smith. In our freshman year, one of the class assignments given by our high school sociology teacher—Mrs. "Sandy" Beach—was for each student to chart his or her ancestry, to the best of their ability. As a way of tracing their ancestral background, Mrs. Beach suggested research methods to the class such as interviewing their mother and/or father, obtaining information from other relatives, and utilizing tools available at the local library including microfilm and archived newspapers. The second part of the assignment was for the students to share their discoveries with the rest of the class. It was then that the class learned of Jessie's Jewish lineage.

Jessie received a favorable response to her thorough background research from the majority of her classmates. However, there were two boys who, after class, decided to tease Jessie by shouting out anti-Semitic slurs and mocking Jewish people in general. Walking with Jessie I was glad when she walked straight ahead and refrained from responding to the two boys. Despite this, I could sense that their words really hurt Jessie.

When we got to her house, Jessie broke down in tears. She turned to me and said, "What would cause people like this to act that way?" Hearing this, I reminded Jessie to recall her father's experience with Tom Smith and her dad's advice to not let hurtful actions like this affect her life.

"Abby you are so right," replied Jessie. "It's people like that who have a problem, not me."

Her father's experience and advice taught Jessie that actions like this only revealed the other person's insecurity, ignorance, and fear. The tears gradually faded and just like her dad, Jessie felt stronger after this incident. She made a vow to herself not to let such actions affect her again. Jessie did confide in me that she was afraid to tell anyone about the Jewish side of her family for fear of being ridiculed or alienated. Hearing this, I just shrugged my shoulders indicating to Jess that it was not a big issue in my mind.

"Jess, you should be proud of your heritage, on both your father's and mother's sides. You obviously know about my mom and dad and I can't say that I'm proud of that situation. But I finally had a chance to read a journal written by my grandfather that my mother shared with me and Brianna. After reading his journal and hearing wonderful stories about my grandmother—who was Polish—on my mom's side, I have a newfound respect and pride for both sides of my family.

"I realized how brave my grandfather was leaving his homeland in Italy to find a better life for himself and his family. I read that my granddad traveled by himself on the Thomas di Savoy passenger ship which left from Naples, Italy, and headed to America. He came to the U.S. to find work so that he could provide for his family when they came later on to America to live with him. It took him two months traveling from Naples to the U.S. Two months—can you believe that!"

Jessie, with raised eyebrows, exclaimed, "Wow, that's unreal."

"I know, and he certainly didn't travel in style. Instead he had to ride in a very uncomfortable compartment in the boat, along with other Italian immigrants. He referred to it as the "steerage" compartment in the boat, near where they kept the cargo. But my mom told us that he never complained.

"Granddad said in his diary that he felt blessed that he was allowed entry into the United States. In his journal, he speaks of the absolute joy and thrill that he and the other passengers felt when they saw the Statue of Liberty for the first time."

"Abby that must have been such a thrill and such a relief for him, especially traveling for so long on that boat. I can't even imagine."

"Yeh, I know. And, my grandfather didn't speak a word of English. He had heard stories that some immigrants who didn't speak the English language were turned away by medical examiners for fear that they may be carrying a disease. He didn't know if that was true but he was determined to not let that happen to him.

"Fortunately, he found other Italians who were able to interpret for him and he was allowed entry. He eventually became a proud U.S. citizen. Unfortunately, he was exposed to a great deal of discrimination, looking for employment and in other matters.

"Jess, I wanted to share this story since many different cultures, like the Irish and Polish cultures, had experienced similar discrimination. I do realize, however, that it was different for the Jewish culture since they were not only discriminated against but, in years past, they were also persecuted. And I believe that discrimination against Jewish people still exists, but to a much lesser degree.

"Well, that's the way I see it. Jess, please don't worry about what a few kids might say. The vast majority of kids in our school really don't care about our backgrounds, which is one of the things I like about this school. Most of us are too busy worrying about our grades and our relationship with boys. And, besides, the few kids who have a problem with something like that are just jerks anyway. If it's not someone's heritage then it's something else that they would complain about. It's just plain old ignorance and insecurity. You and I just need to stay as far away as we can from idiots like them."

Hearing this, Jess thanked me for sharing my background history and promised to take my advice.

***

During our freshman year, we both met and became good friends with a girl by the name of Jane Kenny. Like Jessie, Jane planned to try out for the freshmen basketball team. Jess had heard that she was a very good basketball player at her middle school in Florida. We soon discovered that she also had a great sense of humor and a terrific singing voice.

Jane's family moved from Florida to a very nice—and safe—section of Bridgeport, with their house close to the Trumbull border. On occasion, she invited Jess and me over to her parent's house The three of us shared a lot of laughs, especially about silly things we were involved in at school. With her parent's permission, Jane also hosted some fabulous parties for some of our classmates and friends.

Every once and awhile, Jane and I would sing along to a tune that was playing on her radio. Much to our surprise, we harmonized really well. Jane mentioned that she was thinking about joining the school's glee club and encouraged me to join also. I never received any formal training but I knew how to carry a tune. I told her I would love to have the opportunity to be a part of the glee club and would think about joining. If nothing else, it would be a fun experience.

***

Our gym class was a blast. For reasons unknown to us, Miss "Hershey Bar" Hershey would have us march around the gym floor before she made us do exercises, which we all felt was a waste of time. Miss Hershey was a short, gray-haired, humorless lady who appeared to be physically unfit. Not knowing Jessie's basketball skills, Miss Hershey tried valiantly to teach Jessie how to shoot baskets. Of course, Jessie would play along, which made us laugh hysterically. It became apparent to us that Miss Hersey was not cut out to be a gym teacher and it was obvious that her heart just wasn't into her job.

Every time we had a free moment in the gym, Jessie would desperately try to teach me how to shoot—all to no avail. In a playful, teasing manner, our friends would imitate my shooting "style." I told Jess that I guess I had something in common with Miss Hershey. This caused Jessie to laugh out loud really hard, which brought about a stern look from Miss Hershey.

Jessie had this infectious laugh that all our friends in school got a real kick out of. So the kids would always try to make her laugh—which wasn't difficult.

9

"THE SWEET DREAMS"

I kiddingly told Jess that Jane and I wanted to go out on top as recording artists

At the urging of Jane and Jess, I joined the high school glee club during my freshman year and was happy that Jane also joined the club.

Our teacher, Miss "Gleeful" Gleason actually complimented me on my singing voice, which pleased me. She encouraged me to take private lessons. Of course, that was out of the question given the financial situation at home. Jessie had jokingly given Miss Gleason that nickname but, like Jane and I, she soon found out that Miss Gleason was a very knowledgeable and loving teacher.

Miss Gleason arranged to have us perform outside the school at places such as senior housing, retirement homes, and hospitals in Bridgeport. We figured that with more experience like this, our singing group would sound even better. So we were thankful that Miss Gleason allowed us to perform at different functions. She even encouraged Jane and me to sing a few duets, and we gladly accepted her offer.

Jane and I performed as a duo at school assemblies and local events. All along, my biggest cheerleader was Jess who would always sit in the first row at these events and cheer us on. Jessie encouraged me to continue performing. She constantly told me that I was a "talented singer who was blessed with a wonderful voice." I wasn't completely convinced of that but was so appreciative of her support and enthusiasm.

Jane and I even sang together several times on a local radio station in Bridgeport, which at times featured local unknown singers. We would cover songs like *Let It Be Me* by the Everly Brothers and *Mr. Sandman* by The Chordettes . The host of the radio show liked our singing style. He mentioned that the radio station was about to record a novelty tune and asked if we would like to record a song for the B-side of the record. In those days, vinyl records had an A and B side, with the A-side being the popular tune and the B-side usually being just a filler, which was fine with us. We both agreed to record the B-side of the record.

Jane and I wrote a song together and, surprisingly, the radio station agreed to have us record the song. I guess they figured that since it was only a flip side of their recording it didn't really matter as long as the song was "listenable." We knew they were right since we both had no preconceived notion of stardom.

Jane and I were given the name The Sweet Dreams which would appear on the record. The song that Jane and I wrote was called *Frankie, My Love*. We sang it in a 1950s style, which was simple, charming, and a bit corny. But that was how many songs were sung in those days, especially by female singers. We both grew to like that singing style.

Not knowing what the heck we were doing during the recording session, we did our best to make our song sound at least passable. We had to go through a bunch of takes because Jane and I would constantly crack up in laughter in the middle of the song. The guys in the studio weren't thrilled about the extra takes since any delays cost additional money, but we finally managed to get through our recording. The radio station played their Side A novelty tune constantly and it became their theme song. Jane and I never heard our song on the radio. But that was okay with us.

Our friends were relentless in teasing us about our recording name and the simplicity of our song. Before gym class some of the girls would begin to sing their version of our song, which was hysterical. But they were also very supportive. Our biggest fan, of course, was Jessie who said she bought the record and thought we should cut another song together. Jane and I both agreed that this would be our one and only song. I kiddingly told Jess that Jane and I wanted to go out on top as recording artists.

That whole recording experience was a lot of fun. I still have the vinyl record at home and every time I would see Jane, we would reminisce about our recording experience.

We still couldn't believe we had the audacity to record that song, but it was the source of a lot of fun for the two of us.

It was, indeed, our "fifteen minutes of fame."

10

FRESHMAN BASKETBALL TRY-OUTS

The coaches were instantly in awe once they witnessed Jessie's shooting and dribbling abilities. It was obvious to me that they never saw anything like this in all their years of coaching.

Freshman high school basketball try-outs began on November 30th.

Jessie asked me to come to the gym and watch her try out for the freshman team. She admitted that she was a bit nervous and it would help if I was there. She got the okay from her coaches, so I sat in the gymnasium stands anxiously awaiting her coaches' reactions once it got to be Jessie's turn on the court. It didn't take long for the two coaches to be overwhelmed by what they saw. They were instantly in awe once they witnessed Jessie's shooting and dribbling abilities. At one point I saw the two coaches look at each other with their jaws dropped. It was obvious to me that they never saw anything like this in all their years of coaching.

As we walked back from her first practice, Jessie told me how nervous she was but she felt that she did okay.

"Okay? My goodness Jess, you were amazing! And, judging by the coaches' reactions, I believe you will have no problem making the team."

"Oh, you're just saying that because you're my best friend!"

***

Ten days later, It was no surprise to me when Jessie informed me that not only did she make the freshman team but she was also selected as one of the two starting guards on the basketball squad. The other guard position was given to our friend Jane Kenny, a slim 5'6" fleet-footed basketball player who was a standout at her middle school in Florida. Rounding out the starting five were: Phyllis Riley (forward), Amber Neeland (forward), and Alyssa Ruiz (center). Phyllis Riley, in particular, was a very versatile player as the team's "small forward."

Jess made a point of praising Jane on her basketball knowledge during their practice games. Jane just smiled, knowing this was high praise coming from someone as gifted as Jessie.

Jessie and Jane complimented each other nicely on the basketball court. While her shooting was average, Jane was a terrific playmaker and was outstanding on defense. Her passes to Jess were crisp which enabled Jessie to free herself from her defenders more quickly to take her shots. Jess told me that she was pleased with her progress on the court and was flattered by the kind words from her coaches.

Jessie said she was getting anxious, however, on how she would do in real games once the high school season actually began. She told me that she didn't want to disappoint anyone, especially her dad who had worked so hard to teach her so many basketball skills, and her best friend—me. I assured her that she had nothing to worry about there. Both her dad and I had total confidence in her abilities and, besides, her dad and I were fond of her just as she was—basketball or no basketball.

***

Bridgeport High's opponent for their first official basketball game on December 14th was Wilton High School.

In attendance, of course, was her biggest fan—her dad. He showed up early for Jessie's game and sat in an area of the stands that was visible to his daughter throughout the game. Jessie appreciated this because it gave her a sense of comfort, especially if the game became close. It was yet another way Mr. Darcey showed his support for Jessie. I also showed up early for the game and sat in the second row right behind the team. I too wanted to show support for Jess.

Early on, the score was close. During a timeout, Coach Nichols called the team over to the sidelines to go over several plays she wanted them to execute. While the team was in a huddle and with the score tied, Jessie glanced over to me and made a silly face to make me laugh. This being her first game, I would have thought she would be nervous throughout the game, but I could see that she was in her element. Jess was having fun in a sport she loved and her confidence was growing stronger and stronger. Jane also looked over to me during the game, but was more serious, especially since the game was close at the time.

After the huddle broke, the coach took Jess and Jane aside.

"Okay you two, it's time to show us all what you got. Take charge out there. Let's win this first game!"

Jess gave me a quick nod as she walked back onto the court. From my seat I smiled back at Jess, and shouted "Let's go Jess!"

Heeding their coach's advice, Jess and Jane began to take control of the game. Jane used her leadership skills to direct her teammates on the court.

Jess went into action, dazzling her opponents and fans with her ball handling skills and shooting. She began to score at will. It didn't take long for Bridgeport High to take the lead and quickly widen the margin.

The game eventually ended up being a blow out, led by Jessie who made shots at nearly every area of the court. She also had an amazing 85% average at the foul line. While Coach Nichols had high hopes for Jess, what she saw in Jessie's basketball skills far exceeded her expectations.

The next three games were also blow outs very similar to game one. For all four games, Jessie led the team in scoring, assists, and free throws.

After the second game of the season, word began to spread about this freshman phenom. Beginning with Jessie's third game, the Bridgeport freshmen played in front of sold out crowds—for both home and away games. Fans wanted to see for themselves what all the excitement was about. Jessie did not disappoint them.

Just as he did for the first game, Mr. Darcey sat in the exact same seat in the stands. During the game, Jessie often looked over at him and nodded, purposely showing little expression on her face. Mr. Darcey understood that his daughter didn't want to appear to be a show off by waving or smiling. His only acknowledgement was a smile each time she looked his way. I too sat in my same seat in the second row behind the team's bench.

The Bridgeport High School girls' Basketball team got off to a good start—with a 4-0 record— and all the members of the team were looking forward to a well-deserved rest during the upcoming Christmas vacation.

11

JESSIE'S SINGING DEBUT

"What's a little humiliation in front of the entire school assembly!"

Prior to the school's Christmas vacation break, Miss Gleason arranged

for our glee club to participate in the high school holiday program which was held in our gymnasium. Miss Gleason asked Jane and I to sing several Christmas classics for the program.

Jane and I decided on the holiday songs *White Christmas, Frosty the Snowman, Twelve Days of Christmas,* and end with *We Wish You A Merry Christmas.*

"Abby," asked an amused Jane, "Why don't we get Jess to join us for one of our Christmas songs?"

"You must be kidding! Jess has always said that she has a terrible singing voice. She would never agree to sing with us!"

"Yeh but I have an idea," Jane said with a smile. 'For the song *Twelve Days of Christmas,* let's see if we can get Jess to sing the part 'five golden rings'. We can tell her that we needed a different person for this part and that this is all she would have to perform during the program."

"That would be amazing but I'm not sure Jess will go along with that idea. But let's try."

It took a lot of convincing but we finally managed to coerce Jess to be part of the holiday song we had in mind for her. We even told her she can speak the part if she didn't want to sing. Jess finally agreed, sensing that we were setting her up for a few laughs for the program. Actually, Jess was right. We were hoping that our classmates would get a kick out of their basketball star "singing" her part of the song. So, Jess agreed to play along with our idea since she had a terrific sense of humor. She joked that her "singing" debut could lead to a new career in the music business. Jess knew that she would probably be the source of laughter but thought it would be a fun moment.

"Ok, I know what the two of you are up to," said Jess, "but I'll play along with your gag. What's a little humiliation in front of the entire school assembly!"

Sure enough, when the song reached Jessie's part she spoke the words "five golden rings." Each time she spoke her part, Jess received a big round of applause and a lot of laughter from the audience. I believed that Jess, in her own way, was showing her classmates that all her basketball achievements had not gone to her head and she had no problem being the brunt of our holiday "gag." That was Jess, so talented and yet so modest.

***

At the beginning of our Christmas vacation, I received a call from Jessie.

"Abby, would you like to come with me and my dad to pick out a Christmas tree? My dad takes me to this Christmas tree farm and he cuts down the tree himself."

"You put up a real tree for Christmas?"

"Yeh, my dad brings his truck and uses his saw to cut down whichever tree we decide would look nice in the house. It's a lot of fun. Would you like to go with us?"

"Sure. I never saw anyone cut down a real tree for Christmas."

"Why, do you have an artificial Christmas tree?"

"Jess, we never had *any* kind of Christmas tree. My mom always says we can't afford one."

"Oh, well come along with us anyway. I think you'll enjoy it. My dad really has become good at cutting his own tree."

The next day, the three of us went to this beautiful tree farm in Fairfield. Once there, I followed Jess and her dad to look for their "perfect" tree to cut down. I didn't want to say anything, but I would have been satisfied with any tree on the farm, even the scrawny trees with only a few branches.

Jess called out to her dad that she found a tree that would look beautiful in their house.

"Ok, let me get my saw in the truck. I'll be right back."

As Mr. Darcey walked back to his truck, it began to snow.

"Jess," I said, "I know you and your dad are used to this. But for me, this is such a magical day, especially with the snow falling. It's like being in one of those snow globes you see in gift shops."

Jess instructed me to keep an eye on the tree that she picked out so that nobody tried to claim it. She told me she just had to help her dad set up the truck to put their tree in the back. She promised that she would be right back.

"Dad," Jess said as she caught up with her father. "Would it be possible to cut down a tree for Abby? Her family never had a Christmas tree and I know she would appreciate it. I'm certain that her mom and Brianna would not object."

"Sure Jess, I would be happy to cut down a tree for Abby and pay for the tree myself. Let's go tell Abby."

"Ok, but would you mind waiting here for a minute? I just want to check out something in that gift shop."

Moments later, Jess returned and put a small package in the front seat of the truck.

"Ok, I'm ready," Jessie said excitedly, "let's go cut down our tree!"

Mr. Darcey took his saw from the truck and, with a knowing smile on his face, he said to Jess, "I think I know what you're up to. You're a good friend to Abby, Jess." Mr. Darcey and Jess proceeded to walk to where I stood closely guarding their tree as Jess instructed.

"Abby," said Mr. Darcey, "how would you like me to also cut down a tree for you and your family?"

"Mr. Darcey, I don't have any money, so—"

"Abby, this is on the house. Consider it a Christmas gift from me and Jessie."

Hearing this I bit down on my lower lip in an attempt not to cry.

"Mr. Darcey, you can't imagine how much this means to me! We never had a Christmas tree before because we couldn't afford to buy one. I would love it if you would cut down a tree for us. This is so generous of you and Jess! My mom and Bri are going to love it. I can't wait to decorate the tree with whatever decorations we may have at home."

"Great," replied Mr. Darcey, "pick out whichever tree you think would look nice in your home. Don't worry about the price."

I ran around the tree farm until I found a beautiful tree and pointed to the tree I selected.

"Mr. Darcey, this would look wonderful in our home."

"Great," said Mr. Darcey smiling, "let's cut it down before someone else chooses this tree."

After cutting down the tree, I helped Mr. Darcey carry it to his truck. Mr. Darcey then cut down the tree that he had marked as sold. We then carried the tree back and placed it next to the tree I selected for our house. Once both trees were secured in his truck, he went inside and paid the person at the front desk. He also purchased a tree stand for our Christmas tree. Mr. Darcey told me that he would help bring the tree into our home, if that was okay with me. As Mr. Darcey drove to my house, I kept turning around to look at my new tree at the back of his truck, with a huge smile on my face. Seeing this, Jess would smile back at me knowing how much this meant to me.

As soon as we began walking up the steps to our house, Bri came running out the door.

"Is that for us, Abby? Where in the world did you get this? Did you have enough money?"

"Bri, Jessie's dad cut it down for us at a tree farm—and he paid for it himself!"

"Mr. Darcey," Bri said excitedly, "I can't thank you enough, my mom is going to love this!"

After we put the tree up in our living room I thanked Mr. Darcey, gave Jess a hug and, before she walked out the door, I took my best friend aside.

"Jess, I know you're behind this. You continue to amaze me! This is going to be the best Christmas ever and I have you to thank."

My mom came home late from work that day. When she opened the door she looked very tired. All of a sudden her face lit up with a broad smile.

"Where did you get the beautiful Christmas tree?"

"Mom," I replied, "Jess and her dad cut down a tree for their house. While we were there, Mr. Darcey asked if I would like him to cut down a tree for our house. He said he would pay for the tree. Isn't it beautiful Mom?"

"It's a beauty, Jess. I must repay Jessie's father somehow. I know… I'll bake two pies for Jess and her dad. Do you know what kind of pies they would like?"

"Apple and pumpkin pies," I responded without hesitation.

"Okay, apple and pumpkin pies it is. I'll bake the pies first thing in the morning." My mom then turned to Brianna and me and asked us to sit down.

"I…I have to admit something to both of you. All these years I have been saying that we didn't have the expenses set aside to buy a Christmas tree which is why we never had one before. However, that is not really true. Actually, we always could have managed to purchase one. I know this sounds selfish, but I couldn't bear the thought of putting up a tree in this house. You see, I have very fond memories of your dad and me buying a tree and then decorating it when we got home. That was a fun time for me, and I believe for John also. When your father left us I was devastated to the point where any memories such as that were very hurtful. I couldn't bear putting up a Christmas tree because I thought it would cause me further pain. But looking at this tree that you brought in makes me think how selfish I was, depriving you both of your own happy memories. I ask that you both forgive me for my selfishness and stupidity."

Bri and I walked over to our mom, gave her a hug, and we both told her that we understood and that we love her no matter what.

"You know what," my mom said wiping the tears from her eyes with a tissue, "in the basement are two large boxes that I have hidden. The two green and red boxes contain plenty of decorations, lights, and garland for a Christmas tree. Why don't the two of you go down there and bring them upstairs. You can begin decorating the tree, if you like. I'm a bit tired right now but I can help tomorrow after I finish baking the pies for Jess and her dad. I'm going to bed now but I will help you out in the morning. Goodnight, and I love you both very much!"

Bri and I gave our mom a kiss on the cheek and told her to get some rest.

Hearing about the two boxes in the basement with Christmas decorations, Bri and I looked at each other and made a beeline down to the basement to find those two green and red boxes that our mom talked about. At first we had difficulty locating the two boxes, but then Bri called out "Abby, there they are underneath another box!" When we found the two boxes we began to giggle, treating our "discovery" as if we found a hidden treasure of gold. Actually, to us it was even better than gold. We dusted off the two boxes and carefully brought them upstairs. We both paused a bit before we opened the boxes. To our delight, in the boxes were many old fashion decorations and Christmas bulbs.

"Bri, now I remember these decorations. I was really young at the time but I do remember seeing them spread out on the living room floor. I can't remember seeing a tree in the room though."

"Abby, my guess is that our dad was going to buy a tree but first wanted to make sure he had enough decorations. Dad left us right before Christmas day that year. I'm not even sure if he ever bought a tree since at that time he drank heavily. I always wondered what happened to these decorations."

"Bri, how wonderful that these are mom's actual Christmas decorations! Let's not think about the past. Why don't we decorate the tree ourselves as a surprise to mom."

"Great idea Abby."

Brianna and I were like two kids in a candy shop as we treated each bulb with extra care. We had so much fun decorating our very own tree with all the bulbs, lights, and garland in the two boxes. We even found an angel for the top of the tree. Once we finished trimming the tree, we plugged in the lights and we both stepped back in awe of our very own Christmas tree.

"Bri, this tree is beautiful. I can't wait for mom to see it tomorrow!"

"I know, isn't it gorgeous? Abby, don't forget to bring the two pies over to the Darcey house tomorrow."

"I won't forget. Did you know it was Jessie's idea to convince her dad to get this tree for us?"

"No, I didn't know that but I'm not surprised. You are so lucky to have a best friend like Jess!"

The next day I brought over the two pies my mom baked to the Darcey home. When I gave them the pies Mr. Darcey and Jess were thrilled at seeing the two homemade pies that were still warm since they came right out of the oven. Mr. Darcey asked me to thank my mom for her thoughtfulness.

"You know Abby," Mr. Darcey added, "I have an idea. If you, Brianna and your mom are not going anywhere for Christmas, Jess and I would love to have you join us for Christmas dinner at our house. I'll be making a baked lasagna and carving a turkey."

"I would love that Mr. Darcey! I will ask my mom and Bri. I'm certain that they both will be very happy to come over for dinner. That is very thoughtful of you both, thank you."

My mom, Brianna and myself did have dinner at the Darcey home that Christmas day. Mom brought with her two homemade pies. Mr. Darcey had a huge smile on his face as he was handed the two pies.

"Oh boy," exclaimed Mr. Darcey, "what do we have here? We're in for a real treat after our dinner. These pies are still warm. I can't wait for dessert! A very Merry Christmas to you! Here, let me take your coats and please make yourselves comfortable."

It was so wonderful for me to see my mom enjoying her meal and being so comfortable talking to Mr. Darcey and Jess. Mom opened up about the wonderful Christmas dinners she had with our dad when they first got married. My mother's face lit up when she was sharing her fond memories of those days. I hadn't seen my mom smiling like that for a very long time. I was also so happy to see how comfortable Bri was talking to Mr. Darcey.

After our dinner, Jess invited me into their den to sit and chat. In her hands was a box wrapped in shiny Christmas paper.

"Abby, I think you will like this gift. I bought it in the shop at the Christmas tree farm that we were at."

I unwrapped the present and got so excited when I saw the gift that Jess bought me. It was a Christmas globe showing two girls playing in the snow in front of a Christmas tree. When I shook the globe, snow fell down on the two children. All I could do was giggle and shake the globe again.

"Jess, this is something that I will always treasure. It reminds me so much of that magical day when you helped me pick out my tree. Jess, I feel so blessed to have you as my best friend!"

"Abby, I feel the same way."

"Jess, I don't have a gift to—"

"Abby, having the three of you join us today is our Christmas gift! And, your mom's two delicious homemade pies really made our dinner special.

"Merry Christmas Abby."

"Merry Christmas Jess."

***

After all these years, I still put that snow globe that Jess gave me out on my living room table during Christmas time.

Shaking the globe I see the snow falling down on the two young girls in the globe as they play in front of their Christmas tree. I close my eyes and think of that magical Christmas and think of my best friend Jessie.

I thank God every day that I was blessed to have Jess in my life.

12

EDDIE'S BURGER JOINT

We all laughed at Smitty's antics. All of us except one person—Jessie.

The favorite after school burger joint for many kids who attended Bridgeport High School was Eddie's Best Burgers in Bridgeport. We all thought that was a funny name for this local restaurant since the owner was not named Eddie and since his hamburgers were far from the best. In fact, the burgers were rather terrible. But all the kids from our school would hang out at Eddie's, mainly because it was a convenient place for us to get together after school to discuss our current crisis situation of the day, such as who was dating who or who broke up with who.

The owner—Smitty—stood six feet two, with a muscular built, dark brown hair, and a gruff but kind voice. He had so many amazing and funny stories to share with us, which we loved. Smitty was a former minor league baseball pitcher who was destined for stardom in the big leagues. However, he never made it to the majors.

Smitty's sidekick was a guy by the name of Eddie "EJ" Johnsten. Eddie was a slender, 6'1" individual with short brown hair and long sideburns. He often wore shorts, sometimes even in the dead of winter. Outwardly, he presented himself in a self-assured, fun-loving manner. However, the premature graying around his temples and the wrinkles on his face seemed to tell a different story. EJ was formerly a pitcher for the Stratford Cardinals fast-pitch softball team. The Cardinals were considered the best men's softball team on the East Coast. Eddie was an above average pitcher and a good hitter. But the sport he really excelled in was basketball, specifically high school basketball. He was an exceptional basketball guard for the Stratford High Blue Devils. On the court, EJ possessed outstanding leadership and decision-making skills. Recognizing his leadership abilities, his coaches named him team captain in his high school junior and senior years. Some of his teammates thought of him as a quasi-coach, seeking his advice when the coaches were not available. EJ was offered scholarships from local colleges in Connecticut. However, he decided to forego higher education and concentrate on his full-time job as foreman at a factory in Stratford.

Eddie attended a number of Smitty's minor league games whenever Smitty's team played in the New England area. The two became good friends and would hang out at local bars after Smitty's games. They were both divorced so they would often stay in the bars until closing. He and Smitty traded stories about their careers in sports and life in general. Smitty told us that after one too many drinks they both felt that they solved all the problems in the world.

When Smitty was released from baseball, he decided to open up his own restaurant. Initially, he was planning to call his burger joint Smitty's Restaurant. However, his plan changed after losing a high stakes card game with EJ. Smitty once told us the story of how Smitty's Restaurant turned into Eddie's Best Burgers.

"After repeatedly losing to Eddie at cards for several days straight, I became desperate to recoup my losses, which were substantial. I stupidly put my entire investments on the line for one card game with Eddie. I knew it was a major risk, but I just felt my luck was bound to change. Wrong! EJ asked if I was sure and I responded 'Yep'. EJ was a shrewd and experienced card player. But like I said I was desperate to win back my losses. I mean, I was bound to win one game, right? Well, I was wrong. EJ won our high stakes game and took me to the cleaners. I now owed him a great deal of money.

"EJ thought it would be fun to have a restaurant named after him. Eddie offered to waive all the money I owed him if I agreed to name this place Eddie's Best Burgers instead of Smitty's Restaurant. After a few beers, I agreed with EJ's offer. We shook hands and then we ordered another round of beers—EJ's treat. So that's how this joint became known as Eddie's Best Burgers. It was a stupid wager on my part." Laughing in his familiar gruff voice, Smitty continued, "But it sure wasn't the only stupid decision I made in life! Hey, you win some and you lose some, right?"

After being laid off at the factory, Eddie accepted a part-time job at Smitty's new restaurant. Actually, Smitty offered him a full-time job but Eddie liked spending time at various casinos in and around Connecticut.

EJ would often sit down at our booth when we met at Eddie's. Like Smitty, EJ was a real character and would entertain us with an abundance of funny stories about his career both in basketball and softball. In our private discussions, Jess and I felt that there was more to Eddie than his happy-go-lucky nature, but our fondness of him prevented us from asking any personal questions.

On one occasion, EJ was in a pensive mood and confided in Jessie and me about some of his struggles growing up in Stratford. It was a slow day at Eddie's so he said he had time to talk to us. Besides, EJ said he needed a break from being in the kitchen, especially when Smitty began telling his "tall tales", which EJ knew were only half-true.

"Growing up, my family was very poor. My old man wasn't around very much and even when he was at home he didn't pay much attention to me and my kid brother. He drank a lot and was fired from one job after another. My mom had a low-paying secretary job, so I felt I needed to continue working full-time at the factory so our family could make ends meet.

"My brother and I played sandlot softball for a number of local teams. A few of the teams played fast-pitch softball and it was there that I became a pretty good pitcher. One of the kids suggested that I try out for the Stratford Cardinals and I made the team at 17 years old. But the sport I really loved playing was basketball. I remember that there were times in the winter when my friends and I would actually shovel snow off the outside court to play some games. In the summer months, whenever I wasn't working or playing softball, we would rent out a public school gym and play basketball until late at night. Playing sports helped straighten me out a bit, but I still wasn't happy with my life.

"After two failed marriages, I ended up having a gambling problem. Both divorces were my fault and I knew I wasn't great to be around. And I drank too much. Funny thing is, when I was on the basketball court or on the pitcher's mound, I had all the confidence in the world. It was a different story when I was not playing sports.

"I still like to play cards at the casinos but I somehow managed to lick that awful urge to gamble my life savings. Having Smitty as a friend really helped because he would always lift me up whenever I felt a bit down and out.

"I'm not sure why I'm spilling my guts out like this and I'm sorry for bumming you girls out. I guess I just wanted to tell you what a great guy Smitty is. Of course, you probably already knew that. I—"

Just then, Jess interrupted him saying, "EJ, have you ever thought about coaching high school basketball?"

"Nah, I don't think I got anything to offer those kids. I played a long time ago, so they wouldn't be able to relate to anything I tell them. I do go to some of the boys' games at Stratford High. And, of course, I try to watch you play on the Bridgeport girls' team. But coaching…I don't think so. I ain't got what it takes for that."

Jess chimed in, "EJ, I disagree. Smitty told me all about your accomplishments in basketball. You have a lot to offer kids and they can really benefit from your experience and how you played the game. I know you can do a great job of coaching and know that you'll enjoy being around the kids. They drive us girls crazy sometimes but they're basically good kids. And they have a lot of potential.

"I asked you about coaching," said Jess, "because I heard that the assistant coach of our boys' basketball team is leaving. Why don't you apply for the assistant coach position?"

"Nah, don't think so Jess."

"Well, I'm always talking to the coaches on the boys' team," explained Jess. "How about if I put in a good word for you? Or at least make them aware of your high school basketball accomplishments."

I added, "EJ, I know for a fact that both the boys' and girls' coaches have a great deal of respect for Jessie and listen to her all the time. She is someone that can really go to bat for you. Jessie has a lot of faith in you. How about giving it some consideration?"

"Well Jess, if you think I'm capable of coaching I would consider it. But I don't think it will happen. And, anyway, I'm sure they have someone else in mind to fill that position."

"Well," responded Jess, "let's see what happens. No guarantees."

EJ smiled and said, "Right, no guarantees. Hey, I better get back to the kitchen or the boss may fire me. Always a pleasure talking to you girls." Smiling, EJ said, "Let me see what foods Smitty's destroying back there."

***

Several weeks later, at one of our get-togethers at Eddie's, a smiling EJ came over to our booth and sat down. With a huge grin he turned to Jessie and said, "Jess, guess what? I received a call from the boys' head coach and he offered me the assistant coach position! I know you were the main reason for his decision so I want to thank you. You're amazing! I promise I'll do my best with these kids and won't let you down."

After he left the table, I looked at Jess and remarked, "EJ's right, you are amazing. Once again you made a difference in someone's life. I'm not sure how you do it but you're remarkable!"

"Thanks, Abby," replied an embarrassed Jessie, "Ok, let's order something to eat." Laughing, Jessie asked, "Should we order our usual?"

***

Jane, Jess and I met at Eddie's several days later. When Smitty saw us he sat down at our booth. He was delighted to hear that things were going well in high school for the three of us. During our discussion, Smitty shared with us the reason that he was released by his team. Smitty explained that he had one major flaw which prevented him from achieving his goal of making it to the big leagues.

Smitty was an outstanding strikeout pitcher with a notable strikeout record. However, as he explained, when a ball was hit directly to him, Smitty began having difficulty tossing the ball to the first baseman, especially on simple plays when he had a lot of time to throw the ball to first. By his own admission, this was a play that should have been very simple and which all other pitchers found so easy to make. It got to the point where many times Smitty would actually throw the ball over the first basemen's head and into the stands! His opponents began to take advantage of this flaw by bunting the ball in Smitty's direction for what would inevitably mean that they would be safe at first base.

Neither he nor his manager understood why this was happening. But because this mistake happened so frequently, it eventually would cost the team to lose a few games. Knowing this would just continue, the team had no choice but to release Smitty. Thus ended his promising baseball career and his goal of making the Major Leagues.

Smitty seemed to take his release from the minors in stride. He made us all laugh by demonstrating his flaw of throwing the ball to first base. He asked EJ to pretend he was a first baseman. Of course, EJ hammed his role up and stood with his left arm and leg outstretched waiting for Smitty's throw to first base

"Ok, girls, this is how I would throw to first. Ready EJ?"

Smitty proceeded to toss a crumbled paper cup over EJ's head and over all of us, with the paper cup landing on the other end of the room. We all laughed at Smitty's antics. All of us except one person—Jessie.

While Smitty was telling his story I looked over to Jess who was leaning forward in her chair, listening intently to Smitty's detailed description. Her face was expressionless. At the time, I didn't ask Jess why she didn't see the humor in Smitty's tale, thinking that Jess just didn't find it amusing for some reason. I didn't think anything of that but, in time, I would find out why she took this so seriously.

I decided to change the subject and updated Jess on the glee club that Jane and I participated in. Coming out of her trance, I noticed that her eyes had filled up with tears. I figured I'd ask her later about this. But then, Jess smiled and told me that she thought it was so wonderful that Jane and I shared this common bond. So I just thought Jess had momentarily thought about something at home or with her boyfriend. I was encouraged when I saw that ingratiating smile of hers.

Jane also noticed that something seemed to be bothering Jessie but figured Jess would confide in us if there was a problem. To liven things up, Jane decided to give Jess a laugh.

"Hey Jess," said Jane, "Miss Gleason told me she has room for one more student in her glee club. How about you joining Abby and me in the club?"

"You have to be kidding," responded an amused Jessie, "I am the world's worst singer. I have a terrible singing voice! I think Miss Gleason would kick me out of the glee club after she heard me sing one note!"

Jane knew that would perk Jessie up and figured Jess was just temporarily lost in thought when Smitty was going through his baseball antics.

***

The three of us got together at Eddie's sometimes after school but mostly on Saturdays. On one occasion, just as Smitty delivered lunch to our booth, we heard a loud bang. We quickly turned around and saw that one of the boys at another table had collapsed on the floor. He was holding his throat and had difficulty breathing. Without hesitation, Jess jumped out of her seat, ran over to the boy and began administering CPR. At the same time, Smitty came running over and said he called 911. After several frantic attempts pushing down on the boy's chest, Jessie managed to dislodge an item from the boys throat and the boy began breathing on his own. One of the other boys informed us that the boy—William—was laughing while eating a hot dog and then he collapsed on the floor.

The ambulance arrived shortly after Smitty's call. The EMT congratulated Jess for her quick action and said it was a "life saver." The EMT told Smitty that the boy appeared to be fine but just to be cautious they were bringing him into the hospital for evaluation. Smitty told the ambulance driver that he would call the boy's parents and would tell them what had happened and that he assumed all charges.

As she walked back to our table, Jess received a round of applause from the other customers there.

"Jess, that was terrific!," remarked Jane. "I guess those first aid courses we were forced to take really paid off!"

"Thanks Jane, but I was just glad to help out. Any one of us could have done the same thing. I just happened to be there first."

As a way of congratulating Jess, Smitty walked over and put down another plate with a hamburger and fries.

"This is on the house, I'm sure the customer won't mind me giving this to you. It's the least I can do to say thanks!"

"Why, thank you Smitty," a smiling Jess responded. "That's very thoughtful of you!"

Jane and I covered our faces and did all we could not to laugh when we saw the two plates in front of Jessie.

"Great," an amused Jess said, "now what am I supposed to do with *two* burnt hamburgers?" The three of us burst out in laughter. EJ, hearing us laughing had an amused grin on his face and winked at us with a knowing smile.

We then picked up our conversation where we left off before the incident.

***

Returning from the school's Christmas vacation, Bridgeport High faced a very good Ridgefield basketball team. The first quarter of the game was close with Ridgefield clinging to a one-point lead. Beginning in the second quarter, however, Jessie found her shooting range and began to score at will. The game became a blowout by Bridgeport, with Jessie scoring forty-two points along with twelve assists.

Bridgeport High continued its winning ways and the team was undefeated with a record of 17-0. Each game was played before a jubilant, sold-out crowd.

However, for their next game, Jessie came down with the flu. Mr. Darcey suggested to Jessie that she should probably sit this one out. Knowing his daughter so well, he was not sure she would heed his advice. Sure enough, Jessie responded that she would like to at least give it a try since she didn't want to let her teammates down.

"Jess, you certainly are a chip off the old block! Just don't push yourself, for your own good and the good of the team."

Jessie gallantly tried to play in the game. Seeing Jessie before the game, it was obvious to me that she was not feeling well. Her face was pale and she walked in an unusually slow pace. I tried to talk her out of playing, but to no avail. Not wanting to disappoint her teammates, she told her coach it was only a cold and maybe she can work it off during the game. But that was not meant to be. After several minutes she had to take herself out of the game, feeling very lethargic. Both Mr. Darcey and I were relieved to see this since we were more concerned about Jess's health than this particular game.

Coach Nichols, sensing that Jessie had more than a cold, applauded her efforts but asked Jessie, if it should happen again, to please be more upfront with her so she can factor that in. Jessie promised she would. At the coach's encouragement, she left to go home before halftime.

Without Jess on the court, the team struggled offensively and lost to their opponents 74—67. The team's defense managed to keep the game close for most of the time but fell behind in the final quarter. This was a game they were supposed to win, especially since their opponents had a losing record.

If Jess was in the locker room after the game she certainly would have agreed with what the coach had to say to all her players. Coach Nichols told the team that they should treat this game as a lesson for future games. The lesson that the coach tried to convey to the team was that they cannot rely on Jessie to always have a good game and they needed to step up whether or not Jessie was on the court.

Having fully recovered from her bout with the flu, Jessie was back to her old self for the next game. She put on an outstanding scoring and ball handling performance, leading Bridgeport High to an easy 76—40 win.

Jessie's coach and all her teammates were relieved to have Jess back playing at full strength.

***

There was no doubt in anyone's mind that Jess was the freshman team's standout, leading the squad in points, assists, and foul shooting. It wasn't long until Bridgeport High's varsity coaches began to attend the freshman games to get a close look at Jessie.

During the team's practice session in preparation for the final game of the season, Jane injured her right shoulder. The injury occurred when Jane and another player bumped into each other as they collided in an attempt to retrieve a loose ball. Coach Nichols sat Jane down for the remainder of the practice session. Prior to the team's final game of the season, the coach observed Jane rubbing her shoulder during warm ups. Seeing this, Coach Nichols chose to sit Jane down for the entire game. Jane pleaded with the coach saying her shoulder felt better but the coach overruled her objection fearing that Jane might reinjure her shoulder.

In the final game of the season, the Bridgeport freshman team lost to a very potent Fairfield High team despite Jessie's amazing 44 point output. Jane's leadership skills were greatly missed. The game was a nail biter throughout, with Fairfield High squeaking out a 68—67 victory.

The freshman team ended up with an 18-2 record. Once the season ended, Coach Nichols congratulated the team on an outstanding season and encouraged the players to look upon their two losses as a learning experience to build on. The coach expressed confidence that this team was destined to be a major powerhouse in the next couple of years.

The Most Valuable Player Award for Bridgeport High's freshman team was given to Jessie Darcey. A fully recovered Jane Kenny received the Best Defensive Player Award that year.

***

Once the basketball season ended, several members of the team approached Smitty and asked him if it was possible to have a party at Eddie's burger joint. All the team members, their boyfriends, and coaches would be invited. Smitty graciously agreed and refused to accept payment to rent out his restaurant. Smitty actually closed down Eddie's to the public for the team to have their party. I was honored to receive an invitation to the party. The note in my invitation read, "Abby, you are invited to our party because of all the support you have shown us during the entire season. We feel you are a valuable member of our team."

Eddie's Best Burgers had a great 1950s jukebox which played many wonderful records. This is another reason why all the kids liked to hang out at Eddie's. Smitty even had music "wall boxes" mounted at each booth so kids could drop in their coins and play their favorite tunes while sitting at their booth.

We had a total blast at this party and even danced to some of the tunes played on the jukebox. While I was sitting at one of the tables with Jane and Jess along with our boyfriends, one of the team members stood up and announced, "The Bridgeport High freshmen girls' team would like to play a special song to honor our tremendous season. It's a song that has a special meaning to all of us." As soon as she finished I heard some very familiar opening notes to the song and then Jane immediately turned to me and said, "Oh my Lord Abby, that's our song!" Sure enough, the tune that was selected to honor the basketball season was none other than *Frankie, My Love*. To make matters worse, all the team members stood up and sang along to our song. The expression on Jane's face was priceless. Jane and I both laughed and finally, an embarrassed Jane put her head on the table with both of her hands covering her head and ears. Once the song ended, Jess yelled out, "The Sweet Dreams live on!". Even though Jane and I were embarrassed beyond words we both were very touched by this funny yet thoughtful gesture.

13

BIRDIE RETURNS

Without warning, Birdie ran over and pushed Jane into the front row of the stands saying, "Take that Miss Sunshine!"

Jessie and Jane easily made the varsity squad in our sophomore year. They were both selected as Bridgeport High's starting guards. Jess continued to impress her coaches as well as her growing legion of fans. They all saw ball handling and shooting by Jess that they had never seen before by anyone else.

Jessie welcomed the challenge of playing against the most powerful teams in Connecticut. And she relished the idea of outscoring older female players who were thought to be the best in the state.

As her overall play continued to improve there didn't seem to be any limits on what Jessie could accomplish on the basketball court. Once the word got around about Jess, coaches from area teams frequently attended Bridgeport High's games mainly to see Jessie. I couldn't help but think how much they wished Jess was playing on their team.

It seemed inevitable that Jess would match up again against Birdie Lincoln. This time it was in a regular season game against Wilbur Cross High School. Birdie was now in her junior year. While she did well as a freshman and sophomore for the Wilbur Cross Governors, Birdie fell short of her coaches expectations. Early on in her freshman year, Birdie's coaches were extremely impressed with her performance in her first few games. Her coaches were convinced that she would live up to her nickname "Blazin' Birdie" and felt she was on her way to becoming the greatest high school freshman in the country. When speaking with local media, her coaches were very enthusiastic and predicted that Birdie would become a high school and college basketball superstar. But, for whatever reason, Birdie's performance on the basketball court gradually diminished. She ended up with a 14 point scoring average for the year, much lower than what her coaches and the media had predicted. Her sophomore scoring average was a bit lower at 12 points per game. For some players a scoring average like Birdie's would be very welcomed. However, given all the hoopla surrounding Birdie after she played her first couple of games, her fans and the media alike were unimpressed by her overall performance. Also of concern for her coaches was Birdie's tendency to commit fouls, having fouled out very early in a number of games. Despite her coach's advice and encouragement, her bad temper had a negative impact on her basketball performance and on her team.

Bridgeport High had a 16-2 record going into the game against Wilbur Cross, with Bridgeport High as the home team. The Wilbur Cross Governors' record stood at ten wins and eight losses. Fred Owens was also in his junior year at Wilbur Cross. Fred never forgot about Birdie's dismal performance two years prior against twelve-year-old Jessie during their "horse" contest. Fred continued to be a big fan of the Wilbur Cross women's team. However, his dislike of Birdie grew even greater during the previous two years. Because of this, Fred took great delight in telling his friends at Bridgeport High about Jessie's total domination against Birdie and how nasty Birdie was during that entire "horse" contest. Because of this, the word about Birdie spread around Bridgeport High like wildfire. When Birdie walked onto the court she was greeted by boos from the Bridgeport High fans. Birdie's response was waving her hands in a taunting manner at all the Bridgeport fans.

Birdie was assigned the task of guarding Jessie, who was her opposing guard. As the players took their position in the middle of the court for jump ball, Birdie looked at Jess who was standing next to her. After Birdie looked Jess up and down, she said out loud, "Well, if it ain't Miss Phenom! Are you ready to take a beaten' from 'Blazin' Birdie?" Jessie did not react to this comment which must have irked Birdie because she began her trash talk even before the game began. Ignoring these unpleasant comments, Jess looked over to me and quickly shrugged her shoulders, out of Birdie's view. The gesture by Jess told me all I needed to know—Birdie's trash talk had begun.

The opening tip-off went to Bridgeport High and Jane immediately took charge of directing her teammates. Jane's pass to Jess was sharp, as usual. Standing a bit beyond the foul line Jess shot a jumper with Birdie nearly hanging on her. Jess's shot hit nothing but net. This brought a loud cheer from the Bridgeport faithful.

Jess easily made her next three shots with Birdie desperately trying to defend her. However, in Jessie's next shot attempt, she was deliberately pushed by Birdie resulting in a technical foul and a stern warning from the referee. This caused Jess to limp a bit. As the coach began to walk over to Jess, she was waved off by a smiling Jess.

At half time, Bridgeport had a commanding 20-point lead. I decided to sit next to Mr. Darcey who was sitting in his usual place in the stands. I had to squeeze in tightly since the stands were packed. Mr. Darcey moved over as best he could and gave me a polite smile. However, he had a concerned look on his face. Birdie's trash talking was obvious to everyone so I didn't have to tell Mr. Darcey that her bad mouthing of Jess would only continue in the second half. What was of concern to both of us was the uncertainty of what Birdie was capable of if her frustration continued. We were both relieved when we saw that Jessie was not hurt after being pushed, but we were apprehensive that Birdie's frustration could escalate. Mr. Darcey turned to me and said in a low voice, "I'm so proud of Jessie and how she totally ignored that girl's antics."

The second half started the same way that the first half ended. Jessie easily maneuvered away from her defenders and scored from different areas on the court. By this time the Wilbur High coach had assigned two players to defend Jess, while the Bridgeport fans began their familiar chants "Jessie, Jessie, Jessie." This, I felt, must have humiliated Birdie even more.

Frustrated by Jessie's ability to easily move around her, Birdie fouled Jess two more times, talking trash all the time. Despite being double teamed, Jessie continued to score at will and her point total increased.

As the final quarter began, Birdie managed to score ten points, making only five shots in her eighteen attempts. On the other hand, Jessie's point total steadily increased as Bridgeport High began to further widen its lead. All along, Birdie continued bad-mouthing Jessie in a futile attempt to intimidate Jess. Birdie also committed three fouls. It was very obvious to Mr. Darcey and myself that Birdie's frustration grew even stronger.

After a time out, Jane was ready to take the ball out on the right side of the court and ready to call the next play for her teammates. Without warning, Birdie ran over and pushed Jane into the front row of the stands shouting, "Take that Miss Sunshine!". With Jane still wedged in the stands,

Birdie attempted to punch Jane. Jess immediately ran over and pushed Birdie away with one hand while attempting to free Jane from the stands.

Both refs ran over to hold Birdie back and charged her with a flagrant foul. All the team members stood up ready to defend Jane. Likewise, several boys ran down from the stands to protect the Bridgeport players. The Wilbur Cross coach and several Cross teammates immediately ran over and grabbed Birdie. Once Birdie was subdued, the Cross coach consulted with the referees and agreed with their decision to remove Birdie from the game. Five opponent players surrounded Birdie, preventing her from moving forward. However, her trash talking continued as she defiantly threw her towel onto the court. The boos from the stands were deafening.

Jane managed to get up but began limping. Jessie and another teammate had their arms around Jane to help her walk back to the team, with the crowd cheering when they saw Jane get up from the stands. All the while Jane was grabbing her right knee in obvious pain from colliding against the stands.

As a precautionary measure, the referees walked over to both benches to warn both teams against any further altercations. Seeing that Birdie was being held back by her players, the Cross coach walked over to Coach Nichols for a long discussion. At the end of their discussion, Coach Nichols shook her opponent coach's hand in anticipation of resuming the game. Coach Nichols walked over to console Jane who was sitting on the bench while a school nurse worked on her knee.

With the outcome of the game no longer in doubt and as a precaution, Coach Nichols signaled to her five reserve players to enter the game to replace the starting five. Coach Nichols looked over to her opponents' bench and saw that their coach also removed her starting players. She also noticed that their coach had several of her starting players escort Birdie to the locker room to ensure that no further incidents occurred. This brought another chorus of boos from the crowd.

The game ended in a blowout with Bridgeport High winning by 30 points. Jess was the game's high scorer and Jane was outstanding on defense, as usual.

Leaving the locker room after the game, Jess walked over to me and Mr. Darcey and shook her head.

"I can't tell you how relieved I am that this game is over. I didn't know what that girl was up to. This was one game I didn't enjoy from start to finish."

Mr. Darcey told Jess how proud he was that she took the high road and totally ignored "that Birdie girl." Jess just smiled and gave us both a hug. Mr. Darcey asked Jess how Jane was doing.

"Fortunately, Jane's knee is okay. She only suffered a minor abrasion and appears to be walking better on her own. The nurse bandaged her knee but Jane won't require any additional treatment. I'm so relieved because it could have been a lot worse."

Moments later, Jane walked out of the locker room. She was limping a bit but not as noticeable as before. Many of the Bridgeport faithful stayed after the game and gave Jane a rousing applause as they saw her walking towards us. Jane smiled and gave the fans a quick wave and a thumbs up gesture.

As she approached us, Jane said, "Jess, thank you again for rescuing me and helping me walk back to our bench. If you didn't stop her, she would have begun punching me and I was in no position to defend myself. You saved me from getting really hurt.

"I have to say, that girl has some serious issues. Fortunately, we don't have to play against them again this year. From what I hear there is a strong possibility that she will not be allowed to play again this year or next. She may even be suspended from school but that is just speculation. As much as I love playing basketball, I was so relieved when this game was over."

To our surprise, the Wilbur Cross coach walked over to Jess and Jane. She said she wanted to apologize for the actions by one of her players. She didn't mention a name—she didn't have to. She said that she had a long discussion with Coach Nichols and wanted Coach Nichols to know that Wilbur Cross High School does not, in any way, condone such behavior. The coach told us that she would talk to the school administrators, and as far as she is concerned this was the last game which that player would be involved in.

We all felt it was a very classy thing for the opponent's coach to come over to apologize to us. Jane and Jess assured the coach that there were no hard feelings and thanked her for such a professional gesture.

A relieved Mr. Dacey said, "Well, the main thing is that both of you are okay. Yeh, that was a weird game for sure. Ok, let's put this all behind us and go get a bite to eat, my treat!

Leaving the gym I thought how proud I was of Jessie and Jane and how they both kept their poise throughout the game. It seemed to me that not many people can keep their cool like that under those circumstances.

Jessie continued to amaze me knowing she risked her own safety to help someone in need.

***

The girls' high school basketball team did very well during our sophomore year, with Jessie as the team's leading scorer. The team compiled an 18-2 record and finished fourth in the state tournament that year. The coach congratulated all members of her team for their efforts and praised them for the progress they made throughout their sophomore basketball season.

Leaving the team meeting, Jane gave Jess and me an update on Birdie Lincoln.

"I bumped into one of the players on the Wilbur Cross basketball team. She informed me that Birdie quit school and moved to Georgia with her family."

"Well," said a relieved Jess, "I can't say that I'm unhappy hearing about this. Actually, I'm relieved as I know both of you are also. I have no hard feelings about Birdie and I wish her well. But I do wish she would get help with her anger issues."

"Jess," responded Jane, "you took the words right out of my mouth! I think it's even a relief for all the other Wilbur Cross players and especially their coach!"

***

Jane, Jess, and I hung out quite a bit during our sophomore year in high school. Sometimes we would meet and spend hours at Eddie's, just talking and laughing.

Aside from hanging out at Eddie's, we would go to different places with our dates. When possible, Brianna would drive us to places out of town, which we appreciated.

The three of us tried our luck at duckpin bowling with our dates. Jessie showed her natural athleticism by outscoring both the girls and the boys. Even though she had no experience in bowling, she found it an easy sport to excel in. We also tried indoor ice skating at Waterbury's Fulton Park. Jane and I barely managed to stay on our skates, while Jessie was teaching herself how to skate backwards. Jane and I were convinced that Jess was a gifted athlete who managed to excel in every sport she attempted.

***

At one of our high school parties, Jess asked the star player on the boys' basketball team how he liked playing for EJ as their assistant coach.

"EJ's terrific! We learned a great deal from him throughout the year. All my teammates agree that EJ was a great addition and we look forward to learning even more next season. He certainly has a great basketball background that we can relate to. And, man, does he have a lot of stories to tell! He always has us in stitches with those funny stories, which keeps us loose all the time."

Jess simply replied, "Yep, that's our EJ!"

14

STABBING INCIDENT

After being pushed to the ground, the boy got up and stabbed the other boy in the chest, and then ran away.

Despite giving Jessie some valuable life lessons, Mike Darcey could not shield his daughter from some of the violence that seemed to permeate throughout many of the state's inner city high schools. I agreed with Mike and Jessie's belief that by staying in the upper levels in high school we would avoid many of the problems that existed in the school's lower levels. But Jess and I knew that not all kids at the high school's lower levels were troublemakers, since we were both on friendly terms with many of the girls at that level. Most of them were good kids that we enjoyed being around. But we had to admit that some kids did have violent tendencies. Like other schools in Connecticut's large cities, Bridgeport had its share of violent activities despite the best efforts of the school.

On one April afternoon, Jessie and I witnessed an argument between two boys in the school hallway. One of the boys—Emery—was a classmate of ours. We didn't recognize the other boy. Thinking it was just the usual pushing argument that seemed like a daily occurrence at the school, we just shook our heads and began to walk away. But then things quickly took a different turn which made us turn around and hurry back. We saw the boy we didn't recognize take a knife out of his pocket and threaten Emery with the knife. Jessie grabbed Emery's arm, hoping to pull him away from the boy with the knife, but she lost her grip when the other boy pulled him back. This is when we saw Emery being stabbed in the chest right in front of us and we saw the assailant quickly run out of the school.

Jessie immediately took off her jacket and put it on Emery's bloody body. She was also the first to call out for help from the teachers, while at the same time trying to comfort Emery that he will be alright. The rest of us stood around totally stunned. All Emery could manage to say to Jess was, "Thank you." The EMTs came immediately, responding to the teacher's 911 call. We later found out that, fortunately, the knife missed Emery's heart and that he would be able to fully recover from the incident.

Witnessing this incident at a young age left a lasting impression on both Jessie and myself. We made every effort to try to put this experience out of our minds but it was inevitable that one of us would bring up how scared we both were, witnessing such a senseless stabbing incident. We both recalled the angry look on the face of the boy with the knife. But we knew that violence seemed to be occurring in other schools and in other cities. Agreeing that there was very little that we could do about it, we would change the subject and turn to happier topics, usually about boys that we were both attracted to in school.

A few days later, in the middle of his English class, Mr. Goode heard a knock on the door. As he walked over and opened the door, Jess and I noticed he was greeted by two policemen. Mr. Goode kept the policemen in the hall after closing the classroom door behind him. After nearly 10 minutes, Mr. Goode re-entered the classroom and instructed our entire class to silently read the next three chapters in our English books. He then walked back out to the hallway and was seen walking with the policemen to another area of the school.

Fifteen minutes later, Mr. Goode opened the classroom door and motioned to Jess and me to go out to the hallway. As Jess and I got up from our seats, we heard a lot of commotion and questions from our fellow classmates. In response, both Jess and I turned around and shrugged our shoulders to demonstrate that we had no clue why Mr. Goode had summoned us.

As we walked out to the hallway, Mr. Goode asked if we would meet with the two police officers who were in the principal's office. He assured us that there was nothing for us to be concerned with saying, "The two police officers who are in the principal's office would like to ask what you observed during the stabbing that occurred in the school hallway. The principal wanted me to inform you that you both are not required to talk with the officers if you feel uncomfortable doing so. The principal will be with you during the entire time."

I looked over at Jess and she said, "Mr. Goode, I have no problem talking to the two policemen." Jess turned to me and I said, "I agree." With that, the three of us walked to the principal's office.

Once we entered his office, Principal Rodrigues stood up and smiled at both of us saying, "Jessie and Abby, this is Lieutenant Jansen and Sargent Walker of the Bridgeport police department. They would like to ask you a few questions about the stabbing incident that occurred in our school that apparently you both witnessed. I want to make it very clear that neither of you are obligated to answer any of their questions and it will in no way affect your educational status." We both nodded our heads in agreement.

Lieutenant Jansen was an imposing individual, standing over six feet tall, shaved head, and a very serious no-nonsense facial expression. Sargent Walker appeared to be much younger with short brown hair and a kinder expression as he shook both our hands.

Looking at the two of us, Lieutenant Jansen spoke first. Turning to Jess first, he said, "Are you Jessie Darcey?"

Jessie responded, "Yes I am."

Turning to me he asked, "And are you Abby Girardi?" I replied, "Yes, that's me."

"Ok, thank you. Sargent Walker and I are here to investigate the stabbing incident that occurred in your school recently. We would like to hear from both of you as to exactly what you saw and remember from that incident. But first, I want to ask if either of you know the two boys involved in the altercation that resulted in the stabbing. Who wants to go first?"

Jessie raised her hand. "I'll go first if that's okay.

"One of the boys—Emery—is a schoolmate of ours. I have seen him in the hallways several times but I do not know him personally. I did not recognize the other boy."

Lieutenant Jansen looked at me and said, "How about you Abby, did you recognize the two boys?"

"Like Jess," I replied, "I recognized Emery as one of our classmates but do not know him personally. I have no idea who the other boy was. The rumor going around the school is that the boy with the knife does not even attend our high school, but I can't say for sure."

Lieutenant Jansen asked, "Ok, can you tell us in detail what exactly you witnessed the day of the stabbing incident?"

Jessie responded saying, "Well, Abby and I were walking down the hallway when we saw the two boys pushing each other. We didn't think much of it because it seems like almost a common occurrence that we see boys pushing each other, usually as a result of an argument over a girl. But those arguments usually end with someone breaking up the fight and nothing serious happens. However, this seemed to be something different because we saw the boy threaten Emery with a knife. Once we saw that, Abby and I turned around and walked back. I grabbed Emery's arm with the hope that I could pull him away from the boy with the knife. But I lost my grip on him when the other boy pulled him back. This is when we saw Emery being stabbed in the chest right in front of us and we saw the boy with the knife quickly run out of the school. We both will never forget the angry look on that boy's face before he stabbed Emery. It happened so fast that none of the teachers were able to come out to the hallway to see what was happening."

Sargent Walker asked, "I'm told that one of you girls put their coat over the body of the boy that was stabbed. Which one of you did that?"

I chimed in, "Jess, took immediate action to call out to her teachers for help and also put her own jacket on Emery's bloody body. Fortunately we hear that Emery has recovered from the stabbing."

"That's correct Abby. Ok, Jess, I want to ask you, what did Emery say once you put your jacket on his body?"

Jess responded to the lieutenant saying, "All Emery managed to say was 'Thank you'."

Jess asked the lieutenant, "Did you speak with Emery?"

"Yes, we did have a discussion with Emery, but he didn't have a lot to say. He told us that he doesn't know the individual that stabbed him. Emery said that he accidently bumped into the individual and that's when the pushing began. Other than that we were unable to get much information from him—at least not at this time."

I asked the two officers, "Has the boy who stabbed Emery been located?"

"No he has not been found as yet."

I added, "If it helps, we are told that he was possibly a member of a street gang called The Bloods. We can't say for sure if this is true or just a rumor.

"Yes, we have been informed of his possible involvement with that gang. In truth, we had not heard of this gang up to this point. We are in the process of finding out more about this gang and, hopefully, talk to one of its members, or perhaps one of the members of their rival gang."

Before leaving the room, Jess and I gave the two policemen a description of the boy who stabbed Emery.

As we walked out of the principal's office, Jess said to me, "Abby, I keep thinking how bold that kid was to try to kill Emery in public like that. I hope I'm wrong, but I can't help thinking that if he is not found soon he is bound to kill someone, with his knife or perhaps a gun!"

"I agree Jess. I pray that there are no other victims. But, like you, I think it may be inevitable that he will try to kill someone else. Hopefully, the police will find and punish him before that happens."

Before we returned to our classroom, Jessie stopped walking and said to me, "Abby, I have to confide in you about this crazy dream I had. Actually, it was a nightmare and I woke up in a cold sweat. In my nightmare I dreamt that in trying to pull Emery away I stepped in front of him. In that moment that kid with a knife stabbed *me* in the chest and ran away. That was the extent of the nightmare but it was enough to wake me up, for sure. Fortunately, that nightmare was only that one night. You're the only one I have mentioned this to since you're my best friend. Crazy, huh?"

"No it's not crazy at all Jess. You risked your life trying to pull Emery away from that kid with the knife. So it was bound to affect you more than me or any of the other kids. So it's completely normal that you would have a nightmare like that. I am glad that you only had that nightmare on one occasion. As we discussed previously that knifing incident was quite traumatic for us. I know myself that I think about that incident more than I would like. Hopefully, our description of that kid to the two policemen will help them apprehend that person. I pray that it does and I'm confident he will be apprehended.

"Jess, thank you for sharing this with me. But since that experience is over and the matter is in the hands of the police, let's move on and concentrate on more interesting and happier things—Like our plans once this school year is over. What do you say?"

"I totally agree Abby. Actually, I feel better just confiding in you about that nightmare. You are a true friend. I know I can share anything with you, good or bad. Well, time to move on to happier thoughts, like our summer plans. I'm so looking forward to our get-togethers with Jane and our boyfriends!

"But first, let's get back to Mr. "Notso" Goode's class. I'm sure he will enthrall us all with more boring stories of his family vacations."

Jess and I both laughed since we knew Mr. Goode had a tendency to deviate from the school lessons and share with us— in detail—about his most recent family vacation. While these were interesting experiences for him, our classmates would become bored out of their minds. Our summer vacation couldn't come soon enough for me and Jess!

***

Once school was out and the warmer weather was upon us, we found that Bridgeport's beautiful Beardsley Park was a great place to have a picnic. The three of us took our boyfriends at the time to Bridgeport's popular Beardsley Zoo. Of course, the boys started showing off, imitating monkeys and other animals that were housed there. We just ignored them and continued to talk to each other. We also spent a good deal of time swimming and sunbathing at Madison's Hammonasset Beach.

Jessie continued to work hard on perfecting her basketball skills during the summer. The outside basketball courts became her second home. Jane sometimes joined her and also worked on her basketball techniques.

Jessie loved the idea of playing against the older superstar boys on the outside basketball courts.

15

BRIDGEPORT HIGH'S JUNIOR PROM

As he stepped closer to Jess, Johnny D tripped and lost his balance

I made the cheerleading squad for the boys' basketball team during our junior year. Jess made a point to go to as many games as possible, mainly to watch me do my cheers during the games. Just as in elementary school, Jess was my biggest supporter and always complimented me on my cheerleading. Jane also attended some of the games and, like Jess, was very supportive, which I greatly appreciated.

I also did a lot of babysitting that year and contributed what I could to the household. Fortunately, our dad continued to send mom money for household expenses on a regular basis.

Along with her dedication to basketball and her studies, Jessie volunteered at Bridgeport's Royalty Theatre. Whenever possible, Jessie performed a variety of services at the theatre including box office, marketing, and helping out backstage during performances. She even provided valuable assistance to the directors of the productions held at the theatre. The theatre offered to pay Jess for her services, but she refused payment, saying this was her way of donating to the theatre and showing her love of the musical productions. The administrators at the theatre were very impressed with Jessie's unselfishness. Seeing how dedicated Jessie was in all her assignments, the owner of the theatre told Jessie that there would always be a job there for her after her schooling was finished.

Jess told me that she loved musical plays and wished she had the talent to perform in musicals, especially the famous ones. She convinced Jane and me to attend some of these musicals. We even managed to coax our boyfriends to join us as our dates. Judging by the boys' reaction, they didn't appear to share our love of the theatre.

***

We were each invited to our high school junior prom by our boyfriends at the time. Jess was invited by Johnny D, Carl invited me, and Jane was asked by one of our classmates Kevin Mangini. This, of course, meant shopping for the upcoming prom. We were on a mission to find the perfect gowns, no matter how many stores we needed to check. Even though the prom was still several months away, shopping for our gowns became a very high priority. We also made several not so subtle hints to our boyfriends to ensure that they not only wear a tuxedo but also remember to give each of us a corsage for the occasion.

On the night of the prom, Jane and I met at Jessie's house anxiously waiting for our dates to show up. We were not disappointed as our dates came through for us by showing up wearing a tuxedo and bringing us corsages. Jess was relieved when her boyfriend Johnny showed up wearing a tux. She had kept her fingers crossed, since Johnny had a way of forgetting important things like that. We figured their mothers played a role in purchasing the corsages, but we were all impressed, nevertheless.

We had a blast at our prom, dancing and sharing laughs the entire night. Once again, Brianna volunteered by assisting at the table with the baked goods and non-alcoholic punch. She made every effort to stay out of our way, which I so much appreciated.

After the prom, Brianna asked to take a photo of the three of us with our dates. The restaurant where our prom was held had a beautiful water fountain outside. So we decided to have our photo taken in front of the fountain. Brianna asked that we move in closer to each other so she could get all of us into the picture.

As he stepped closer to Jess, Johnny D tripped, lost his balance, and fell backwards into the water fountain. We couldn't help but laugh when we saw Johnny D standing up in the fountain completely soaked! I immediately looked over at Jess to see her reaction.

Jess had her hand over her face and said, "I don't even want to look!"

As he stepped out of the fountain, Johnny D walked over to Jessie with an embarrassed look on his face.

"Sorry 'bout that Jess. I guess I lost my balance or something."

"Johnny, how in the world do you manage to do these things?" responded Jess still laughing.

"Well at least I didn't rip my tuxedo!", said a shivering Johnny D.

"C'mon let's get you inside before you catch a cold."

We all had to admit that the Johnny D episode made the night even more memorable. We wondered if we would have this much fun next year at our senior prom. The consensus was that we would.

***

In her junior year, Jessie broke Bridgeport High School's basketball records in scoring and assists.

Two games in particular stood out in my mind. In one game, Jess nearly broke the single-game scoring record in a game against the North Haven High School team. Jess scored 50 points. Her point total became the third highest in the state's high school history, behind the men's record of 52 points and the women's 51 points.

In another game, Jessie put her playmaking skills on full display. Since her freshman year, it became a common occurrence that nearly every time Jess handled the ball the chant "Jessie, Jessie, Jessie" arose from the Bridgeport fans. But there was one game in her junior year when this chant intensified to the point where the cheering was deafening.

In a close scoring game, Coach Sara Johnson asked Jess if she could eat up some time by using her ball handling skills in a game against Ridgefield High. The coach asked Jess to dribble around the court as much as she could without passing the ball. Of course, if she saw one of her teammates under the hoop with no defender, she should pass the ball to that player. Since her team had a slight lead and it was late in the game, Coach Johnson hoped that this move would tire out the defensive players and even cause them to make an unnecessary foul in desperation. Jessie agreed to do as her coach suggested.

Once the ref blew the whistle to begin play, Jane passed the ball to Jess. Receiving the ball, Jess went to work. Her playmaking skills were phenomenal. Jess began dribbling around the court at will, occasionally looking at the basket for an open player. Seeing what was going on, the Bridgeport fans began once again chanting her name. But because of the length of time that Jessie was dribbling the ball past her defenders, the chanting became deafening. I was sitting next to Mr. Darcey but we could not hear each other speak because the sound in the gym was so loud.

Mr. Darcey had a smile on his face when he saw Jess demonstrating some of the dribbling techniques he initially taught her and which she had perfected on her own. She alternated dribbling low to the floor, around her back, and through defenders' legs. At first, two defenders tried to stop her but then that increased to three defenders. Coach Johnson's strategy worked as the opponent players became frustrated and tired. Finally one of the defenders bumped into Jess creating a foul. Because Jessie ate up enough valuable time and managed to tire out her opponent players, Bridgeport had a much easier time widening their lead and eventually won the game by 12 points.

Bridgeport High's overall record at the end of our junior year was 19-1. Their only loss was against a very tough and undefeated Hartford High basketball team, which went on to win the state championship.

Jessie had perfected her basketball skills that junior year, much to the delight of her coaches and her proud father. Jessie's teammates and fans all believed that there were no limits to the skills Jess displayed on the basketball court.

Together with her coaches' training, her dad's extra training and encouragement, and her God-given talents—Jessie became a local star.

I couldn't wait to see how Jess would perform her "magic" on the basketball court the following year, as she would finish out her high school years.

***

Hanging on the wall in my hallway at home is the photo that Brianna took of us in front of the restaurant's water fountain after the junior high school prom. She gave it to me as a memento of that memorable night. Shown in the photo is Johnny D standing soaking wet in the fountain. In front of him is a bewildered Jess with her hand over her face while Jane and I were laughing hysterically. All of us, so very young and so very happy.

It's one of those moments I will cherish forever.

16

"THE HAIL MARY"

Towards the end of Jessie's junior year, Mr. Darcey asked his daughter if it was possible for her to reserve the Bridgeport High basketball court for the entire morning at some point. Curious, but not saying anything yet to her dad, Jess walked into her coach's office.

Jess asked her coach if it was possible for she and her dad to schedule the court at some point. She told the coach that she and her father would like to spend a little time together and would just like to shoot around. Jess and the coach walked over to the office where the basketball court schedule was kept. Fortunately, the volleyball team had to reschedule their practice so the court was free on that coming Saturday. The coach gave Jess permission to use the court without interruption from 8 a.m.-12 noon.

After she informed her dad, Jess called and asked me to come to the gym to watch her practice. She was also going to call Jane but remembered that Jane had a prior commitment that she couldn't reschedule. I said I could free myself up and would be there at 8 a.m. as Jess mentioned. I asked Jess about this special practice session and Jessie replied that she had no clue but would find out from her dad once she hung up the phone.

After her phone call with me, Jess told her dad that she was curious as to why her father requested the court for the morning.

"Dad, what did you have in mind?"

"Jess, when you were in fourth grade, I promised you and your mother that I would teach you all I know about the game of basketball. I've done everything in my power to live up to my promise.

"However, there is one play that I know about but I do not have the ability to teach you. In all honesty there are not many people who can even begin to teach you this play so that you can use it successfully, should the need arise.

"Jess, I would like you to meet a guy who might help you with a particular shot which is only used in certain last minute, dire situations in a basketball game.

"Let me explain by giving you a little background and then let you know why I asked to reserve the court for the entire morning.

"When I was in high school, I made friends with a guy from an opposing team. His name is Ed Carlson, but he goes by the nickname "Downtown." He—"

Jess interrupted. "Why was he nicknamed that?"

"Well, you'll see for yourself on Saturday."

"I'm intrigued. Was he a great basketball player?"

"Well, not really great. Overall, I would say he was average at best."

Seeing that Jess had a confused look on her face Mr. Darcey said he wanted to continue.

"When I played High School basketball, Ed played on our opponent's team. He was very young at the time. I believe he was a freshman. Ed was a 6'9" center for their team. He since has grown to 6'10" in height."

"Wow, said an astonished Jessie, "Ed must have been tough to score against!"

"Well now that's the thing Jess. Before the game against Ed's team we began taking our usual layups. One of my teammates looked over at the other team and told us to check out that "tall guy." We all turned to look at the team practicing their pre-game layups. The guy that my teammate was referring to was Ed Carlson. Keep in mind a 6'9" player can be a big deal, especially when I played high school ball. Collectively, we all became instantly intimidated once we saw Ed. We just stood there in amazement at what we saw. Our coach came over to us and asked us why we were just standing around.

"When we told this to our coach, he laughed and briefly explained that Ed was very tall but most of us had the ability to move around him to get our shots off. Our coach advised us not to be intimidated by Ed's size, and assured us that we would have no difficulty playing against this team. He told us that if we just played our usual game, we should win easily, but we had to put aside any feelings of intimidation.

"Sure enough, we easily defeated Carlson's team despite Ed's presence on the court. Ed could not keep up with my playmaking and my other teammates scored very easily off him and his teammates.

"You see, despite his height, Ed was just an average ballplayer. He was very good at blocking shots, but he didn't have the lateral movement necessary to keep up with good ballhandlers. For players who were not good ball handlers, Ed could be a bit difficult to get around since he had a very long reach. But for our team it wasn't an issue, since most of us were able to handle the ball properly. Ed was a below average shooter and was terrible at the foul line.

"Ed's teammates were also just average shooters and defensive players. Once we figured out how to maneuver around Ed, we easily won the game.

"By his own admission, Ed clowned around throughout his high school years and failed most of his subjects, which didn't seem to faze him. He also didn't take his basketball practices seriously. He constantly clowned around during practice.

"I bumped into Ed one day and he asked if I would join him in getting a cup of coffee at the local diner, which I happily agreed to.

"Ed is a real character and always made me laugh. He said that several weeks after our high school game his coach threatened to bench him because he wasn't taking his basketball practices seriously. He told the coach "Don't bother benching me, because I quit." Ed told me that he had a tryout for a an NBA team. But he also goofed around during their practices and was eventually let go before the players were selected for the team. I was curious about what happened to him after being let go by the professional team. Ed gave me an update.

"Well, Mr. Mike, it was like this. I knew I wasn't cut out for high school or learnin' in general. I mean, can you picture me behind a desk at some big shot company? So I joined a travelin' basketball team"

"What team was that?"

"Mr. Mike, ever hear of the Maryland Dunkers?"

"Is that the team that performs around the country like the Harlem Globetrotters?"

"Yes sir! I made the team and have begun travelin' around with them and having fun. I don't have to worry 'bout no basketball rules like in high school or pro ball. We just do our thing, which is to entertain the crowd, 'specially the little ones. I learned to perfect certain difficult shots that fans love to see."

Jessie listened intently but seemed a bit perplexed.

"So dad," interrupted Jess, "what makes this guy 'Downtown' so special and how is he able to help me with this new basketball technique that you mentioned?"

"It's not so much a technique as it is a basketball play that is seldom used. But if and when it's used it could be a game-winner.

"Jess, what I'm referring to is a very seldom used play in sports such as football and basketball. It's referred to as the 'The Hail Mary'.

"The 'Hail Mary'? What's that?"

"Many fans and sports critics refer to 'The Hail Mary' as a desperation play. Take for instance football. If a team is losing by let's say six points and the ball is on the forty-yard line with only several seconds left in the game, the quarterback has no option but to throw the ball high into the end zone and hope that one of his teammates catches the ball for a touchdown. Ninety-nine out of a hundred times it results in an incomplete pass and a loss for the team. But every once in a while, actually very rarely, the team lucks out and the teammate will catch the ball for a touchdown and win the game. The same thing in basketball. There are games when a team is down by one point with only a few seconds left on the clock. The ball would be passed to a player at the half-court line and the ballplayer would desperately attempt a shot from that distance. The play would in all likelihood end in failure, especially if the shooter did not have the ability to shoot at that distance."

"Half-court, I should say so!" Jess exclaimed. "I don't know anyone who could make that shot, especially in a pressure situation."

"Enter Ed Carlson," Mr. Darcey proudly proclaimed.

"I've done a lot of research on 'Downtown'. Ed was given the nickname 'Downton' because he has this uncanny ability to make half-court shots at a phenomenal pace. I've read that he can make a half-court shot over sixty percent of the time!"

"Sixty percent, dad that's unreal!"

"It is Jess, but he told me that he practiced the shot a great deal. 'Downtown' has now incorporated the half-court shot during his antics playing with his team called the Maryland Dunkers.

"The Dunkers are a team similar to the Harlem Globetrotters who put on a show for the audience. They usually don't play by strict rules since the audience pays to see them make unusual shots such as standing on a teammate's shoulders during the game and placing the ball in the hoop or dunking the ball backwards. The team they play against normally lets them score at will since the fans are only interested in the antics performed by the Dunkers. In Ed's case, one of his specialty shots is the half-court shot. As I mentioned he makes this shot at an alarming rate.

"And so, Jess, I would like 'Downtown' to help you shoot a half-court shot if, by any chance, you need to attempt taking that shot in a game."

That Saturday the three of us—Jess, her dad, and myself—waited anxiously for 'Downtown' and a couple of his friends to arrive at the court.

Just before 8 a.m. we saw three men walk into the gym. Jess and I looked at each other with amazement as we saw three extremely tall men all dressed in purple outfits from head to toe. That included purple hats and purple sneakers. One was an older man and the other two seemed much younger. But at first glance, the older guy appeared to be in great physical shape and quick on his feet.

Once they got near us, the older man had a huge smile on his face and bounced on the tip of his toes as he walked over to us. Jess and I instantly thought that this must be "Downtown."

"Mr. Mike, here we are! Is that your daughter Miss Jessie?"

"Hi Ed, yes it is. Jessie say hello to 'Downtown' and his friends."

Shaking hands, Jess asked him, "Should I call you 'Downtown' or Ed?

"Whichever you prefer. You know, I heard a lot 'bout you Miss Jessie. *You* have a gift."

"Downtown" then looked my way.

"Are you one of Miss Jessie's teammates?"

"No, good grief, I don't know anything about basketball. I'm just a friend of Jessie's," I said laughing

"Just a friend huh. Well, do you want me to teach you a basketball play too?"

"Are you kidding? I wouldn't even be able to make a shot if you lowered the basket to four feet!" Downtown got a kick out of that.

"Well, Miss Jessie, your dad here says that he would like me to show you how I make my half-court shots. They call me 'Downtown' because I learned how to shoot from long distances like at half-court. It took me a long time but I managed to finally get the hang of it. You do realize that those shots are my bread 'n' butter 'cause the fans really like watching me shoot them?"

"My dad tells me that the half-court shot is a 'Hail Mary' desperation shot."

"Well, it's like this Miss Jessie. First of all, I never refer to this half-court shot as a 'Hail Mary' shot?"

"Why is that?" asked Jess.

"Because Miss Jessie, the term 'Hail Mary' in sports is used by folks as a desperation shot. I don't see it that way. I refer to this shot as a 'My Goodness' shot."

"Why 'My Goodness'?" asked a smiling Jess.

"Well, it's like this. The way I look at it is that this shot is no different than any of your other shots, 'cept at a farther distance. I —"

"You're kidding right?" Jessie interrupted. "How can I possibly consider this extremely long shot the same as my regular shots?"

"Good question. That's why I'm here.

"Most people are just plain 'fraid of taking this shot and have a negative vibe about shooting the shot. No wonder they can't make it no matter how good they are. If you are 'proaching something with that negativity, it just ain't gonna work.

"I know I can make this shot. I don't believe I can make it. I don't hope I can make it. I *know* I can make it. The reason is because I have practiced this shot for a long time and I'm confident and comfortable with this. So to answer your question, it's all about practice and positivity.

"So instead of this so-called desperate 'Hail Mary' business, I refer to this shot as a 'My Goodness' shot. Reason I call it a 'My Goodness' shot is because every time I make this shot, folks look shocked and say to each other 'my goodness, did you see that'?"

Jess and I got a kick out of what "Downtown" was saying, but we were beginning to understand.

"Ok, enough of my preachin', let's see what ya got. Oh, first let me introduce my friends from the Dunkers. The big guy's name is 'The Wall' and the other guy is 'Shotgun'."

After the two friends were introduced, the expression on Jessie's face was priceless. She turned to me with a strange look on her face.

"Abby, I can see why 'The Wall' was given that nickname. He's as big as a wall. And I'm frightened just looking at his death stare!

"Ok, before we start," said Jess, "I just want to have my dad take care of this bracelet"

As she walked over to Mr. Darcey, Jess whispered, "Dad, these guys are enormous! How in the world am I going to get a shot off?"

"Jess, just listen to 'Downtown' and have confidence in yourself. I know you can do it. Go out there and show them."

As Jess walked back onto the court, I asked Mr. Darcey, "Do you really think she can do this?"

"I don't think she can. I know she can. Remember, Abby, positive vibes!"

"Ok Miss Jessie," said 'Downtown', "from what I read, most teams double or triple team you during the game. Right? So with only a few seconds on the clock, they will likely triple team.

"Your dad's gonna take the ball out at half-court and pass it to you. The three of us are going to defend you. Your dad has a stopwatch to set at eight seconds. You need to find a way to get around us, free yourself and get a good shot off before the end of those eight seconds.

"Be prepared because we ain't gonna make it easy on you. That's the only way you're gonna learn this 'My Goodness' shot."

Mr. Darcey then took the ball to the half-court sideline, set his timer to eight seconds, and passed the ball to Jess. As soon as Jess began to move, "Downtown" slapped the ball away. The second time Jess tried, "The Wall" quickly stood in her way and the eight seconds ran out. The third time was no better because it was "Shotgun" who got in her way. This went on for over a half hour, with no success. I could see Jessie becoming frustrated and confused.

"I don't think I can do this. You guys are just too tall!" Jessie stopped for a moment and "Downtown" approached her.

"Positive vibes, Miss Jessie, positive vibes. I know you can do it. We may be tall but we ain't no different than the other people you easily fake out and get a shot off. You see, Miss Jessie, I've been readin' all 'bout you. You ain't gonna tell me you can't get by the three of us. Concentrate and remember, positive vibes. You'll get the hang of it. We got all morning. We ain't going no place."

Jessie looked over at her dad who told her to remember her playmaking practices. Smiling, he made the letter "D" with his two hands, referring to "Downtown."

The next time she got the ball, Jess quickly faked to her right, moved to her left, dribbled the ball around her back and quickly got the shot off. Her shot hit the rim and fell down to the court.

"That's the idea Miss Jessie. Keep it going."

Jessie finally figured out a way to get around the three men. As "Downtown" said it was no different than what she has been doing all along when defended by three opponents. She began to understand that these three guys may be a lot taller but if she managed to fake them out and free herself for a shot, it really would be no different. Now the challenge would be making the basket from the half-court distance. On her next three attempts, Jess hit either the hoop's rim or the backboard. But I could tell Jess was beginning to be more comfortable and confident.

Finally, Jessie's shot hit nothing but net as she made the basket.

"Yes!", exclaimed Jessie as she pumped her fist.

As several hours passed, Jess began to increase the number of times she made the basket. "Downtown" looked at his friends and they all had smiles on their faces.

After three hours of practicing her "My Goodness" shot, Jessie began to make her half-court much more frequently, averaging over fifty percent of her shots.

As noontime approached, "Downtown" came over to Jess and Mr. Darcey and told them that he felt that Jessie had learned the knack of making her half-court shots. He said that if the situation ever arose where Jess had to shoot a half-court shot in a game, he was confident that Jessie would have a good chance of making this "My Goodness" shot.

Jess walked over to "Downtown" and told him that she was now comfortable and confident to make this shot if called upon to take it. She thanked him for taking so much of his time to teach her this play.

"Don't thank me now Miss Jessie. Thank me after you win a game using that shot."

"Downtown" turned to me with a huge grin.

"Miss Abby, you sure you don't want me to show you a trick like this? You look like you can do it." As he asked me the question, "Downtown" spun the basketball on one finger, making it twirl around and around.

"Maybe if we reserve the court again for like four months!" I replied. All three of the guys laughed at that.

After shaking Jessie's hand and wishing her good luck, "Downtown" put his arm around Mr. Darcey in a teasing manner, bouncing on his toes as he walked.

"Mr. Mike, you have one helluva daughter. She has the gift. If she doesn't go to college we would be pleased to have her try out for our team. I think she would be a good fit."

With that the three teammates walked out of the gym, purple outfits and all.

After the three men left, Jess gave her dad a big hug.

"Thank you, dad, I appreciate this so much.

"You were right, 'Downtown' is a real character. But, you know what, he's such a nice guy. For him to take so much time out of his busy schedule and teach me his 'My Goodness' shot speaks volumes about what a great guy he is. It also tells me how much he thinks of you as a friend!

"The important thing now is for me to continue practicing this 'My Goodness' shot. So in the event that I'm ever called upon to use this shot, I would be prepared. So, who knows?"

17

HISTORY IN THE MAKING

"The single most amazing feat in Connecticut basketball by 'our girl' Jessie Darcey."

Senior year began on a high note for the three of us. I found a job at a

music store, where I would work part-time during school and full time in the summer months. Jane, who loved to read, worked at a popular bookstore in Fairfield on a part time basis. Jess continued her volunteer work at the theatre whenever she had free time. The three of us really enjoyed working at our part-time jobs and liked the idea of being productive employees.

***

Jessie refused to rest on her junior year basketball accomplishments, feeling the need to focus on certain areas that she felt needed improvement. Plus, she wanted to stay sharp for the senior year basketball season. Jess asked Jane if she could join her at the outside basketball court. Jane had a good deal of flexibility with her job and the store owner was very understanding. So, Jane agreed to join Jess with their basketball practice. To ensure a spot on the court, they met at 6:30 a.m. Their practices were fairly intense as they tried to simulate specific strategic defensive lineups that they would encounter during the season. First, they talked about various ways they could work around any obstacles they may face with by their defenders. Jane wrote down all of the strategies they discussed. As the point guard who would call these plays, she wanted to first run them by their coaches.

After talking and visualizing these strategic plays, Jess and Jane then went out to the court and practiced each and every play they discussed. All along, they visualized where their teammates and opponents would be situated on the court. They practiced their strategic moves over and over again until they were satisfied that they addressed all the possible defensive scenarios that their opponent teams would try to execute against them.

***

It was during her senior year at Bridgeport High that Jessie really excelled. She maintained a scoring average of 32 points per game, an average unheard of at that time. In addition, Jessie averaged 14 assists per game.

Taking notice were a number of colleges that had begun to express interest in recruiting Jessie. Her local legend status grew even further when, unbeknownst to Jessie, the legendary Bobby Steed came to see her play. He received a round of applause as he took his seat. Jessie's dad was impressed that he took the time to attend the game. He wondered if Steed was there to watch his daughter play or if maybe he was invited for another reason. Jess was concentrating on going over a particular play with Jane. Neither one of them noticed that an NBA star was in the gym.

Mr. Darcey had a friend who was an acquaintance of Bobby Steed. At half time, his friend walked over to Mr. Darcey and informed him that he had a brief discussion with Steed in the gymnasium hallway. Steed privately told him that he was most interested in Jessie's ball-handling. His friend wanted Mr. Darcey to know why Steed was at the game. Being one of the greatest NBA ball-handlers, Steed was not disappointed once he saw Jessie displaying her basketball skills on the court.

Not knowing that the NBA great was in attendance, Jessie turned in another great shooting and ball-handling exhibition in a game that Bridgeport High easily won. At one point, Steed was seen to have a big smile on his face, as he watched the feeble attempts of Jessie's defenders who tried in vain to take the ball away from her. Steed appeared to be very impressed and was seen leaving the game before it ended to make a phone call, presumably to report what he had seen.

Despite being a prolific scorer, what had gone unnoticed was Jessie's one inexplicable flaw. For whatever reason, Jessie had difficulty making easy layups, especially in pressure situations. For this reason, she would shy away from attempting a layup and revert to a turnaround jump shot close to the basket, many times using her left hand. This became her trademark move, although the crowd and her coaches never realized the real reason. As I became aware of Jessie's flaw, I suddenly realized why Jess was so serious that day when Smitty was clowning around about his own personal flaw of not being able to throw the baseball properly to first base. In an effort to resolve this one basketball problem that Jess had, her dad included in her home schedule shooting layups for forty-five minutes straight.

Even with the new addition to her home basketball schedule, Jessie still shied away from taking layups during her high school games, reverting instead to making jump shots near the basket. None of us were able to figure out why this was the case, including Jessie. But we were at least pleased that it didn't affect her scoring average at all.

Not only did Mike attend every one of Jessie's games, but he was even allowed to watch Jessie in practice—from a distance. The understanding was that he would never interfere in the practice and would not try to upstage the coaches. As a matter of fact, Mr. Darcey made a point of always taking the side of the coaches when driving Jessie back and forth to her game. This made Jessie very happy and so proud of her dad. Jess always made a point of thanking him for getting her started in basketball, teaching her how to effectively handle the ball, and mostly to love the game. At all of Jessie's games, Mr. Darcey sat in the same seat so Jessie could see him, which she always made an effort to do.

***

On a cold and wintry February night, an overflow crowd at the New Haven Arena witnessed state history. On that night Jessie Darcey turned in a performance for the ages in what the local newspapers referred to as the "single most amazing feat in Connecticut basketball history by 'our girl' Jessie Darcey." For on that day, Jessie Darcey set a single game basketball record in grand fashion. It was a record that many fans and experts felt would last for a very long time.

The game featured Bridgeport High and a very good Trumbull High School basketball team.

At one point during a timeout in the game, Jessie quietly took Coach Johnson to the side.

"Coach I'm going to break the scoring record," she said in a non-boastful, matter-of-fact way, "I just know it. All my shots are falling in for me."

"Jessie, go for it," was her coach's only response.

As she was closing in on the record, Jessie looked up at her dad who had a very proud grin on his face. The girls single game scoring record stood at 51 points, while the boys' record was 52 points. Jess was about to easily shatter both of those records.

Jessie didn't appear to be fazed by what she was about to accomplish. She seemed so relaxed and so confident throughout the entire game. Each time the team got into a huddle on the sidelines, Jess would look over at me and make a silly face at me. It's an image that I have always treasured.

Jessie proceeded to break both the boy's and girl's state scoring records when she made a foul shot which gave her 53 points.

The scoreboard displayed the news: "Jessie Darcey has just broken Connecticut's single game scoring record." Seeing the scoreboard's display, the fans erupted, chanting "Jessie, Jessie, Jessie."

But Jess was far from finished since there was still plenty of time left in the game. Towards the end of the game, with the clock showing only five seconds, Jessie got the ball under the basket for an easy layup. Instead, Jessie took the ball in front of the hoop for a turn-around jump shot right at the buzzer. That shot gave her a stunning total of 71 points for the game, and the state record. The fans all knew that they were witnessing state history. Her teammates and her coach knew this as well. Once the game ended, they joyfully ran to congratulate Jessie on her amazing achievement. In a classy show of admiration, every member of the Trumbull team, including the coach, walked over to Jessie to congratulate her on this amazing achievement. Her father stood applauding and, when he saw Jessie looking his way, he raised his hands in a jubilant manner.

One devoted fan seemed to sum up Jessie's performance the best in speaking to a local reporter saying, "I have seen a lot of high school basketball players, men, and women, but I have never seen anyone like this before and I doubt I will ever see it again."

I accompanied the team on their bus for their next game as they traveled the short distance to Stratford to take on the Stratford Red Devils basketball team. At one point during the bus ride, Coach Johnson walked back to where Jess was sitting. Standing in the aisle, the coach addressed the entire team while looking directly at Jess.

"Jessie, I just found out from the U.S. Athletic Commission that you not only broke the state scoring record, but your 71 points also set a *National* high school scoring record. Congratulations!"

This brought a cheer from everyone on the bus. An embarrassed Jessie smiled and could only say, "Thank you, coach."

In each of her games, Jessie dominated the basketball court with her dribbling ability, reminding many fans of the great Marcus Haines of the Harlem Globetrotters. In an effort to guard her from totally controlling the game on the court, many teams would double and even triple team Jessie—all to no avail. She simply dribbled around her defenders. Jessie would even sometimes dazzle the crowd by skillfully performing techniques she learned from her dad years ago — dribbling the ball behind her back, through the arms and legs of her defenders, and finally taking the shot or passing the ball to an unguarded player for an easy layup.

The fans were witnessing the culmination of her years of dedicated practice beginning at age nine—they were witnessing basketball perfection, plain and simple.

As the season progressed, the Bridgeport High team continued to dominate their opponents behind Jessie's high-scoring game totals, and Jane's brilliant defensive play.

***

Bridgeport High had an unbeaten record going into their final regular season game. For this game, they faced a very tough and much improved Xavier High School team. The Xavier team lost two games but those two games were at the very beginning of the season. Since then, Xavier easily won all their remaining games. They had a very good offensive team and their defense had improved greatly.

The game was a real nail-biter throughout the entire contest. Despite Jessie's pinpoint shooting, Xavier matched Bridgeport basket for basket. With 19 seconds left in the game, Coach Johnson called a timeout. The coach looked up at the scoreboard and saw that her team had a one point lead, 87—86. The coach called on her team to not take a shot but rather to run out the clock which would win the game.

Once the team left the huddle there seemed to be some miscommunication. Instead of Jane Kenny taking the ball out at the sideline, one of the forwards stepped in to take the ball from the referee. Her pass to Jessie was not as sharp as Jane's passes. This resulted in the Xavier guard stealing the ball before it got to Jess and then quickly passing it to a fleet footed Xavier player for an easy layup. Now the score stood at 88—87, in favor of Xavier.

Jane managed to get the ball to half-court and immediately called their remaining timeout. Looking up at the scoreboard Coach Johnson saw that there were only 5 seconds left in the game

"Well girls, it looks like we are going to have to try a desperation shot."

When she heard the term "desperation shot", Jessie smiled to herself and thought of the lesson that "Downtown" conveyed to her during their four-hour training on that Saturday morning. She could hear his words in her head.

"Miss Jessie, this shot is not a desperation shot if you have the confidence, trainin', and skill to treat it like all your other shots. I call it a 'My Goodness' shot and that's how I want you to think. If you're ever in that situation, you just can't think you can make the shot, you must know that you can make the shot. Positive vibes, Miss Jessie, positive vibes"

A despondent Coach Johnson looked directly at Jessie, with a pleading look on her face. The coach seemed a bit startled when she saw Jessie with a bit of a smile.

"Jessie, can you try as best you can to take this shot?"

"I will coach."

The Xavier fans were ecstatic knowing it would take a miracle for them to not upset the unbeaten Bridgeport High team. Xavier was about to end its season on a high note. It was a completely different feeling over on the Bridgeport High side. Their fans were despondent, seeing the reality of the situation. They had resigned themselves to the fact that their team was about to go down to their first defeat. In fact, a few Bridgeport fans began to get up and leave the game.

While in the huddle, Jessie looked up at her dad. As he stood up, Mr. Darcey made the letter "D" with his two hands, holding his hands high above his shoulders for Jess to see. Jess smiled and knew exactly what the gesture meant. It was a clear message to Jessie to remember everything that "Downtown" taught her. This was the shot that "Downtown" had perfected. Now it was her turn. When I saw Mr. Darcey making that "D" gesture, I immediately stood up and made the same gesture that I hoped Jess would see.

Realistically, Jess knew her chances were fifty-fifty but she refused to think in a negative way. She told herself to be positive and visualize making the shot going into the hoop. While still in the huddle, Jess looked over at me standing as I made the "D" gesture just like her dad. Seeing me, Jess smiled and made a silly face.

"*Oh my word*," I thought to myself, "*she really does believe she's going to make this shot!*"

Leaving the huddle, Jessie mumbled to herself, "*Positive vibes Jess, positive vibes.*

As they began to walk to their places on the court, Jane noticed how calm Jessie seemed.

"Jess, do you think you can make this shot?"

"I don't think I can make this shot. I *know* I can make the shot! Jane, just give me a crisp pass and I'll take it from there."

The Bridgeport fans were quiet and subdued, thinking that not even Jessie Darcey could pull off this miracle.

As expected, three Xavier defenders met Jess at half-court. Their coach told them to stand in the way of Jessie but made it clear to them that they must not foul her. She reminded her players that if they were to foul her, they would most likely lose since Jessie was nearly perfect at the foul line all year long. She had confidently told her players, "With only five seconds left and three players standing in her way, even Jessie Darcey couldn't pull off this miracle. There is no way they can win this game!"

As the buzzer sounded to begin play, Jane threw a sharp pass to Jess. When she received the ball, Jessie made a quick move, dribbling the ball behind her back and faking out all three defenders. This freed her for a clear look at the basket. She then took her half-court shot—just as the buzzer sounded signaling that there was no time left on the clock.

As it was in mid-flight, the ball seemed to sail in slow motion. The crowd was on their feet, hoping against hope that the ball would reach its target.

Finally, I saw the ball heading into the basket and heard that wonderful "swish" sound.

Jessie made the half-court shot!

Jessie's miracle shot gave the Bridgeport High team an unlikely 89-88 victory.

As soon as the basket was made, pandemonium set in. All of Jessie's teammates piled onto Jess in a moment of jubilation. The noise in the gym was deafening as the Bridgeport fans erupted in sheer euphoria, chanting "Jessie, Jessie, Jessie!"

Once Jess climbed out of the pile, a barrage of reporters ran over to her for her reaction. Jessie explained to the reporters how she approached this situation.

"This was a shot that I practiced over and over again in anticipation of a situation like this. A very wise basketball player impressed upon me the need to not look at this as a desperation shot, because that has a negative feel to it. He taught me to be in control, be confident, be positive, and to think of it as any other shot despite the long distance to the basket. I am eternally grateful to him for teaching me all of this."

As she saw me running towards her, a jubilant Jessie exclaimed, "My Goodness Miss Abby!"

Running full steam with my arms stretched wide open, I screamed to be heard above the crowd—"My Goodness, Miss Jessie! I then gave her a huge hug and exclaimed, "I think our good friend 'Downtown' was channeling through you! Won't he be proud when he hears about this?"

"He sure will be Miss Abby. I never could have made that shot without our friend 'Downtown'. What a wonderful man! I can't wait to call and thank him when I get home."

As promised, Jess did call "Downtown" to tell him about her "My Goodness" shot, He was ecstatic when she told him how her half-court shot won the game.

"I knew it, I knew it! So proud of you Miss Jessie, so proud!"

From that moment on, Connecticut sports fans referred to Jessie as "The Wonder Girl", and her last-second basket as "THE Shot."

The next day an article about her winning basket appeared in newspapers throughout Connecticut. Her incredible achievement even made the newspapers in many states across the country.

The Shot

Last night, Jessie Darcey electrified the Bridgeport High faithful in what can only be described as "THE Shot." With only 5 seconds left in the game, Jessie turned a certain defeat into a stunning one-point win for Bridgeport High.

How? Well, you almost had to be there to believe it. But suffice it to say, Jessie pulled off one heck of a miracle play by freeing herself from three defenders (that's right, not two but three defenders) and made an improbable shot at the half-court line, right at the buzzer!

Her jubilant teammates all converged on Jessie who found herself on the bottom of the pile. It was pandemonium time as the ecstatic fans chanted "Jessie, Jessie, Jessie" for nearly ten minutes. Jessie Darcey lived up to her nickname "The Wonder Girl."

Led by Darcey's 48 points the win enabled the Bridgeport High women's basketball team to maintain its regular season unbeaten record.

Jessie is now set to lead her team to compete in the State Championship.

18

THE STATE CHAMPIONSHIP GAME

It was a Championship game that Jessie performed with a flourish — and with a broken heart.

For basketball fans throughout the state of Connecticut and beyond, Jessie Darcey became affectionately known as "our girl Jessie."

Aside from her dad, I was proud to also be Jessie's biggest fan. I told her how amazed and proud I was of her many successes on the basketball court. Jessie's response always made me smile.

"Well, I would never have had this success if it wasn't for my 'bucket girl' when I first learned how to play!"

The Bridgeport High School girls' team ended the season undefeated as did the very powerful and defending champions, the Hartford High School Falcons. So it seemed inevitable that the two teams would meet for the state basketball championship, to be played on Hartford High's home court.

It was a Championship game that Jessie performed with a flourish—and with a broken heart.

On the day of the big game, Jessie and her dad had their usual game day lunch at home together. The two had a nice meal and a long discussion about the Championship game that day. It was a pleasant discussion and they both admitted that they were a bit nervous but very excited. With a kiss on her father's cheek, Jessie picked up her gym bag, turned around and gave her dad a big smile.

"I love you Dad, see you at the game, right?"

"I love you too Jessie, and I wouldn't miss your game for the world!"

As the championship game began, Jessie looked up to get a glimpse of her dad. She noticed that his seat was empty. *"Maybe he was running late,"* she thought. The game was a defensive duel and was close throughout the first two quarters. It had the makings of being a real nail-biter.

At half time with the score tied at 41—41, Jessie noticed that her dad's seat was still empty. Jess quickly ran over to me while I was sitting in the second row and asked if I knew why her dad was not there. After hesitating, I looked at Jessie and tried as best as I could to hold back my tears.

"Jessie, I just found out that your dad is in the hospital, he was involved in a car crash. I will be glad to drive you to the hospital whenever you tell me."

A stunned Jessie immediately thought to tell her coach that she needed to leave the game. But she then remembered what her dad always told her, *"Stay focused on the game and then worry about things later."* Jessie knew that her teammates really needed her and, like her father, she was a true teammate. Jessie decided not to tell her coach and would have me quickly drive her to the hospital once the game ended.

At the 2:59 minute mark, Jessie's team held a very slim one-point lead, 78—77. Timeout was called by Bridgeport High. While in their huddle, Coach Johnson looked at some of her players and could see that they were visibly exhausted, mainly because of the pressure of the game. It was then that the coach asked Jess to do something incredible. Fearing her team was losing steam and that Hartford High would overtake the lead, Coach Johnson asked Jessie to try to run out the clock by dribbling the ball for the remainder of the game. Thinking of her dad in the hospital and feeling a bit despondent, Jessie lowered her head and meekly told her coach that she would do it. If this worked, her team would hold on to the slim one-point lead and win the state title. This was a risky call by the coach since there were still 2:59 minutes left on the clock. The coach also noticed a change in Jessie's facial expressions, especially since half time. But Jessie told the coach that she was just trying to stay focused since this was a big game.

In basketball, 2:59 minutes can be a very long time with timeouts available and plenty of opportunities for a team's opponent to score and win the game. But Coach Johnson had seen what Jessie could do with her ball handling. She knew that the opponent team members did not want to foul Jessie, who in this game was perfect at the foul line. If they were to foul Jess, it would almost certainly increase the lead to 3 points, which would require two possessions by Hartford High to take the lead. The hope was that Jessie could eat up most of the remaining time and, if the opportunity presented itself, for Jessie to get the ball to a teammate if the player was unguarded under the basket.

Once the referee blew the whistle to resume play, Bridgeport's Jane Kenny took the ball from the referee at the far left sideline of the court and quickly threw the ball to Jess. As expected, Jessie was met by three defenders. Unfazed, Jess put on a show for all the fans at the game. Jess began to work her ball-handling magic, dribbling around her defenders who tried desperately to force her to give up the ball. With the Bridgeport High fans cheering at a crescendo level, the defenders were unable to get the ball from Jessie or at least force her to pass the ball. In fact, two of her defenders actually fell to the floor in a feeble attempt to steal the ball. This aroused the crowd even more, with some fans actually cheering when the players fell to the court. All along, the Bridgeport High fans were chanting "Jessie, Jessie, Jessie" to spur her on. By then the fans knew what was going on and this made Jessie even more confident to pull off this "miracle."

Finally, with the scoreboard clock showing 59 seconds, the lead scorer for the Falcons was forced to foul Jessie. By doing this, the Falcons' star fouled out of the game. But what choice did she have? The referee signaled that it was a "1 and 1" at the foul line, meaning that if Jessie made the first shot, she would then be allowed to shoot another foul shot.

Jessie confidently strolled to the foul line. Her first shot hit nothing but the net, giving her team a 2 shot advantage. Her second foul shot was just as good, giving her team a 3-point advantage, 80-77. Hartford High immediately called time out. At the other end of the court, Bridgeport's Coach Johnson instructed her team members to in no way foul any of the Hartford players. She instructed her two guards to meet their opponent at half-court which would force Hartford to use up valuable seconds by having to dribble around the guards. As instructed by their coach, the Bridgeport players allowed Hartford to drive down the rest of the court and score an easy layup. This closed the score to 80—79.

Coach Johnson called her final time out and looked directly at Jessie.

"Jessie, can you do it one more time, run out the clock for us to win?"

"Yes, I can Coach."

Taking the ball at the far end of the court, Jane waited for the referee to blow the whistle and then passed the ball to Jessie. With the clock ticking down the final seconds, Jessie once again dazzled the crowd by giving the Hartford players a basketball clinic. Dribbling the ball around her back, between her legs, and between her opponents' outstretched hands, Jessie dribbled the length of the court while the Falcons frantically tried to stop her. Looking up at the clock, Hartford's coach saw that only 14 seconds remained and immediately yelled out "Foul her!" This they did, with 12 seconds left. Now it was up to Jessie again to continue her perfection at the foul line and make the next two foul shots, two points that would ensure a Bridgeport High victory.

As she strode to the foul line, Jessie knew what needed to be done—make BOTH foul shots. First, she needed to tune out all the noise and excitement coming from the stands. She had learned from her dad how to relax her body and visualize making her shots in key situations.

Once Jessie got to the foul line, she gave Jane a quick nod as if to say we were about to become state champions. The first foul shot she scored made the score 81-79, a two-point lead. Even though there were only 12 seconds left, it was still enough time for a miracle shot by Hartford High to put the game into overtime. So this next shot was crucial. Incredibly, the sound in the gym had gone from pandemonium to complete silence. At that moment, Jessie remembered what her dad had told her, *"Jessie, if you play your game, no one can stop you. But the main thing is to relax and be in total control."* Jessie exhaled briefly and in an inaudible whisper, said to herself, *"This one's for you Dad."* Jessie effortlessly made the second foul shot, *swish*. Now Bridgeport High had a 3-point advantage at 82-79.

Hartford immediately called its last time out. Back in the huddle, Coach Johnson once again implored her team NOT to foul and to allow the Falcons to run the ball the full length of the court and score. The coach knew at that moment that even if a shot was made, there would be no time left for Hartford to score again, especially since they had run out of time outs. And she was right.

The Hartford fleet-footed guard received the ball from her teammate and easily dribbled by the two defenders who were first to meet her. The guard quickly raced to the basket and made an easy layup, unencumbered by any of Bridgeport's players who heeded Coach Johnson's advice and did not try to stop the shooter, fearing they would commit a foul. The layup brought the score to 82-81. However, just as the layup was made the official buzzer sounded, signaling the end of the game.

Bridgeport High School became the Connecticut State Champions!

***

After the game, Jessie was met with a barrage of reporters who wanted to get her thoughts about the Championship game and her incredible basketball achievements during her four years of high school basketball. Instead, Jessie politely excused herself and frantically ran over to me to ask for a ride to the hospital.

I dropped Jessie off at the hospital's front entrance and proceeded to find a parking space. Running at full speed into the hospital, Jessie was told by the nurse at the front desk that her father was being closely monitored after he was in a car accident. The nurse explained that her father hit his head on the dashboard and the doctors were checking for any signs of a concussion. The nurse went on to say, "That is all I know. I will have the head doctor, Dr. Billings, see you in the waiting room and give you an update."

Soon, Dr. Billings came out to the waiting room and gave Jessie an update on her dad's condition.

"As you may have been told by nurse Jackson, your father sustained some head trauma as a result of a car accident he was involved in. Given his age and his history of heart problems, we are taking extra precautions and are running a few additional tests to make sure there is no underlying or sustained head injury. We believe he will be okay but we'll wait to see the test results.

"Your father is in good spirits and you can pay him a brief visit if you'd like. He is a bit groggy from the medication. Your dad strikes me as a real fighter so that certainly works in his favor. We will provide you with an update after the test results come in, which should be fairly soon."

"Thank you, doctor, I appreciate this and will keep my fingers crossed that the test results are negative. And, by the way, your hunch is right, my dad is a real fighter!"

The doctor's words gave Jess a sense of relief but she remained anxious knowing her dad was not quite out of the woods yet. Rushing into the waiting room, I gave Jessie a hug.

"How's your dad doing?"

"They're running some tests and will let me know when they receive the results. The doctor believes he will be okay but won't know until he sees the results of the tests. They told me they would contact me as soon as they heard. Abby, would you come with me to visit my dad? The doctor said I could.

"Absolutely Jess, I would love to see your dad."

When we got to Mr. Darcey's room, he smiled at the sight of both of us.

"Jess, I'm so sorry I missed your game."

After giving him a big hug, Jessie responded, "Dad, being here with you means so much more to me than any basketball game."

After I gave him a hug, Mr. Darcey said to me, "Abby, thank you for being such a good friend to my Jess. That means a lot to me.

"Jess, I bought you a little something that I hope you will like. I had it in my jacket pocket and wanted to give it to you myself for all your amazing achievements. But then I got into that accident. The nurse at the front counter can give it to you. I'm a bit tired now. Can you visit me soon?"

"I'll visit you tomorrow Dad and I'll check with the front desk nurse. You get your rest and know that I'm always with you. I love you, Dad."

"Love you too Jess," responded Mr. Darcey as he drifted off to sleep.

Before leaving the hospital, we stopped at the front desk and Jessie asked the nurse about the gift that her dad said was kept there. Sure enough, the nurse knew what she was referring to and said it was in with the rest of his belongings when he was admitted to the hospital. When she returned, the nurse held up a piece of jewelry.

"This is so beautiful and thoughtful of your father. He mentioned to me that he had purchased this for you. It was difficult to understand him because he was a bit groggy from all the medication. But I believe he said he wanted to surprise you with it. I didn't look inside the small locket but it must be something special."

Jessie took the necklace from the nurse and noticed the locket that the nurse referred to. She delicately opened the lock, put her hand to her cheek, and was overcome with emotion.

"Oh my God Abby, look at this! The photos in this locket are of my mom and dad when they were young. I will treasure this forever. I love my dad so much. "

"Jess, it's beautiful. I can only say it is truly a gift of love. You are so blessed to have a father like Mike."

Later that day, Jessie received a phone call from Dr. Billings' assistant. He told Jessie that her father's test results came back negative and he was doing much better. The doctor said that they were keeping Mr. Darcey overnight as a precaution but that he saw no reason why he cannot be released after that.

Mike was all smiles when Jessie and I picked him up at the hospital and drove him back home. When we got back to Mr. Darcey's house, Mr. Darcey asked Jessie if she was excited about the prospect of applying to colleges. Jessie responded that she was very much looking forward to that.

In recognition of Jessie's numerous basketball achievements, she received significant accolades from national news media outlets. Many newspapers across the country declared Jessie Darcey to be "the greatest female basketball player in high school history." National newspaper and television basketball critics agreed.

Jessie was now a national treasure, and I couldn't be more thrilled!

19

A VERY SPECIAL LETTER

In early Spring of her senior year, Jessie began receiving letters of interest

from various schools to attend their colleges. Jessie was overwhelmed and couldn't make up her mind. But, with a little assistance from me, she narrowed it down to three colleges that she would be interested in attending. All three letters were from major universities located in different parts of the country. And all three had very competitive basketball programs. One day, Jessie opened a letter that sparked her interest. She was quite sure it was a recruitment letter, but it seemed to arrive fairly late in the process since she had already narrowed her decision down to three colleges.

The recruitment letter was from Boston College. Included in the letter was an offer of a full scholarship based on both her academic and athletic accomplishments. Not only was Jessie a gifted basketball player but also would soon graduate high school with high honors. Jessie asked me to stop over to her house, saying that she wanted to show her dad the recruitment letter and ask both of us for our feedback. After I was at her house for a few minutes, Jess gave her dad the letter and asked for his opinion. Mr. Darcey was about to read the recruitment letter when he saw the school's letterhead.

"That's the college that Bobby Steed attended and became a basketball star. Do you girls know who Bobby Steed is?"

"No, not really, only from the little you told me when I was growing up," replied Jess.

"Ok, let me read the letter."

After reading the college recruitment letter, Mr. Darcey said, "Jess, I see they are offering you a full scholarship much like the other schools you are interested in.

"I know it's your decision on what school to choose, and I want it to be that way. But since you asked, I would recommend that you give this college your serious consideration. I know it's smaller than some of the other colleges you are considering, but I do know that this school has an excellent reputation, for its academic and athletic programs.

"Jess, regardless of the college you choose, this is your opportunity to escape this very unsafe environment. That would be such a relief for both of us!"

"Dad, I promise I will give this school consideration along with the other three college recruitment letters I put aside."

The following day, Jessie thoroughly researched all four colleges. She admitted to herself that playing for the three major universities she set aside initially could possibly further her national recognition. But she asked herself, *"Is that what I'm really looking for?"* Jessie kept going back to the Boston College recruitment letter. She found something intriguing about this school but wasn't exactly sure what that was. Maybe it was the noted reputation of the Jesuit teaching there or maybe it was something else. She decided to put all four letters aside for the time being.

Several days later, I visited Jess at her house. She had said she wanted my thoughts on a correspondence she received earlier that day. As we sat in her living room, Jessie asked me to read a letter that she just received that morning. I looked at the letter and read it aloud.

Hi Jessie,

You may not know me. My name is Bobby Steed. I was delighted to hear that you received a recruitment letter from my Alma Mater, Boston College.

Boston College is a fine school and, it seems to me, it would be a very nice fit for you, in all respects. While the decision is entirely yours to make, I am secretly hoping that you choose Boston College.

Sincerely,

Bobby Steed

P.S. I attended one of your games recently. I must say that I was extremely impressed. I did pass on my thoughts to a few people and I hope that factored into their decision to recruit you. I'm not sure, but I'm keeping my fingers crossed. You should be very proud of your many accomplishments. I wish you all the best in deciding on the school that best fits your needs, whether or not that includes Boston College.

"Wow!," I blurted out. "This is the athlete that your dad always talks about. I'm amazed that someone that famous took the time to write this. Did you know that he attended one of your games? I had heard that Mr. Steed showed up at one of your games but I didn't pay any attention."

"No, I had no idea. I'm kinda glad I didn't because that may have made me nervous knowing he was in the stands. So what do you think?"

"First of all, I think you should show this letter to your dad. I'm sure he'll get a kick out of it. But like he always said, the final decision is strictly yours. Neither your dad nor I want to make that decision for you."

"Well, I now know the right decision to make. My research showed that Boston College is a great school both academically and athletically. And for Mr. Steed to go out of his way to send me such a meaningful message, I—"

Interrupting Jess, I excitedly blurted out, "So you decided to accept Boston College's full scholarship?"

Jessie nodded with a huge grin. "Yep, that's exactly what I'm going to do. The other three schools are much larger with high national recognition, but I believe Boston College is the right fit for me.

"Abby, my dad will be home from work later. Would you be able to stop by when I show him this letter?

"I would love to. Just let me know. I can't wait to see his reaction not only to this letter but also to your college selection."

"Me too, Abby."

Jessie's decision to attend Boston College meant that she could stay close to her father and she would be able to easily drive to Connecticut to visit him. Personally, I was also glad and relieved. Knowing that Jess felt that the college she chose would be a good fit for her made me feel good. I knew there was a chance that Jessie would choose a college thousands of miles away. So, selfishly, I was relieved that she settled on a college fairly close to where I was living in Connecticut and I would see her more often. It also meant that I would be able to see many of her home games.

Boston College was about to witness what I personally witnessed ever since elementary school—a gifted athlete who was about to perform her magic on the school's basketball court. In my mind, Jessie was more than capable of turning the Boston College team into a major contender.

When she stated her intention to attend Boston College to her father, he was ecstatic about her choice.

An excited Mr. Darcey admitted, "Jess, I was secretly hoping that you would choose Boston College. As I mentioned, Boston College was the school that one of my basketball idols Bobby Steed attended. More importantly, this is a school that will be a good fit for you—with excellent academic and athletic programs. As much as I was hoping this would be your choice, I wanted this to be your decision, which is why I tried very hard not to persuade you to decide on this school. And you will receive a full scholarship, how wonderful Jess!. You can't imagine how proud I am of you! Do you realize you will be the first one in our family to attend college?"

"Yes, I remember you saying that you hoped I would have the opportunity to go to college. And I owe it all to you because you were the one who encouraged me to put a high value on education and always maintain good grades throughout my elementary and high school years. I am so thankful for all your encouragement and support you have given me not only in school but also during my basketball career. I look forward to having you attend some of my games at Boston College."

"Well, you can certainly count on that Jess! I can't wait to see you perform your magic with your college team."

Jessie had to admit that making the college decision was a load off her mind. She told me that even though it was her decision, she was excited that her dad was happy and couldn't wait to have him visit her and go to her games.

I decided to stay in Connecticut and was thrilled to receive a full scholarship from Southern Connecticut State College in New Haven, with the intention of majoring in dramatic arts. Looking at my scholarship letter, I smiled and couldn't help but think back to the inspiration and encouragement I received from that nine-year-old girl who became my very best friend.

I told Jess that I was excited to see the variety of courses Southern Connecticut had to offer, especially classes dealing with my dramatic arts major. Jess said she was so thrilled that I chose a major in the arts. She said that whenever I was ready to use my major and perform on stage, she would reach out to the owner and artistic director of the Royalty Theatre. Jess told me she would be glad to recommend that they consider me as a performer in one of their productions. Jessie also reminded me of her goal of becoming an owner of a local musical theatre.

"I know it's a very ambitious and challenging goal, but someday I would like to pursue it. Hey, who knows?"

"Jess, thank you for your very generous offer to reach out to Royalty Theatre at some point. I will let you know when I may be ready to perform onstage. How cool it would be if your wish came true and you became an owner of a musical theatre!"

Later that day, Jane called me. I could hear the excitement in her voice as she told me that she received a full scholarship from New Britain's Central Connecticut State College. Jane said she planned to play basketball on their team and was keeping her fingers crossed that she would be selected as a starting guard on Central's basketball team.

I told Jane, "Knowing how talented and confident you are, I have no doubt that you will be selected for a starting position."

Having made her college selection, Jessie told me she was looking forward to playing basketball at the college level. She was confident that she would make the squad and hoped to be a contributing factor to the success of the college's basketball program.

***

While things were going great for Jess on the basketball court, what mattered most to Jessie was that she found her one true love early on in our senior year at Bridgeport High. His name was Paul Mari and things became very serious between the two. Paul was a longtime friend and neighbor of mine. I had invited Paul to one of Jane Kenny's parties and it was there that Paul and Jessie met. They began dating soon after. Much to Jessie's surprise and delight, Paul said he really liked musical plays, not knowing that Jess also loved musicals and always wished that she had the talent to perform in a play. So, their favorite dates were attending musicals at various theatres within Connecticut. Paul was several years older, attended Yale University, and was already offered a very good, steady job once he graduated from Yale. Paul possessed all the qualities Jess dreamed of. He always was impeccably dressed, and polite, and took his work and education very seriously. Just as important for Jessie was that her Dad really liked Paul and always told her that she and Paul were a perfect match. Attending Boston College meant that she would see a great deal of Paul during the school year since he would have a fairly short drive from Connecticut.

***

One day, Jess bumped into Johnny D in the school hallway. She asked Johnny how he was doing since she hadn't heard from him in a while. Johnny D said he became friends with a classmate by the name of Claudia Marchent. The two sat next to each other in Science class and they instantly became good friends and began to hang out together outside of class. He told Jess that he has become very fond of Claudia and they have been dating ever since and became inseparable. Claudia was a transfer student from Newport Beach, California, which is an affluent city in Orange County. Claudia's family moved quite a bit because of her father's work.

Johnny confided in Jess a concern that he initially had about Claudia. For the most part, they were very compatible and seemed to like the same things, such as food and their tastes in movies and TV shows. However, from the beginning, it was obvious to Johnny that Claudia had no interest in education. She was a year older than him and mentioned that she already had to stay back a year because of her poor academic record. Johnny found out that she was flunking several courses at Bridgeport High and her graduation was in jeopardy. Claudia admitted to Johnny that her goal was to be a model and, if successful, to travel the world. She had done a little modeling in California and thought that might be a cool path for her to pursue.

Johnny was a bit shocked to hear that she was not passing all her courses. He was surprised to hear this since outwardly she seemed to have it all together, and the last thing he would have thought was that she was not doing well in school. As for her modeling goal, Johnny sensed that her heart was not really into that but she had convinced herself that this could be her career since she didn't seem to have anything else to fall back on. Her mother and father didn't get along for a long time and finally got divorced once they moved to Connecticut. Her father graduated from a prestigious university but was never around the house to give Claudia the support that she desperately needed. Her mom tried but was unsure how to advise her daughter knowing she was failing high school. Hearing Claudie explain all of this Johnny initially did not know what to say or do. But then Johnny recalled how Jessie told him, in no uncertain terms, that he needed to concentrate on his studies if he hoped to graduate. He admitted to Jessie that those talks got him back on the right track.

"Jess, I remembered the 'tough love' discussion you had with me and how it straightened my life out. So I had the same kind of discussion with Claudia at the beginning of the year. And, Jess, guess what? It worked! You're not going to believe this, but I actually helped Claudia—and myself—study very hard for her exams. I also convinced her, as you have always advised, of the importance of a good education. By helping her study, she managed to improve her grades significantly, especially in the subjects that she was in danger of flunking. Actually, for the subjects that we both took, our study sessions also helped me improve my grades.

"At one point during one of our study sessions, Claudia admitted that her goal of modeling was not something she was actually serious about. She used that more as a crutch since she didn't believe she was ever going to graduate from high school and maybe she didn't need a high school degree for that career. She secretly asked around and found out that most modeling companies prefer potential models with high school diplomas.

"Since her grades dramatically improved, Claudia and I hope to apply to local colleges, even if we are accepted only to a two-year program

"Jess, I can't wait for you to meet Claudia. She is such a sweet and wonderful person."

Jessie couldn't help but smile saying, "I'm very much looking forward to meeting Claudia and I'm so happy to hear that you found someone very special."

Johnny responded, "Yeh, we have a lot of fun going out to concerts, movies, and dances. Claudia suggested that we brush up on our dancing before the prom but I don't think that's necessary, do you?"

Jessie didn't want to laugh so she quickly changed the subject, saying "I'm so thrilled that both of you turned your lives around and now see the importance of a quality education."

"Well, we both have you to thank for that!"

***

With our high school prom quickly approaching, Jess called Jane and me to ask if the two of us would be able to join her in shopping for a gown to wear to the prom. We both said that we would love to join her since we both were excited about choosing our gowns as well. Jess was going to the prom with Paul, I was invited by Carl, and Jane was going with a one of our classmates named Brian Hawley.

The three of us felt so fortunate that our three boyfriends got along so well. Because of this, there was no awkwardness for us at any point during our prom. It was so great to talk to many of our classmates and their boyfriends outside of the school setting. We shared so many great stories and fun experiences that we encountered during our four years of high school. It was also interesting to find out which colleges our classmates were applying to and what career paths they were considering. We tried to make a point of not excluding our boyfriends from our discussions so we tried our best to also include topics that they would be interested in.

Brian and Jane were voted King and Queen of the Prom and received a nice receptive applause from all the attendees. When the high school administrators put the tiara on Jane's head, she turned to us with an embarrassing look on her face.

While talking to Jess at the prom, I noticed Johnny D dancing with his girlfriend and pointed it out to Jess. Looking at the two of them in a slow dance, Jessie burst out in laughter.

"Oh man, I hope Claudia doesn't get her toes stepped on too much when they're dancing. I think my feet still hurt from those dances with Johnny! But, seriously Abby, I hope things work out okay for Johnny. He's actually a nice kid. Clumsy, but nice!"

"I agree Jess, he basically is a good kid with a big heart. I guess he never did take those Arthur Murray dance lessons!" Jessie, with her infectious laugh, put her hand to her mouth to try not to continue laughing and just nodded her head in agreement.

After she calmed down, Jessie said, "Claudia seems like a very nice person and a good fit for Johnny. I'm glad we all got to meet her. I wish them all the best." Jane and I both agreed.

We had a great time at our prom and it was so nice getting all dressed up and being with our other classmates. As we were leaving the prom, I turned to Jess and said, in a kidding fashion, "Jess, do you think we will still be allowed to hang out with the "queen"? With that, Jane gave me a jab on the side and said, "Be careful or I'll make both of you curtsy every time you see me!" Once again Jess burst out in that wonderful laugh of hers.

20

BRIDGEPORT HIGH GRADUATION

Kind of strange that after graduation tomorrow the three of us will be going our separate ways, attending different colleges.

As high school graduation approached, Jess and I went to a nearby formal wear shop to get our graduation gowns which we were told were ready to be picked up. Jane was unable to join us due to a family commitment.

Jess and I picked up our gowns and decided to try them on when we got back to Jessie's house. Once we tried on our gowns, we both looked at each other and laughed hysterically. Jessie's gown was so long that she stepped on it as she tried to walk. I had the opposite problem as the sleeves on my gown were so short they showed part of my arms. Needless to say, we took the gowns back to the shop and picked out gowns that fit us properly. This time we had the good sense to try on our gowns right there in the shop.

Jane, Jess, and I attended driver's education classes together. Jess challenged Jane and me to quizzes designed to accurately answer the driver's ed test questions. Just as Jess and I did with our "study buddy" sessions in elementary and high schools, the winner was treated to a chocolate sundae. As a result, the three of us aced our driver's ed exam. All three of us also did well on the driver's part of the test and we received our driver's license with very little difficulty. Obtaining our license gave us a sense of freedom. For me, personally, I would no longer have to rely on my older sister for a ride for shopping, school, or events. Even though she didn't say it, I'm sure this was a major relief to Brianna.

***

On the day before high school graduation, Jessie, Jane, and myself met at our favorite hangout, Eddie's Best Burgers. Once we got there, we were so excited to see each other that the three of us began talking all at once. I guess we were a bit loud giggling and talking at the same time because

Smitty shook his head and had that "here we go again" look on his face. So we decided—as best we could—to talk one at a time. We each wanted to update each other since we hadn't talked in days.

Jane began and said that things were going very well with her boyfriend Brian and they were having a lot of fun just being together. She said that she enjoyed working at the bookstore and got along really well with the store manager. Jane began to make up a list of books she intended to read based on all the books she found in the bookstore. Every once in a while, Brian would stop in and they would have coffee together and discuss some of the books they both had read or would like to read. As Jane found out, Brian was an avid reader just like Jane.

When it was my turn, I mentioned like Jane, things were going very well with my boyfriend Carl. It was nothing serious but we did enjoy each other's company. I was pleased to say that after dating Carl for a while, I found that he was as nice to me as the first day that I met him at Johnny D's party. Hearing Johnny D's name brought about a chuckle from the three of us, especially from Jess with that amazing laugh of hers.

I also mentioned that my job at the music store was going well. I had to admit that my goal was to get more involved in the field of music, but I wasn't quite sure what route to take to achieve my goal.

I then asked Jessie for an update. She told us that things were still very serious between Paul and herself and she felt that she found the true love of her life. Jane and I were so happy to hear this, knowing that we felt Jess and Paul were the ideal couple.

Smitty eventually came over to our table with our lunch.

"This is on the house", said Smitty, "Congratulations on your graduation!" As he put the plates down at our table, Smitty smiled and said proudly, "Enjoy!". We looked at each other and we broke out in laughter.

All three of us had ordered hamburgers, and all three of us had clearly specified to Smitty that our burgers were to be cooked at a medium temperature. But, as usual, all three hamburgers were cooked well-done, actually they were nearly burnt. Of course, this didn't surprise us as this was customary and something he had become "famous" for.

We then began to reminisce about our high school days. The first thing that was brought up was Jessie's incredible high school scoring record. As she had done so many times before, Jess downplayed the whole thing, changing the topic and asked about the glee club that Jane and I belonged to. Jane said how much fun it was being in that club, especially the times when Jane and I sang as a duo at various events.

"Of course, the two of you became recording stars with that hit record of yours," said Jess. "I forgot to bring that record with me so the two of you can autograph it for me."

Jane responded, "Oh darn, I've been practicing my autograph since that record came out and you would have been my first signing!"

"Do you think the station ever played *Frankie, My Love*, at least once?" I asked

Jane chimed in, "I sure hope not!", causing us to laugh once again.

The conversation turned serious when Jess brought up that awful stabbing incident we witnessed in our sophomore year.

"Sure hope they found that kid. I'm told he was only 13 years old. Hopefully, they will find and punish him so he never hurts another person again! Luckily, Emery survived."

Shaking her head, Jess changed the subject again and began talking about our high school teachers.

"I wonder if Miss 'Hersey Bar' will stay at Bridgeport High or find a job she would be good at, whatever that might be."

All Jane and I could think of was the time Miss Hersey tried to "teach" Jess how to shoot baskets. Jessie began laughing with that infectious laugh of hers which caused some of the other kids in the burger joint to look at us and join in our laughter.

"Kind of strange," said Jane in a soft voice, "that after graduation tomorrow the three of us will be going our separate ways, attending different colleges."

"Yeh," responded Jess, "but we must promise here and now that we will keep our close friendship going and be in touch as often as possible."

Without hesitation, the three of us made a solemn oath that we would remain friends no matter what.

"How are the burgers?" asked Smitty as he walked by our table.

"Same as always," replied Jane with her keen sense of humor. "Keep up the good work Smitty!"

Jess and I recounted to Jane our fun experience trying on our graduation gowns.

I sure wish I was there for that one!", replied Jane. "By the way Jess, how's your dad doing?"

"Fine. Thank you, Jane, he's really looking forward to attending my college games."

I chimed in, "What an amazing dad you have Jess. I really love that guy!"

Jess, choking up a bit, responded, "Yeh, me too. He certainly has been my rock!"

After staying at Eddie's for nearly three hours we figured it was time to leave. As we got up to go, Jane said in a kidding fashion, "Are you two going to ask Smitty for a doggie bag to bring home our leftovers?" We all got a kick out of that.

As we got to our cars in the parking lot, Jess turned and shouted, "See you both tomorrow at our graduation!" We nodded in agreement and left Eddie's and got in our cars.

***

On a beautiful, warm day in the spring of 1970, we all gathered outside for our graduation ceremony.

In the audience seated next to each other were Jessie's dad, Paul Mari, my mom, Brianna, and Jane's mom and dad. It was great seeing them sitting together.

Jess and I got a big hand once it was announced that we received high honors. While we were proud of our accomplishments, we both felt more happy for our family than ourselves.

I was so happy when Brianna told me that our mom was feeling well enough to attend our graduation. I couldn't help but think that maybe this would give her the lift that she needed to stop drinking and begin to get better.

The graduation ceremony went smoothly as planned, with only one exception. The one exception was when Johnny D tripped and collided with the line of graduates in front of him who were about to get their diplomas. This almost caused a domino chain reaction on stage. Fortunately, one of our fellow graduates prevented that from happening.

I looked back at Jess who was standing in line in back of me and asked, "Isn't he your former boyfriend?" I jokingly asked in a whisper.

"Don't remind me!" responded Jess with her hand covering her face as she tried not to laugh, "At least he didn't fall on his face. Well, at least not yet!"

21

NEW ADVENTURES

Jane and I both knew in our hearts that Jess would soon be on her way to become a college basketball star.

The summer after graduation was filled with mixed emotions. Jane, Jess, and I continued to hang out as much as we could, but there were many times when we were not able to get together. Jane and I continued to work at our jobs, while Jess continued her volunteer work at the Royalty Theatre.

Jessie often told me about two nine-year-old girls who reminded Jess of her and me. The two girls' names were Gina and Debbie.

"They were two outgoing kids like you and me," said Jess. "When they were not practicing or performing in a play, they both would follow me around everywhere I went. I loved being around them because they were so cute and, like I said, they reminded me of you and me. Depending on which musical was being performed, one or both of them would appear on stage. They were great little actresses and had beautiful voices for their age.

"They knew I was a basketball player and would ask me a million questions about sports. They also had that same curiosity about school that we had at that age, which made me so happy.

"One musical that featured both Gina and Debbie was a play called *The Two Of Us*. It had a successful fifteen performance run. I was invited to the after-party following the finale. At the after-party, the director praised both Gina and Debbie and as a memento gave them both a shiny bracelet with the name of the play on one side and their names on the back.

"Immediately after they were presented the bracelets they both ran up to me at full steam, giggling and shouting, 'Jessie, Jessie, look what we got!' They were so excited to show me the special gifts in honor of their performance. I told them, 'These gifts are so well deserved. I'm so very proud of you and love you both very much!' Even though it was a bit awkward for me, I have to admit that I felt honored that they both ran immediately to me even before they showed their immediate families who were also in the room."

Even though we were busy with basketball, cheerleading practices, working, volunteering, and babysitting, the three of us made every effort to hang out together at Eddie's, even if it was for only an hour or two.

Jane and Jess also found a need to spend more time practicing their basketball techniques in preparation for college, knowing they would be facing stiffer competition once their college season began. I fully understood this. I was quite busy not only working my summer full-time hours but also taking care of my mom along with Brianna. But, I made every effort to go to the basketball courts to watch them both practice.

Despite our busy schedules, the three of us vowed that we would find the time to get together as much as possible, especially since we would soon be going our separate ways. So, Eddie's burger joint and local ice cream shops took on a special significance for us. We spent hours just talking, sharing memories, and laughing all the time. Our high school days were filled with many fun experiences and so much laughter. It was a very nostalgic time for us and the three of us admitted it was sad to see those happy moments come to an end.

And, so, with our high school years behind us, it was now time to turn the page and look forward to new adventures that the future had in store for us.

We had mixed feelings about joining the college ranks. On the one hand, the three of us admitted to being excited about the prospect of becoming college students, but on the other hand we felt sad that we would not be attending the same schools. With this in mind, we vowed to keep in touch by phone on a regular basis.

Jane and I both shared the same feeling about Jessie's basketball future—that Jessie's talent was not just a high school phenomenon. We knew in our hearts that Jess would soon be on her way to becoming a college basketball star.

My first day at Southern Connecticut State College went rather smoothly and the transition from high school to college was not as difficult as I thought it might be. My course schedule did not look imposing and I talked to a few students about upcoming tryouts for the cheerleading team. In speaking with Jane, she too found the transition to college not as frightening as she anticipated. She had a few questions about her class schedule but the guidance counselor answered them to her satisfaction. In the coming weeks Jane hoped to find out about basketball practices at Central Connecticut State College.

After I spoke with Jane on the phone, Jessie called me. She said that she received a call from the Boston College Athletic Director on the first day of school. He said that he heard all about her and that he wanted to personally give her a tour of the campus, especially the sports facilities. She found the AD very cordial and accessible, which she appreciated. Jessie told me that she had a very good first impression of the school and could not wait for the basketball practices to begin. I was very impressed that on the very first day, the Athletic Director actually reached out to *her*. I told her that it spoke volumes about how they felt Jessie would fit into their plans of becoming a top-ranked basketball team. Jessie thanked me and admitted she was surprised that the AD contacted her so soon.

As promised, the three of us kept in touch by phone nearly on a daily basis. During one of the calls, Jessie excitedly told us about a special date she had with Paul during a break from college.

Jess told us that one evening, Paul took her to an upscale restaurant, which impressed Jessie very much. During their meal, Paul clumsily dropped his fork on the floor and they both began to laugh. When Jessie looked up she noticed Paul's chair was still empty. She looked down and thought it odd that Paul was still down on the floor. Looking again, she noticed that Paul was kneeling on one knee holding a ring up to her.

"Jessie Darcey, will you marry me?"

A totally ecstatic Jessie responded, "Yes … yes I will."

With that, the entire restaurant clientele began to clap and cheer.

I could hear the excitement in her voice. Sheer joy! During our calls, Jessie asked if I would be her maid of honor and asked if Jane would agree to be one of her bridesmaids. Jane and I both told her we would be honored.

Jess and Paul both decided to wait a few years before getting married since Jessie was only a college freshman and wanted time to settle in with both her school and basketball schedules. Paul agreed and said he too needed time to complete his studies and graduate from Yale. He also wanted to concentrate on getting off to a good start with the job that was waiting for him upon graduation.

Paul told Jess that his goal outside of school and work was to get a pilot's license and someday purchase his own small airplane. He said that if that were to happen he would fly both of them to the Caribbean for their honeymoon. Jess replied that she never flew in a small airplane but that she would trust Paul as a pilot.

22

COLLEGE

"I don't believe what I'm seeing!"

It didn't take long for Jessie's college coaches to be blown away by Jessie's

skills on the basketball court.

During one of my college breaks, I drove up to Chestnut Hill, Massachusetts to visit Jessie at Boston College. Jane had wanted to go but decided at the last moment that she needed to concentrate on two important school assignments. She said she planned to visit Jess soon and would contact me at that time.

Jess had just begun her basketball practice sessions at the college and asked if I would like to attend one of her practice games. She said she would get permission from one of her coaches for me to go to her practice. Her coach said it was okay for me to attend her practice providing I didn't interrupt their sessions in any way. I assured Jessie I would not.

The coaches split the team in two for a practice game. I sat by myself somewhat near where the coaches were standing to observe their players during the practice game. Once they saw Jess in action on the court, I overheard the head coach say to his assistant, "I don't believe what I'm seeing!"

As I have seen many times before, Jessie's ball handling and shooting were flawless. Her defenders had a very difficult time keeping up with her as she easily dribbled past them and made shots at all different areas on the court. The coaches were all smiles as they witnessed for the first time Jessie's wizardry on the basketball court.

Once practice was over, I noticed that the head coach walked the full length of the court to catch up to Jess.

"Nice job out there Jessie", said the coach, "Keep up the good work!"

"Thank you, coach, I will. "

Once Jess got dressed and came out of the locker room, she asked if it would be okay for her to bring along one of her teammates to the local hangout for a bite to eat. I told her of course.

Julie Edmonds was a college recruit from Palo Alto, California. Jessie introduced me saying "Julie, this is my best friend Abby." Her reference to me as her best friend made me very happy. Once we sat down at the Townline Diner, Jessie turned to me and said, "Abby, the food at this place isn't as 'good' as Eddie's but it will do for now." Laughing, Jess explained our inside joke. Julie smiled and said that, obviously, that was a fun experience for both of us. We agreed.

Changing the subject, I asked Julie what high school she attended in California. She responded that she attended Palo Alto High School. Jess commented that Julie was the star player on the girls' Palo Alto high school team. Julie nodded in appreciation and returned the favor by saying, "Well, we all heard about Jessie's basketball accomplishments 3,000 miles away!" Julie admitted that she had hoped to attend Stanford University in nearby Stanford, California but her grades weren't that great. When she was offered a full scholarship from Boston College she jumped at the opportunity. "Now that I'm here", Julie continued, "I believe we have a strong basketball team, especially with the addition of Jessie." This brought a smile from Jess.

Julie informed us that when she arrived at Boston College it was the first time that she was in New England.

"I'm trying to adjust to this cold weather you have out here," Julie said with a smile.

"Well, Jess and I have lived in New England all our lives and we're still trying to get used to the cold weather."

Jessie agreed and said, "It's just something we expect but we still have to adjust to the harsh winters."

Later, Jess and I decided to go to a nearby community theatre for a performance of Shakespeare's *As You Like It*. I suggested that we invite Julie to go with us. Jessie thought that was a good idea. Julie said that she had never seen a play so this would be a new experience for her. The three of us thought the performance was very good.

After the play, we stopped at a local diner for a quick bite. As our food was served, I asked Jess how things were going with her and Paul.

"Great! Paul comes up here quite a bit. We have so much fun together going out to dinner or movies, going for walks, things like that.

"So Abby, how are things going with the guy you met in school?"

"Very nice. His name is Roger Anderson and he's a freshman at Southern Connecticut. He's a good looking guy with a great sense of humor. I can't wait for you to meet Roger. "

Turning to Julie, I asked, "So Julie, how about you, are you seeing anyone in particular?"

"No, not at this time. I broke up with a guy in Palo Alto before leaving and I'm just getting adjusted to things here."

"Well, we'll have to see about that," said Jess smiling at me. "I'll be on the lookout for you Julie!"

Julie said she would appreciate that since she's a bit shy around guys. Jess and I just looked at each other remembering quite well how shy we were when it came to dating.

The next day I told Jess that I had to go back to Connecticut but that I would call her when I got back home. After giving me a quick hug, Jess asked if I would be able to attend any of her home games. I replied, "Absolutely, I can't wait to see as many home games as I can. You can count on that!"

Days later, a very excited Jess called me to say she was informed by the head coach that she would be one of the starting guards on the Boston College varsity team. She knew this was a big deal since freshmen normally were not selected for the varsity squad. If it were another player I would say I was surprised since the season was still nearly a month away. But because it was Jess, I was not surprised.

After giving me the good news about herself, Jess told me that she was a bit concerned about Julie's status on the team. For some reason, her shooting and playmaking skills were not going well. Before the fall off in her shooting, the coaches were seriously considering making Julie the starting guard along with Jess. However, seeing how Julie's shooting and playmaking were not as sharp as they were in earlier practice sessions, she was benched a few times and the coaches seemed to be leaning towards another player to become the other starting guard. It seemed that something was bothering Julie and it was affecting her play on the court.

Jess told me that she was going to spend some additional time with Julie. She said that Julie was a very good shooter and playmaker and it showed in the first few scrimmage games. But then it all fell flat for some reason.

Two weeks later, Jessie called to let me know that Julie's play on the court had improved greatly. She was now performing as well as she did during her first few practice sessions. Jess said that she did spend time privately with Julie to go over her basketball techniques. But, in Jessie's opinion, it seemed like Julie had lost her confidence and motivation and eventually found a way to get back to her real self. I could hear the excitement in Jessie's voice during our call.

"Abby, I'm so thrilled that our coaches seem to be very happy with Julie's performance on the court and, hopefully, she will win back her starting position once the season starts. I hope that our coaches are seeing how well Julie and I complement each other on the court. Even though we are both freshmen, I'm keeping my fingers crossed that Julie will join me as a starting guard on the varsity team."

As opening day of the Boston College women's basketball team was approaching, I checked my schedule and saw that I would be free on the day of the opening game. Jane called me to say that she would be able to go with me.

I called Jess and told her Jane and I would be going to her first game. Jessie said she was thrilled hearing this and was looking forward to hearing updates on what was happening in our lives. Jess mentioned that her father was going to the game also but had some concerns about him going by himself.

"Abby would it be possible to drive my dad to the game?" asked Jess. "He's also planning on going, but I worry about him driving, especially at night."

"Absolutely! I will be delighted to drive your father to the game. Actually, it will be a nice opportunity for Jane and me to talk to him since we haven't seen your dad in a long time."

Jess told me that Paul had also planned to go to her game but had prior commitments which he was not able to reschedule. She said that Paul would be visiting her during the week and they made plans to attend several cultural events in the area.

The opening game was against a much improved Loyola team. As Jessie had hoped, Julie won her starting position on the team.

We got to the game early to get good seats. During the team's warmup before the game, Jess saw the three of us sitting together and briefly smiled.

The game was close during the first few minutes as the Loyola Ramblers matched Boston College basket for basket. It was then that Jessie displayed her magic on the court.

With the score tied early in the game, Jessie sensed that Loyola was gaining momentum. Knowing this, Jess took matters into her own hands. She began by easily dribbling past her defender to free herself up for open shots which she made three straight times.

After a time out, the Loyola coach put two defenders on Jess, all to no avail. As taught by her dad years ago, Jessie developed excellent court vision, knowing all the time where her teammates were situated on the court. Once she easily dribbled past her two defenders she would take the shot or pass the ball to a player very near the basket.

The Loyola team seemed stymied as Boston College began to widen the lead. This time, the Loyola coach had three defenders to prevent Jessie from shooting or passing the ball. This strategy also failed as Jess dribbled past all three defenders with relative ease. The Boston College fans took notice and began to cheer Jessie on, with chants of "Jessie, Jessie, Jessie." Those were the same chants that I heard when Jess thrilled her fans in high school.

Jessie began to put on a basketball clinic and the game became a blow out in favor of the Boston College team. Jessie ended up with 58 points and 14 assists. Julie did very well in the game, scoring 24 points and did an outstanding job directing plays for the team's offense.

After the game, we waited for Jess and Julie to come out of the locker room. Julie came out first, saying Jessie was still being congratulated by her teammates but she would be out shortly. While waiting, Julie took me to the side.

"Abby I have to tell you something. I owe everything to Jessie for helping me regain my confidence. It's a long story, but my ex-boyfriend from Palo Alto came up to see me at my dorm. He was very loud and belligerent to me to the point where I had to call the campus police to escort him out of the building. I was so embarrassed and hurt by that and it affected me mentally. I withdrew into my shell and completely lost confidence in myself. This had an immediate impact on my basketball play. I began losing interest in my studies and in basketball."

"Julie, I'm so sorry to hear that about your ex-boyfriend. That must have been so difficult for you. But you shouldn't feel embarrassed. He's the one who was being a jerk! Please try not to keep something like that to yourself. Jess and I are here to help you, so please don't hesitate to contact us, even if it's just to talk it out."

"Thank you, Abby, I will do that if something like that happens again. I want you to know that it was Jessie who got me to believe in myself again. She was so kind to stay with me after our basketball practices and go over certain basketball techniques that she saw I needed help on. But mainly she got me to open up about what had happened when my ex-boyfriend said some very hurtful things to me. I don't know how she did it, but Jessie got me to believe in myself and to let go of my negative emotions. She didn't tell me, but I'm sure Jessie was instrumental in having our coaches see that we worked well together on the court and for me to have the opportunity to be a starter on our team.

"Abby, Jessie has been such an inspiration to me, and watching her play is the most amazing thing I've ever seen. I just wanted you to know since you are her best friend."

Biting down on her quivering lower lip trying not to tear up, Julie then said, "I'm sure Jessie will downplay all of this but she is the reason why I was the starting guard tonight and why I had a good game."

Smiling I responded, "Sure sounds like the Jessie we know and love! Wait…here comes Jessie now…Thank you for sharing all of this with me."

I quickly thought about all the people that Jess has inspired—including me. Just then, Jessie approached us and apologized for the delay. When she saw Julie she smiled and gave her a quick hug

"Now, that's the Julie I know!" said Jess.

Looking over to her dad, Jess gave him a big hug.

"Thank you Dad for being here for our opening game, you know that means a lot to me, right?"

"I do Jess, and it was a pleasure to see how well you and Julie worked together on the court. Way to go Julie!"

"Thank you, Mr. Darcey. I too want to thank the three of you for all your support!"

Jess nodded and said, "Yeh, Julie and I work together very well on the court." Putting her arm around Jane, Jess remarked, "Julie's passes to me are really crisp, just like Jane here!" This brought a huge smile on Jane's face.

"Okay," said Jess, "let's get something to eat. I'm famished!"

The next game was an away game against a tough Maryland team. We were unable to attend this game, but the local newspapers in the Boston area told us all we needed to know. Julie called me the following day. She read me an article over the phone that was in one of the popular local newspapers up there.

Jessie Darcey Shines for Boston College

Jessie Darcey of Boston College put on a basketball clinic last night for the Maryland faithful, scoring 64 points with 20 assists. Jessie wowed the fans during the game, leading Boston College to an upset victory over Maryland.

Darcey seemed to score at will and the fans were mesmerized by Jessie's ball handling exhibition on the court. It reached the point where even many Maryland fans began cheering for Jessie as they saw first-hand the magic she displayed.

Judging by Jessie Darcey's performance in her first two games and speaking with her coaches, we are witnessing the emergence of possibly the best female freshman basketball player in the country.

After speaking with Julie on the phone, I then called Jess to congratulate her. In true form, Jess thanked me but immediately changed the subject. She asked me how things were going at college and wanted an update on Roger and myself. She told me that Jane also called her and they had a nice conversation. Jess said she was looking forward to the three of us getting together soon.

As we expected, Jane did make the starting team at Central Connecticut. She called both Jessie and me to tell us how thrilled she was on her selection as the team's point guard.

***

Several weeks later I received a call from Jess about a party at her college.

"Abby, our college is hosting an informal party next Saturday. Would you and Jane be available to come up to the party? Of course, please feel free to bring your boyfriends."

"I'd love to. Let me check with Jane and get back to you."

Fortunately, all four of us were available to go to the party at Jessie's college. I called Jess to confirm that we would meet her at her dorm and go to the party from there. Roger drove and Brian and Jane sat in the back. It was a wonderful opportunity for the four of us to chat about a host of things during our drive to the college. I especially liked how Roger and Brian got along so well as if they knew each other for many years.

Once we got to Jessie's dorm, she introduced her boyfriend Paul to Roger and Brian.

At the party, Jessie introduced Julie to our boyfriends as well as several other people Jess had made friends with. From the very beginning of the party, we all found it very comfortable being together with no one feeling awkward or uncomfortable.

Despite the loud music and all the talking going on, we all heard a loud thud. Looking towards the room's entrance, we noticed a man stumbling his way across the room, knocking chairs over as he appeared to walk towards us. He was obviously intoxicated and began to yell out "Julie.... Julie, where are you?"

"Oh my God, it's Jeff," cried Julie as she slumped in her seat and swiped the back of her hand across her eyes which had started to tear up.

"Who's Jeff?" asked Roger.

I quickly responded, "Jeff is Julie's former boyfriend when they lived in Palo Alto." Turning to our boyfriends I asked that they help me get Jeff out of the main room. "Guys, he doesn't belong here. Julie already told him that she doesn't want to see him again.'"

As Jeff began to make his way to Julie with a vase in his hands, our boyfriends stopped him. Jeff took a szq1wing at Roger but his punch missed its mark. Jeff eluded Roger's grasp and rushed to Julie in a threatening manner. Before Jeff had a chance to hit Julie, Roger hit him with both fists from behind and Jeff fell to the floor. The guys then grabbed a hold of Jeff and dragged him to the lobby, with Jeff's feet dragging on the floor the entire time. As they pushed Jeff into a chair in the lobby, campus police showed up and our boyfriends explained the situation. A call was made to the police department and Jeff was arrested for aggravated assault and threatening with a weapon.

Jeff was escorted out of the room by the police, with the guys keeping a close eye on the perpetrator. Jess had hurried over to Julie who was crying uncontrollably.

"Julie," urged Jess as she took her hand, "listen to me. This is NOT your fault. You already made it crystal clear that he is not to see you. The police will take care of this matter now. This is entirely his fault and you should not be upset or embarrassed by his actions. You have nothing to be ashamed of Julie, do you hear what I'm saying?"

"Yes, I do Jess. I'm sorry to put you all through this. Jeff was never like this when we were in Palo Alto. He never even drank at the time. I'm frightened now, Jess. That…that evil look on his face. What should I do?"

"Well, the first thing is to compose yourself. Tomorrow you and I will make a trip to the police station to explain the situation and ask that a restraining order be placed against Jeff. That way he wouldn't dare try to get near you."

Jess stood up and addressed all the shocked onlookers at the party.

"Everyone, can I have your attention please? Thank you. Everything is under control. The man is now in police custody and will not be returning. So let's get back to enjoying our party. Thank you."

The music began to play again as did the loud chatter and laughing.

Wiping the tears from her eyes with tissues that Jess gave her, Julie said to our group, "I'm going back to my dorm. I'm so…" Julie's voice trailed off.

"By no means are you returning to your dorm," insisted Jess. "Julie, you are going to stay here and once you're settled down we are going to enjoy the party. We are all here for you. The worst is over and now it's time for all of us to get back to having fun." Looking over to our boyfriends, Jess smiled and said, "Thank you guys, you were amazing."

The following day Julie and Jess asked the police to place a restraining order on Jeff. We were told that the court would have to issue a restraining order.

In the next few days, Jess watched over Julie like a mother hen ensuring that Julie didn't withdraw like she had done when her ex-boyfriend showed up uninvited at her dorm.

I was relieved when Jess told me that the court did issue a restraining order to deter Jeff from going near Julie. I was also happy to hear that Julie did not withdraw and she got back to living her normal life.

Jane suggested that it would be great if we can schedule a party and invite Jess and Julie. Jane said that she spoke with her parents who gave her permission to host a party at her house.

Jane told me that one of her classmates—Art Spensor— was a basketball player on the men's team at her college. She mentioned that he and his girlfriend split up on an amicable basis. She described Art as tall, good looking, and a lot of fun to be around. I knew exactly what Jane had in mind.

"So, Jane, why don't you invite Art to our party?

With a slight giggle, Jane responded, "Why, Abby, you read my mind!"

Jess and Julie agreed to come down to Jane's party. Of course, Jane also invited Jess's boyfriend Paul. Jess didn't mention anything about Jane's friend Art just in case Jane's matchmaking scheme didn't work.

At the party, Jane introduced Art to Julie. At first, there appeared to be some awkwardness between the two. However, once the topic turned to basketball the awkwardness seemed to disappear. In fact, the two talked nearly the entire time we were there. Towards the end of the party, Julie whispered to Jess and me that Art asked her for a date and she accepted. We were all very happy for Julie, especially after that traumatic episode during the college party.

Julie began dating Art on a regular basis. Jess and I were thrilled to hear that they got along very well. Art visited Julie on campus whenever he managed to find free time in between his basketball practices and school assignments. In turn, Julie made every attempt to drive down to Connecticut to attend as many of Art's basketball games as possible.

On one occasion, Julie invited Jess and me to Art's game against Holy Cross. Jess and I freed up our schedule in order to attend Central's game which would be played on Holy Cross's home court. Early on in the season, Central was having a less than stellar year with what Julie described as "erratic play" by the team. Sometimes the team looked very good while other times the team looked flat. Central hoped to turn things around beginning with an upset victory over a very strong Holy Cross squad.

Sitting next to Jess and me, Julie confided in us that Art was not off to a very good season. His shooting was average but, as Julie saw it, his lateral movement needed a good deal of work. His coach worked with him on this but Art was still having difficulty freeing himself up to score more points. Julie thought that maybe it was because of Art's lack of quickness

He seemed to be unable to shoot without one of his opponents blocking his shot or forcing him to change his shooting in mid-air, which caused him to miss many of his shots. Julie told us that she gave Art a lot of encouragement but did not want to give him any shooting advice since she didn't want it to ruin their relationship.

As the game progressed, the three of us saw exactly what Julie was talking about. Even I, with my limited basketball knowledge, saw the difficulty Art was having attempting shots that were either blocked or missed because Art was not in the right position. With Central's offense struggling, Holy Cross began to take a commanding lead.

I turned to Jess with pleading eyes, and Jessie knew exactly what I was going to ask her.

"I know that look, Abby," Jess said, "and no, I will not get involved. That's up to his coach and I don't want to step on anyone's toes. Besides he may not even want my advice, which I fully understand."

"Jessie," I asked, "do you see what Art is doing wrong?"

"Yes, I do. But that doesn't mean I can help him. It's mid-season so there may not be enough time for him to turn this around even if he agreed to accept my advice."

"Jess," said Julie, "Art thinks the world of you and respects your basketball skills. Would you mind if I at least ask him? If he says no, I promise I won't pursue it further. If you're not comfortable with this, I completely understand. But if he's not getting help from his coach that he needs, maybe an outsider such as you can be of help to him."

"Julie, if it was before or after basketball season, I would love to help out. I just don't want to interfere. I'm not sure if I…" Jessie's voice trailed off.

Seeing Jessie's indecision, I asked her, "Why don't you at least let Julie ask him in a non-threatening way? If he says no, that would be the end of that. But at least we would have tried."

Jessie responded, "Ok, but Julie please be honest with me. If he says no or if he hesitates in any way let me know, ok?"

"I promise I will," said Julie.

After leaving the locker room, Art came up to us and, with an awkward smile, said, "Man that was some shellacking that we took!"

Jessie tried to put things into perspective for Art, saying, "Well, you're not the only team that Holy Cross has beaten like this. I've read that they are a very powerful team this year and many of their games are lopsided like this one. You shouldn't feel discouraged by this game but rather you should learn from any mistakes made."

Art nodded his head in agreement. He then suggested that we all go get something to eat. Julie had promised Jess that she would suggest having Jessie give him some basketball tips during a private discussion when they got home. So, there was no talk of having Jess help out Art during our meal.

Two days later, Julie walked into Jessie's dorm room with a smile on her face.

"Jess, I spoke privately with Art and asked him if he would be comfortable with you giving him some basketball advice. Surprisingly, Art said, 'Sure! I was going to bring that up during our meal but didn't want to put Jess on the spot. Any help I can get from Jess would be much appreciated. If there is anyone who could help turn my basketball performance around, it would be Jessie.' Julie continued, "Art even mentioned this to his coach. At first, the coach was a bit hesitant, but then told Art, 'If it was anyone other than Jessie Darcey, I would have a problem with this. But knowing Jessie's incredible basketball skills, especially her playmaking ability, I really have no problem. Just keep me updated.'"

Jessie, shaking her head, said, "Ok Julie, I'll give it a try but I can't guarantee anything. I'm only doing this because you are such a good friend."

Julie gave her a quick hug and said, "Jessie Darcey, you're the best!"

"Well, let's not get ahead of ourselves. These lessons may not pan out quite like you imagine. Anyway, with my school studies and basketball practices I only have a limited amount of time to help Art out." Shrugging her shoulders Jess said, "But who knows? Let's see what we can do to make this work."

Jess told Julie that she was in the best shape of her life. She had been keeping up with her school studies and felt physically fit. All this helped her to practice in a good frame of mind, so now may be a good time to spend some time helping Art out.

Art traveled up to Boston College as much as he could to get some private lessons from Jess. The lessons began to pay off for Art, as Jessie taught him some very important playmaking moves. During Art's private lessons, he hung on Jessie's every word. With a great deal of encouragement and heeding Jessie's basketball advice, Art began to effectively maneuver around his opponents which would free himself for more open shots.

Once Art began to effectively employ Jessie's playmaking strategy in his games, Art was a completely different player on the court. His scoring average began to increase substantially. With Art leading the way, Central ended up with a respectable won-loss record, having won the last four games of the season and winning praise from their coach.

To his amazement, Art ended up receiving Central's MVP award. Later that day, he called Jess to thank her for all her valuable assistance.

***

Whenever possible, Jess and I attended Jane's home games to cheer her on. She did not disappoint her coaches. Just as in high school, Jane demonstrated her leadership abilities on the court as well as her outstanding defensive skills. After her games we would make a point to get together at a local diner to update each other on college life, and life in general. Jane made a point of saying how much she appreciated our support and our friendship.

***

As weeks went by, Jessie noticed a sudden change in her physical status. She became aware of the fact that she began to gain weight. She also began feeling nauseous just about every morning, which was unusual for her. At first she chalked this up to eating more junk food than usual since she was a bit nervous about the change in her class schedule at the college. Knowing this, Jessie made a point to sign up for exercise classes that were available at the school. She knew that being on the college basketball team would require her to be in top physical condition.

Despite her rigorous training, Jessie noticed that her weight gain continued. She casually mentioned this to me during one of our daily phone calls. Hearing this, I encouraged Jess to make an appointment right away with the school nurse to make sure everything was okay. Privately, I became very concerned about Jess's health knowing how physically fit she always was since the first day I met her years ago.

So, Jessie saw the school nurse as I asked, probably knowing I would haunt her if she didn't make an appointment. Jessie was totally surprised when the nurse said she had a hunch that Jessie might be pregnant. Saying it was only a hunch, the nurse advised her to have an examination by a doctor as soon as possible. Heeding the nurse's advice, Jessie made an appointment that day to see a nearby doctor. To her astonishment, the doctor confirmed that Jessie was indeed pregnant.

Jessie had mixed emotions once she heard that she was pregnant. On the one hand she was very excited to know that she was going to have a baby with Paul. On the other hand, Jessie was well aware that she would have to put her basketball ambitions temporarily on hold. She also was not sure if her pregnancy would affect her scholarship in any way. However, once she thought this through, Jessie felt that giving birth at this time was so much more important than playing sports.

Jessie couldn't wait to tell Paul the good news, knowing that Paul would be just as excited as her. Sure enough Jessie told me that when she called Paul to tell him they would be having a baby, Paul sounded very excited. He said he would take time off from school so they can celebrate the "great news" in person.

When Jessie was several months pregnant she decided to drive to Connecticut to visit her father during a break in her school schedule. As soon as Mr. Darcey looked at Jessie's belly, he told Jessie how ecstatic he was at the notion of becoming a grandfather. It was an emotional experience for both Mr. Darcey and Jessie.

***

Several days after her visit with her dad, Jessie received a call from Bridgeport Hospital. She was told on the phone that her father had suffered a heart attack and he was in very serious condition. Hearing this news, Jessie ran to her car and rushed to Bridgeport Hospital, hoping against hope that her father would still be alive when she got to the hospital. She was a bit relieved when the receptionist told her that her dad was being treated by the doctors in his room. The receptionist told her that she would call the nurse on the floor who can give her more details. As she waited for the nurse to come down to the waiting room, Jessie called me. After explaining what occurred, Jess asked if I would be able to come down to the hospital to be with her. I told her I would immediately come down to the hospital. A few minutes later, Nurse Donohue met Jess in the waiting room and explained, as best she could, Mr. Darcey's status. The nurse said that the cardiologist—Doctor Connors—was busy treating her father in his hospital room. She said she would have Doctor Connors come down to see Jessie and provide her a status report as soon as he is finished in Mr. Darcey's room.

Rushing down to the hospital, I met Jess in the waiting room and gave her a big hug. Jessie explained that she was waiting for Doctor Connors to come down and give her an update on Mr. Darcey's condition. Seeing that Jess was crying and appeared exhausted I went to the water fountain and came back with a cup of water, which Jessie said she appreciated.

Soon after, Doctor Connors arrived in the waiting room and addressed us.

"I'm looking for Jessie Darcey?"

"I'm Jessie," said a beleaguered Jess.

"Jessie, my name is Doctor Connors. I'm a cardiologist and I have been treating your father. Mr. Darcey had a heart attack, and he is in serious condition. We had to perform emergency surgery and he is currently on a breathing tube. Jessie, I must tell you that although we managed to keep your father alive his heart is very weak. Together with my assistants and the nursing staff, we are monitoring your father on a 24/7 basis. I do need tell you that his condition is grave and we fear that his heart may give out at any time. We are doing our very best to not let that happen. You may visit your father for a few minutes. He may have difficulty responding but

I feel you should visit him now just in case. Just inform the attending nurse that I gave you permission to see your father."

"Thank you doctor. I appreciate all that you and your staff are doing to help my dad. I promise to keep my visit short as you suggest."

With that, Jessie turned to me and said, "Abby, would you be able to come with me to visit my dad. I feel a bit weak and I would appreciate your support."

"Of course, Jess, let's go tell the nurse that you would like to visit your dad."

As we entered Mr. Darcey's hospital room, we were both shocked to see the life support system that Jessie's dad was hooked up to. As Jess approached her dad, she immediately doubled back and walked to the hallway. Fortunately, Mr. Darcey did not see us enter his room. Walking into the hallway, I saw that Jessie had burst into tears and was trying her best to compose herself.

"Abby, I didn't expect to see my dad like this. I need to collect myself before I go back into his room. I hope he didn't see me crying." I assured Jess that he did not see her walk in his room.

"Okay Abby, I think I'm ready to go back into the room. Thank you for being here with me and for your understanding."

The first thing we noticed was how the color seemed to disappear from his face and also his labored breathing. Jess immediately walked over and gave her dad a kiss on his forehead. Her dad did not turn in her direction. However, as she held his hand, she smiled when he responded by lightly gripping her hand.

"I love you, Dad. Abby and I are here with you." Just as she said that, Jess felt him grip her hand again, which was his way of telling her that he understood.

After sitting down in a chair close to Mr. Darcey's bed, I signaled to Jessie to have a seat. However, Jess shook her head and said that she preferred to stand, as she continued to hold his hand.

Minutes later, a nurse came into the room and said that she needed to check his breathing tubes and intravenous. Jess said that she would leave so that the nurse can treat her. At that point Jess gave her father a kiss on his forehead. Once she did that, she felt his grip on her hand again. I too gave Mr. Darcey a kiss on his forehead and said, "I love you Mr. Darcey." Just as I said that I could feel his grip as I held his hand.

Once in the hallway, Jess and I both broke down in tears. Gaining her composure, Jess said to me, "Abby, I know my dad is a fighter, but it doesn't appear to me that he is going to win this fight. Based on what his doctor told me and from what I saw, this may very well be the last time we see him alive. I love him so much, but I just have a feeling that he's not going to make it this time."

"Jess, please know that your dad is in my thoughts and prayers that he will recover from this. I don't think I have to tell you that you can call me at any time day or night."

"Thank you, Abby. Yes, I know that. I don't think I told you this but during the last time I visited him when I was a few months pregnant, my dad gave me the combination to his safe. He showed me the important documents he kept in the safe in the event of his passing. Even though he was healthy at the time, it was like he had a feeling that something like this was going to happen to him."

Jessie's feelings about her dad turned out to become a reality. Jess decided to stay at her dad's house while he was in the hospital. The next day, as she prepared to visit her father in the hospital, Jess received a call from Doctor Connors. He gave her the sad news that her dad passed away shortly before his call.

When Jess called me to tell me about her dad's passing, I could barely make out what she was saying because she was crying so hard. As soon as I figured out what she was saying I told her I would call Jane and, if Jane is available, we would both go over to Mr. Darcey's house right away. When Jane and I got there, Jessie gave us a big hug and said she appreciated us coming over to the house. It was obvious to us that she had been crying very hard for some time and bravely tried to gain her composure when we entered her room.

Of course, Jane and I told Jessie that we would always be by her side. We assured Jess that we would both be available to help out with all the logistics of the services held for Mr. Darcey and all matters that needed to be attended to after Mike's services were over.

Mr. Darcey's wake was held at a nearby funeral home.

Jess was amazed at the never ending line of people who came to pay their respects. There were former classmates, teammates, and the many friends whose lives were touched by Mr. Darcey's generosity and kindness.

Jessie was told by one of Mr. Darcey's friends at the service that one of the mourners who came to pay his respect was Tom Smith, the man she heard so much about. She remembered how her father so graciously forgave him after being a victim of Tom's anti-Semitism.

During Mr. Darcey's burial, Jane and I stood next to Jess and made every attempt to console her the best we could. When we got back to Jessie's house, the two of us tried to cheer up a tearful Jessie by recounting many of her dad's wonderful accomplishments and his generosity not only toward Jess but also towards so many others that he encountered in his life. This made Jess smile. It was a smile of a very proud daughter.

***

Weeks later, Brianna and I began to see a deterioration in my mom's condition. Her alcoholism finally began to take its toll. Not only did it affect her mentally, but it had a major effect on her physical condition. Each day my mom's condition grew worse and worse. Brianna and I did what we could to feed, clothe and tend to all her physical needs. But it got to be too much for us. Finally, it reached the point where we had to admit my mother to a nursing home since she needed 24/7 care. The nurses did what they could, but it was to no avail. Shortly thereafter, our mother died in the nursing home.

Knowing that Jess was still dealing with occasional morning sickness due to her pregnancy, I wasn't sure if she would be able to make it to the services. So, I was so happy when she arrived at my house and said she would be attending my mom's services. I made sure Jessie was at my side at all times—along with Jane and Brianna—during my mother's service. After Mom's wake, her funeral mass was held at St Michael's church. Jane sang several wonderful hymns at the church service, which brought tears to my eyes.

Unlike Mr. Darcey's services, there were not a lot of people who attended my mom's wake or church service. Being so preoccupied with her two jobs and then her alcoholism, she only managed to have a couple of friends.

While sitting at the wake with Jess and my sister, I suddenly noticed a startled look on Brianna's face as a tall, handsome man with salt and pepper hair walked towards us. With a solemn look on his face, the man approached Brianna.

"Hello Brianna, do you remember me?"

"Yes, I do. I'm surprised to see you here Dad."

Brianna's words hit me like a ton of bricks. The man looked towards me.

"And you must be Abigail. Gosh, you look a lot like your mom!"

Not knowing what to do, I began to stand up but the man told me to please stay seated.

"I just wanted to offer my condolences and see my two daughters."

Not knowing what to say, I introduced him to Jess and Jane.

"Yes, I've been reading all about you two as has everybody else in this state. Congratulations on your outstanding basketball careers."

In almost a whisper he said to my sister, "Brianna, besides offering my condolences I wanted to say how sorry I am for putting you and your mother through such hell. I know I can never make up for my actions but wanted you to at least know that I have gotten help for my condition and have been sober for a number of years now.

"I know this is not the time or place but maybe when you are both ready we can meet somewhere for dinner or a cup of coffee. Here is my phone number, if you ever decide to call.

"Before I go I wanted to let you know that I will continue to help you with expenses until you both are financially settled, if that is okay with both of you."

As I looked closer, I noticed he had tears in his eyes. I kept asking myself, were those heartfelt tears, or was he putting on an act? Much to my amazement, when my father finished talking, Brianna stood up and gave our dad a big hug.

"Thank you for coming Dad, please take care of yourself. Maybe we will take you up on your offer someday."

Following Brianna's lead, I stood up and gave my dad a hug. With that, he walked away with his head slightly lowered. Jess and Jane, who remained silent, both got up and gave Brianna and me a hug.

"Abby," said Jess, "please know that Jane and I will always be here for you if you ever want to talk about all of this."

Brianna turned to me and whispered, "Abby we'll talk about this at some point." She then quickly changed the subject.

***

With a grueling school schedule including time-sensitive school projects, the months seemed to fly by. Being nearly nine months pregnant, Jessie felt an urgent need to get together with me. She wanted to go over her childbirth plans and other baby related matters. On the phone, I told her that I was so excited that she was coming back to Connecticut and said I couldn't wait to see my "very pregnant best friend."

23

BABY LAND

"Oh my God, what is happening?"

J essie and I decided to meet in Bridgeport at a baby shop to look for baby clothes that would soon be needed. The name of the shop was Baby Land and was widely known throughout Bridgeport as having the finest quality and most reasonably priced baby supplies in the city. Plus, next door was Eddie's Best Burgers, the burger joint that was the local hangout we both frequented on numerous occasions during high school. We thought it would be great to treat ourselves to one of Smitty's burnt hamburgers which he became "famous" for. And maybe we would also bump into one of our former classmates there. Neither of us had heard of any criminal activities in that area for a long time. So we both were not afraid to take our new cars to that location. I had purchased a used metallic blue sports car but it was in beautiful condition and actually looked brand new. It was my first car and I tried to keep it meticulously clean.

Before she left, Jessie called and told me on the phone how wonderful things were turning out, and how lucky she was to have a friend like me and to have Paul as her future husband.

Jessie knew that I also found the love of my life. I confided in Jessie that things were beginning to get very serious between me and Roger and that we had been talking about getting married. Hearing this, Jessie said she was so happy for both of us. I asked Jess to be my maid of honor. Jess replied, "I would be honored. Just let me know when that will be and I will be there for sure."

Jessie said she always smiled when she thought of how I would laugh at the nickname she gave me, "Abby Gabby." She also thought of how Paul would always refer to me by my given name, Abigail. She found that to be so typical of Paul because he always tried to act and speak in a professional manner

Jessie also wanted to tell me about some of the great musicals she attended at theatres near college. She wanted me to know that she was taking music courses at school and was still pursuing her goal of one day becoming a co-owner of a musical theatre. She said she realized that it was a lofty goal and it would take a great deal of resources. Still, it was a goal she wanted to pursue one day. Jess asked me what I thought and whether or not Jane and I would consider possibly being co-owners of a small musical theatre. I told her that I would definitely be interested and suggested that we run it by Jane also. Jessie thought for a few seconds and said, "Legacy Theatre has a nice ring to it." We both thought that would be a dream job since the three of us loved musicals.

"Abby, how cool would it be if you and Jane produced a musical play in our very own theatre!"

"Now that would be awesome! Let's see what Jane has to say about this.

We both knew, realistically, that to achieve our goal, it would take a great deal of money, a lot of research, and hopefully find some donors along the way who would make our dream a reality. But, in our mind, it was a venture worth pursuing in the not so distant future.

"Let's talk about our plans to become theatre co-owners after I give birth and settle back into normal school life," Jessie said. "We have so much to look forward to. I'm so psyched about this! Ok, I'm getting into my car now and I'll see you very soon."

When she arrived at the parking lot in front of the Baby Land store in Bridgeport, I was already waiting for her. I parked in a parking space near the street in an effort to keep someone from banging into my beautiful sports car. Once I saw Jessie, I leaped out of the car and ran to give my friend a big hug. We both laughed at my look of excitement seeing Jessie's pregnant belly.

"I see you are wearing that beautiful necklace and locket that your father gave you," I said.

"I wear this necklace every day and it gives me such comfort."

"C'mon Jess, I want to show you a little gift I bought for your baby. I purchased it at Baby Land. It's in my car."

Jessie followed me to my car and began to laugh at how far away I parked my car in the parking lot.

"I can see why you parked so far away from the shop, your new car is gorgeous! But, you're practically in the street!. I guess I would do the same if I had a cool car like this!"

The two of us began to giggle with excitement as I handed her the baby gift I bought. Standing by my car, Jessie turned to me and her face just lit up.

"Abby this is the happiest moment in my life. And guess what? I'm having a baby girl!

"Jessie, that is such wonderful news. I can't wait!"

"Me too Abby! After our lunch, I want to bring you up to date on everything including the wonderful plans I have for my baby. I am so excited to become a mother and for Paul and me to raise our child as loving parents. I want my child to be exposed to a world of opportunities and become successful in all phases of life.

"Abby, I was so thrilled when you agreed to be my maid of honor for our eventual wedding, but I do have another question. Would you consider being the godmother of my child?"

"I would truly be honored Jess."

"Abby, I can't tell you how much I treasure our friendship. You mean everything to me. I can't wait to see what life has in store for both of us in the future. We have so much to live for!"

Just then, I felt a sharp sting on my neck. Looking down, I saw Jessie lying on the ground. A pool of blood was flowing all around her body.

"Oh my God, what is happening?" I screamed.

In total shock, I did manage to call the emergency number but then froze at the sight of my best friend lying still on the ground. I dropped down next to her, crying uncontrollably. I could feel the blood around my knees as I knelt on the cold, hard ground. I put my jacket around her motionless body. My entire body became numb.

"Please don't leave us, Jess!" I cried out. "Please Jess don't leave me!"

***

The ambulance arrived within minutes and took Jessie on a stretcher and signaled for me to come into the ambulance. I could hardly move but managed to will myself to walk into the ambulance. Looking down at my best friend I felt myself becoming faint and told myself I needed to be strong for Jess.

On the way to Bridgeport Hospital, the medics quickly performed medical treatments on Jessie in a valiant effort to try to get Jess to regain consciousness. All along I held my best friend's lifeless hand.

Jessie was immediately wheeled directly into the operating room. I was treated for a superficial wound and was told I would be all right, words that had no meaning to me. My thoughts and prayers were focused solely on Jess. I remember being led to the waiting room. Once there I asked the nurse at the front desk if she could possibly call my friends because I felt too weak to call. Seeing my trembling hands, the nurse agreed, and I gave her the phone numbers of Paul, Jane, and Roger.

To my amazement, Smitty and EJ were already seated in the waiting room when I got there. I could tell that both Smitty and EJ had been crying and still had tears in their eyes when I gave them both a big hug. Smitty said in a barely recognizable voice that he and EJ ran out to the parking lot but the ambulance was just driving off. They got up and sat next to me and Smitty held my hand without speaking, seeing the weaken condition I was in.

After many hours, I noticed the nurse at the front counter having a discussion with a doctor. During her conversation the nurse pointed in my direction. The doctor then proceeded to walk towards me. As I got up from my chair I felt my legs shaking as I anticipated that the doctor wanted to talk to me. As he approached, he took me to a less crowded area of the waiting room.

"Are you Abby Girardi?"

"Yes…I am." I said nervously.

"My name is Dr. Grayson, I'm one of the hospital surgeons.

"Abby, I'm told by the police that both you and Jessie were hit by a stray bullet as a result of gunfire between two rival gangs. The police are still looking for the people responsible.

"I'm afraid I have some terrible news," he said in a solemn voice. "We have made every effort to revive Jessie, but I'm sorry to tell you that she didn't make it. She died on the operating table."

Hearing the doctor's words, I became weak and nearly fainted. Dr. Grayson signaled the front desk to quickly get me a cup of water. My worst fear had been realized. This all seemed like one big dream. No, it was more like a horrible nightmare.

When he saw that I was a bit more alert after drinking the water, the doctor looked directly at me and continued his conversation.

"While we were not able to save Jessie, we were successful in saving the life of the baby."

"Can I see the baby?" I asked.

"I'm afraid it's much too early for that. The baby is being closely monitored, and it's still touch and go. However, we are optimistic that the baby will pull through this ordeal. The next few days and weeks are crucial since the survival rate for babies in situations like this is not very high. But please know that we are doing everything in our power to ensure that Jessie's baby pulls through. The nurse will call you with an update on the baby's condition. Again, I am very sorry for your loss."

As he got up to leave, I asked, "Doctor, is it a boy or a girl?"

The doctor turned around and responded, "It's a girl."

After a few minutes, Jane came running over to me in the waiting room, her face was white as a ghost. As she gave me a hug, I felt her whole body shaking

"Jess, is she—"

"Jess died on the operating table," I whispered.

Jane cupped her hands over her face and collapsed in the chair in the waiting room. I sat next to Jane and we both broke down in tears.

Soon Paul and Roger came over to us and gave us both a hug.

Paul lowered his head and said in a very low voice, "I just can't believe this. I love Jessie so much!"

Seeing the bandage on my neck and the blood stains on my jeans, Roger asked if I was okay. I explained that I was just grazed by the bullet and the blood stains were from kneeling on the ground next to Jess.

I tried to explain what had happened.

"I gave Jess this gift and I ..." My voice trailed off and I just couldn't finish my thoughts.

Jane put her hand on my arm and suggested that we just sit for a while.

After spending a long time in the waiting area, we realized there was nothing else we could do. Jane said that she would drive me home.

"Abby you're in no condition to drive. Leave your car where it is and we'll pick it up tomorrow. I'll give you a ride home."

Jane turned and blew a kiss to Paul, Roger, Smitty, and EJ. I was unable to turn around and barely was able to walk.

Holding my arm, Jane walked with me to the door of my house. When Brianna saw me she had a terrified look on her face.

"Oh my God Abby, what happened?"

"Can…Can we talk about this tomorrow, Brianna? I need to wash up and go to my room. I just can't talk right now."

Jane tried to compose herself and explained to Brianna the little she knew of what happened.

"Jess was shot and killed earlier today."

"Oh my God!" shouted a bewildered Brianna as she put her hands to her face.

Jane continued, "We don't know who or how it happened. We just came back from the hospital where Jess was pronounced dead. Abby is okay physically but needs your support right now. I will call you in the morning after I, hopefully, get some rest."

"And the baby?" Brianna asked.

"The baby survived, thank God, but is being closely monitored."

"Thank you, Jane, please get some rest. I will definitely take care of Abby, you can count on that. I'll talk to you in the morning.

"Abby, we'll talk in the morning. Try to get some rest if possible," Brianna said as she gave her sister a hug.

"Ok, love you Bri"

"Love you too, Sis"

The following day, I recalled a brief conversation that I had with Jessie's father a while back. For whatever reason he felt confident that Jessie was going to have a baby girl. It had something to do with the shape of Jessie's belly or something like that. He said that his wife Kathleen taught him that "trick."

Mr. Darcey had asked me if Jessie would consider naming the baby "Bobbie" in honor of Bobby Steed. He explained that her full name could be Roberta Darcey, with the nickname "Bobbie." Knowing it would please Jessie, I agreed that it would be a perfect name for the child but at that time I told Mr. Darcey that I would first need to talk to Jessie about that. I never did get a chance to mention this conversation with Jess but knew in my heart that she would totally agree with naming the baby "Bobbie." I asked for Paul's permission, and he agreed.

Still rattled by all that had happened, I called Jane to ask her thoughts on what the proper thing to do in terms of services for Jessie. Such a thing was never brought up in our discussions.

"I really have no idea what Jessie would have wanted," replied Jane. "She was so young, I'm sure she never thought of that herself. But I do know that many people would want to pay their final respects because she had such a profound effect on many peoples' lives, including her teammates, classmates, and so many others. For that reason, I believe there should be services with a wake and a public mass the next day."

Hesitating a bit, I finally agreed with Jane. Once that was decided, Jane asked if I would feel comfortable giving the eulogy during the church services. I told her that it would be very difficult but that I would do my best. I then asked Jane if she would be willing to sing a few hymns during the church proceedings, and she agreed. Jane thought of a couple of hymns which Jess had heard and was very fond of.

The wake took place at DeGenua's Funeral Home in Bridgeport. Jane and I sat together at Jess's wake. We both made the tough decision to have an open casket, thinking that is what her friends would want as they paid their last respects to Jess.

Seeing my best friend just lying there in the casket was almost unbearable. I kept walking up to the casket to take a look at her beautiful but still face. I guess I just needed confirmation that Jess had really been taken from my life. At one point I remember getting close to Jess and wishing I could just give her one last hug.

Before the doors opened for the public to pay their respects, I cried out to Jane, "Oh my God, look out the window!" When Jane got up to look out the funeral home's window, she saw what I saw—the line was forming around the block in anticipation of seeing Jess for the last time.

Even after the doors were open, there seemed to be an endless number of people waiting to get into the funeral home. We recognized many of Jessie's former classmates and teammates from Bridgeport High School and Boston College. We were a bit startled to see all five starting players of the Hartford High School women's basketball team in line, along with their coach. It was a very classy thing for them to do, especially since Jessie's team had beaten them in the State Championship game.

Once Julie paid her respects at the casket, Jane and I signaled for her to sit next to us for the remainder of the wake.

It was so nice to see Smitty and his sidekick EJ standing in line to pay their respects. Despite their clowning around, Smitty and EJ were such thoughtful people who we thought of as close friends. Jane whispered to me that she heard that Smitty closed down Eddie's for the entire day in Jessie's honor.

Johnny D showed up in line with his current girlfriend and a few of his former band members.

"Abby," said Jane, "I hope Johnny D doesn't trip on the carpet!" This gave Jane and me a much needed laugh.

After paying his respects to Jess, Johnny proceeded to head our way and gave us both a hug.

"Hi guys, I really don't know what to say. Jessie was such a wonderful person. I know I sometimes acted immaturely, especially around girls. I guess I felt I had to be someone I'm not. I think you know what I'm talking about. But I really liked Jessie. While dating, it was Jessie I have to thank for telling me straight out that I wasn't fooling anyone, to get my act together, and to act more mature. I guess it was like tough love or something. But because of Jess, I feel I am now more of a grown-up person. I'm dating a real nice girl who would never accept the immature way I acted before. So thanks to Jess I now feel I can have a normal relationship and not have to worry about impressing anyone. Anyway, I just feel that I should tell you this and how amazing I think Jessie was."

After Johnny left, Jane and I looked at each other in bewilderment.

"Abby," Jane said, "did you hear what I just heard? I never thought the words maturity and Johnny D would ever go together. Abby, I remember you saying that Jess had a serious discussion with Johnny. Do you know what Jess told Johnny to make him turn around his life like this?"

"I knew she wanted to have a serious discussion with him when he was skipping class with his friend Emmett and he must have listened to her because he started attending class again and raised his grades. But I never asked Jess about her discussion because I knew she wanted to keep it private. But whatever she said to him certainly straightened Johnny out. Sounds like Jess worked her magic on Johnny D. We all knew he had a kind heart. It's so nice to hear him say he has turned his life around. And it's all because of Jess. Truly amazing!"

Entering the funeral home along with others were three very tall individuals, each wearing a bright purple outfit. It was an amazing site for people in line who stared at them with their mouths wide open. I immediately recognized "Downtown", "The Wall" and "Spider." The Dunkers had come all the way up to Connecticut to pay their respects. After stopping at the casket to say a prayer, the three men walked over to us. Downtown spoke for the three of them.

"We are so sorry to hear of the passin' of Miss Jessie. She was such an amazin' person, inside and out. I have such a good feelin' when I think back at how excited she was when she called me about her game winning 'My Goodness' shot. I will never forget that! We drove up from Maryland to pay our respects because Miss Jessie left such a lastin' impression on us. Miss Abby, I got to know many very talented basketball players in my career. But I got to tell you I never met anyone with the determination and confidence of 'our girl'. But more 'mportantly is that she was such a sweet person."

I introduced Jane to the three Dunkers.

"Oh yeh, I heard all 'bout Miss Jane too. So talented! If either of you are lookin' for more basketball techniques, the Dunkers here will be glad to help out. That 'speially goes for you, Miss Abby. I still would like to have you try that basketball trick I showed you.

"Miss Abby, we are staying overnight in Connecticut. Would it be possible for me to be one of those pallbearers?" I responded, "Jess would love that Downtown." This brought a huge smile to his face as he said, "Well then, we will see you tomorrow."

I replied to Downtown saying, "Thank you for everything you did for Jess. You sure are an amazing person."

"Aww… don't go talkin' like that. I'm just tryin' to pay it forward. Well, we best be goin'. Miss Abby, Miss Jane, love and peace to both of you." As the Dunkers left, I noticed that Downtown still bounced on his tip toes as he walked out the door. This brought a brief smile to my face.

A tearful Paul Mari was one of the mourners and gave Jane and me a big hug. He found it difficult to speak but said he would be honored to be one of the pallbearers for the funeral.

The line continued to grow, there were so many people that we did not know. Of course, this didn't really surprise us given how much Jess had meant to so many people, both inside and outside the state of Connecticut.

Once the wake was over I asked the funeral director if it would be possible for Jane and me to have a private viewing before they closed the casket. The director agreed.

For a few minutes Jane and I sat still and just stared at our good friend Jess in the casket.

Finally Jane walked up to the casket.

"Jess, thank you so much for all that you taught me both in basketball and in life. I love you my friend and will never forget you!". Jane then gave Jess a kiss on the forehead and walked back to her chair crying.

I finally worked up the courage to walk up to the casket. I remember leaning over and kissing Jess on the forehead. I was surprised to find that her forehead was cold as a stone, but I didn't care.

I whispered in Jessie's ear, "Jess, why couldn't it be me instead of you in that casket? You have been my best friend since we were nine years old at Webster School. You've been my inspiration for so many years. You have been and will continue to always be my very best friend. Goodbye Jess, I love you so much and will miss you dearly." As I started weeping uncontrollably, Jane came over and helped me back to my chair.

At that moment, one of the workers asked if it was okay to close the casket as they were ready to close the funeral home for the night. Jane and I both nodded and the man walked over and closed the casket lid. It was a moment that I will never forget as we said our final goodbyes to our good friend who we both loved beyond words.

The mass the next day was held at St Michael's Cathedral in Bridgeport. Although the church was rather large it could barely hold the huge number of people who came to the mass. Besides all the pews that were packed, people were lined up in the hallway in the back of the pews and also packed the area towards the church entrance.

Carrying the casket up the stairs of the church and accompanying it down the aisle were Roger, Brian, Paul, Art Spensor, Smitty, and "Downtown." The sight of the casket in front of the altar brought tears to my eyes.

The entire service was such an emotional experience for myself and others. Jane's hymns were sung with such passion and in a flawless manner. When it came time for my eulogy, I did the best I could to keep my emotions in check, but I broke down towards the end of the eulogy and was unable to finish. To this day, I have no recollection of what I said during the eulogy, but friends approached me afterward and told me they were very touched by my words before I broke down in tears.

***

Once the condition of Jess's baby was stable and one or two visitors were allowed, Paul and I visited the child in the baby ward. We both agreed that the baby looked so much like Jessie. We smiled as we each delicately held the newborn baby for the first time.

Paul and I were asked to meet with the hospital's Discharge Department. Agnes in the Discharge Office brought up a sensitive matter that completely escaped both Paul and me. Agnes explained that in cases like this, it was standard policy for the hospital to release the baby to the Child Services Department. She said she wasn't quite sure what would happen next and didn't want to speculate about legal matters since she wasn't a legal expert. Agnes told us that it was her understanding that

Jessie's only next-of-kin would have been her father but she had been informed that Mike had passed away recently.

I explained to Agnes that Paul is the father but they were never married. In response, Agnes suggested that Paul consult with his lawyer to determine Connecticut's custody law in cases like this. Agnes thought the court would possibly have to decide but could not say for sure. She did advise us both, "Please act on this quickly. It's in your best interest." With that, Paul and I left the hospital.

Walking to our cars, Paul assured me that he would contact his attorney as soon as possible and determine what was needed to gain custody of the baby. He promised that he would get back to me as soon as he talked with his attorney.

***

Several days later, I received a knock at my door. It was Paul Mari. After sitting down, Paul said he wanted to talk to me about an important matter.

"Abigail, I have given this a lot of thought. I loved Jessie very much and I know I told her I was excited to become a father. The truth is I know I am not prepared or have the ability to raise a child. Once I graduate from Yale in a few months I have decided to pursue a master's degree at Stanford U. in California. I —

Interrupting, I asked " But what about the job you said was waiting for you when you get out of Yale?"

"I decided to not accept that job and pursue my graduate degree instead.

"Abigail," Paul continued, "I need to ask you an important question.

"If the court allows, would you consider adopting Jessie's baby? I will fill out whatever legal papers that are needed.

"With Jessie gone, I know I would not be able to properly care for the baby, and as I have said I feel a need to pursue a graduate degree at Stanford. While this is my decision, I must say that my entire family supports my decision. They are very old-school in matters like this and I don't want to disappoint them. They told me that they would not want to

168

adopt the baby. However, both my mother and father told me that they fully support my decision to have you file for adoption if that is possible. But the main thing is I know you would be a much better provider than me and I trust you with all my heart to properly raise my daughter.

"I know that I am asking a lot of you, but I can't think of a better person to take care of my child. Please know that I love you dearly as a friend and I ask that you give this your consideration."

I sat back in my chair a bit startled. I then leaned back, closed my eyes, and thought in silence for a minute.

"Paul, if that is your wish, I would be honored to adopt Bobbie. Can you come with me when I consult with my attorney in person?"

"Yes, I promise I will go with you."

"Ok, I'll set up an appointment with him right away.

"Are you absolutely sure about this Paul?"

"Yes, I am. I know you're the best person to give her the love and attention she will need, especially throughout her formative years."

After what seemed to be a long and arduous process, the court granted me legal custody. Bobbie was now my adopted child, and I couldn't be more thrilled! I immediately called Paul in California, who was visiting the campus of Stanford University. Paul was quite pleased and relieved to hear that the adoption was made official.

As it turned out, adopting Bobbie was made even more special after I was informed by my doctor that I would be unable to give birth myself.

***

Roger and I became engaged and we purchased a new house in Branford. Our new place was rather modest but Roger and I didn't care. We were just happy to have a home of our own.

We began making plans to be married, debating whether we should have a large or small wedding. Jane agreed to be my maid of honor.

Driving Bobbie home to our new house, I was determined to bring her up as my own child. Bobbie soon became the love of my life. I had already purchased some baby necessities and more would follow.

I asked Jane if she would consider being Bobbie's godmother. Jane happily agreed and began showering her godchild with every conceivable baby gift that the store had on display. Amazed at the beautiful selection of outfits, I asked Jane where she bought all these items.

"I bought all of these outfits at that wonderful baby store next to Eddie's called Baby Land."

Seeing the stunned look on my face, Jane asked me, "Abby what's the matter?"

"I just need to sit down for a second." Putting my hand to my face, I whispered, "Jane, would you…would you be able to get me a glass of water?"

Jane quickly went to the kitchen sink and rushed back with a cup of water.

"Abby, did I say something wrong?"

"Jane, hearing the name of that baby store just brought me back to that horrible incident. That's where Jess was killed, right in that parking lot."

"Oh Abby, I'm so sorry. I knew she was shot in a parking lot but I didn't realize that was the spot where Jess was murdered. I certainly can return those baby gifts if you wish."

"Don't be silly Jane," I replied. "It just brought me back momentarily to that horrific moment, but it certainly has nothing to do with that baby shop. In fact, all the items you purchased for Bobbie are adorable and I treasure all of these gifts. I can't wait to see my baby wearing these outfits!"

I assured Jane that I was honored that she agreed to be Bobbie's godmother and I could think of nobody better for baby Bobbie. Jane was relieved to hear this.

Jane was a frequent visitor to my house and she provided Bobbie with a lot of love and attention. She would also babysit for Bobbie whenever I had to go to the grocery store or hairdresser.

It gave me great comfort to have Jane as a close friend. We confided in each other many times on important matters in our lives.

***

During the time that I was bringing up Bobbie as a young child, Jessie's

words and actions continued to inspire me. I often thought back at the first time I met Jess in fourth grade. Just as she did at the early age of nine,

170

Jessie continued to be my inspiration as I impressed upon Bobbie the importance of a quality education once she was of school age.

While elementary school was still a few years away, I couldn't help but wonder if Bobbie would choose to follow in her mother's footsteps and become interested in sports. But that was not even something I would bring up to people I was close to, including my good friend Jane. Only time will tell, and I was determined to have Bobbie make the final decision on whether or not to participate in sports once that situation came up in the future.

But still, I wondered. I would eventually find out in the coming years.

COURT TRIAL

One morning, as I was having breakfast, a headline in the local newspaper caught my attention.

Youth arrested in shooting death of basketball star.

Fifteen-year-old Jacob Simmons was taken into custody yesterday in connection with the shooting death of local basketball star Jessie Darcey.

Surrounded by two court appointed attorneys, Simmons made a brief, tearful statement in which he pled not guilty.

The arrest occurred after Bridgeport Police apprehended a member of a rival street gang known as The Savages. The fourteen-year-old gang member, whose name was withheld, was arrested after a botched robbery attempt of the Diamond Jewelry Store on Main Street. During his interrogation, the fourteen-year-old stated that he knew all members of the rival street gang known as The Bloods. When questioned, he stated that Jacob Simmons was a member of The Bloods and that Simmons was the person who shot Jessie Darcey. He also directed the police to a possible location where the Simmons' "murder gun" may be found.

The Simmons' case will be held in Bridgeport court and the accused is expected to go to trial soon.

If found guilty, the accused will be sentenced to 10 - 25 years in prison.

Reading the article brought tears to my eyes. Once again, I relived the horrific moment when I saw my best friend lying helplessly in a pool of blood on the ground. My eyes filled up, still in disbelief at what had occurred.

"Fifteen years old," I whispered to myself, *"how can that be and what made him do such a horrible thing?"* Confused, I began to rationalize to myself, *"Was Jessie a target or did we both just get in the way of a gang war that the hospital had referred to?"*

I then recalled the knifing incident that Jessie and I witnessed and the rumor that the person who pulled the knife was allegedly a member of a gang called The Bloods. I noticed that the article mentioned the name of that gang. I wondered to myself if there was any connection between that stabbing incident from one of the members of that gang and this shooting. I was told that after two years the person who stabbed our schoolmate was never located.

Two days after reading the article about Jacob Simmons, I was summoned to appear in court as a witness for the prosecution. I was asked to meet with the prosecution attorney—Attorney Reynolds—to discuss my role as a witness. My boyfriend Roger showed some concern about me appearing as a witness in this murder trial.

"Abby, I know you are determined to be a witness in this case. But, please keep your statements brief and factual. And also, please be careful what you say or do so that you don't jeopardize yourself or the case against this shooter."

"I promise I will be careful Roger."

Brianna and I met with Attorney Reynolds in his Bridgeport office. The first thing that Attorney Reynolds impressed upon me was to just tell the truth while I was on the stand. I appreciated him saying this because, in my mind, it made things simpler for me and I had no intention of not being truthful in court. He told me that when I take the stand that I should describe in detail what occurred just prior to and during the shooting.

During the hour-long questioning, I happened to notice a mugshot photo on the attorney's desk. I asked him if that was a photo of the accused. The attorney's response was that it was. He then handed me the mug shot photo.

Taking the photo from the attorney and looking at the mug shot I immediately exclaimed, "Oh my God!"

The attorney asked me what startled me.

Still shocked I said, "This is the boy that stabbed our schoolmate in Bridgeport High's hallway two years ago!"

"Are you sure about that Abby?" asked the attorney.

"One hundred percent! This is the boy who stabbed our classmate Emery in our high school hallway two years ago. I will never forget this face. After stabbing him in the chest this kid quickly ran out of the school before being seen or caught by any of the teachers. If Jess was here she would also identify this individual since Jess was the first one to react by trying to separate the two boys and then by placing her coat on Emery's bloody body. At the same time, she called out to alert one of the teachers."

Attorney Reynolds responded, "Amazing. Ok, I will mention to the defense attorney that this may come up in trial to show a prior criminal past. However, I'm not sure the judge will allow this to proceed in court, but we can at least try."

***

Walking into my home, I sat down by myself and just fell into my favorite chair in our den, emotionally exhausted after our meeting with Attorney Reynolds. Thinking of the mug shot I saw on his desk, I immediately sat up as I recalled my discussion with Jess after meeting with the two policemen about the stabbing incident in our sophomore year.

I suddenly was haunted by Jessie's words. I vividly recalled what she said about the nightmare she had after the stabbing incident, *"In my nightmare, I dreamt that in trying to pull Emery away I stepped in front of him. In that moment that kid with a knife stabbed me in the chest and ran away."*

Just then, it dawned on me as I tearfully said out loud, *"Oh my God Jess, that nightmare you had that night of the stabbing was actually a premonition of your death at the hands of the same person—Jacob Simmons!!"*

***

"The court will come to order. In the case of Jacob Simmons in the shooting death of Jessie Darcey, the prosecution may call its first witness." So declared Judge William McCray to begin Day 2 of the trial. When the murmuring continued in the standing room only audience, Judge McCray banged his gavel again and called for everyone to immediately take their seats and to do so in an orderly fashion.

Hearing Jessie's name in connection with this shooting sent shivers throughout my body.

"Your honor, I call Miss Abby Girardi to the stand." After being sworn in I took my seat on the stand. As I looked at the accused, I felt my entire body shake with anger as I visualized my best friend lying helplessly on the ground in a pool of blood. But I told myself that I must maintain my composure. *Keep calm Abby. Keep calm. Do this for Jess.*

As soon as he saw me settled, Attorney Reynolds spoke. "Miss Girardi, do you recognize the defendant Mr. Simmons?"

In a shaken voice, I responded, "Yes, I do."

"How so?", asked Attorney Reynolds.

"I definitely identify him as the person who stabbed one of my schoolmates in the chest two years ago in the hallway of my high school." My statement set off a loud commotion in the courtroom from the audience in the room, and also the newspaper reporters who were reaching for their cameras.

I barely finished the sentence before the defense attorney quickly jumped to his feet and shouted, "Your honor I object and ask that this line of questioning be immediately stricken from the record. There is absolutely no evidence that my client was questioned, convicted, or tried for this alleged incident.

Hearing this, Judge McCray summoned both attorneys to approach the bench.

Once the two lawyers stood in front of the judge, he turned to Attorney Reynolds and said, "What is the purpose of this line of questioning?"

"Your honor I want to show that contrary to what we were told, the accused does have a criminal background."

The judge countered by emphatically stating, "I am directing you to inform this witness and all your other witnesses that they will *not* bring up any prior criminal allegations which are not directly related to the purpose of this trial. If you do not do as I order, you can be sure that I will hold you in contempt. I will be telling the jury to disregard this line of questioning. Do you understand?"

"Yes, your honor."

The judge turned to the jury and said, "The objection of the defense is sustained. The jury is to disregard the most recent line of questioning. I have instructed the prosecution to not bring up any possible prior criminal allegations and you are to disregard any such allegations."

Attorney Reynolds came back to me on the stand and said, "Abby please describe to the court in detail what occurred prior to and during the murder of Jessie Darcey."

Again I felt chills throughout my entire body hearing Jessie's name. But I knew I had to be strong for Jessie's sake, and my own.

I responded in a shaken but clear voice.

"Jessie Darcey was my best friend. We had been friends since fourth grade and she was my role model and inspiration ever since. In fact Jess continues to be my inspiration. Jessie and I spoke nearly every day. When she became pregnant she asked me to be her baby's godmother. When she was nine months pregnant, Jess called me and asked me to meet her so we could go over her plans for her baby. We decided to meet in the parking lot in front of the Baby Land store in Bridgeport. When Jess showed up I gave my very pregnant friend a big hug. I then asked her to come over to my car because I had a beautiful gift for her baby that I purchased at Baby Land. She…" As I began to choke up. Lowering my head, I took a deep breath and tried to regain my composure. *Keep calm Abby. Keep Calm. Do this for Jess.*

Attorney Reynolds spoke, "Please continue Abby."

Biting my lower lip and trying not to cry, I continued, "Her last words to me were 'Abby, this is the greatest moment in my life'. It was precisely then that I felt a sting on my neck and when I looked down I saw my very best friend, who I loved with all my heart, lying on the ground in a pool of blood."

Looking directly at Jacob Simmons, I said in a shaken but forceful voice, 'The person who pulled the trigger and killed my best friend Jessie Darcey, when she was nine months pregnant, is nothing short of a vicious monster and he should be locked up forever!" Exhausted and distraught I suddenly broke down in tears. Attorney Reynolds walked over and handed me some tissues.

"That is all your honor," said Attorney Reynolds.

I was then approached by the prosecutor who asked, "Abby, did you see the individual who shot you and Jessie Darcey.?" Did you have any knowledge as to who may have shot you and Jessie Darcey?

"No, I did not."

"That is all your honor."

At that point, the judge said, "The witness may step down." Banging his gavel, the judge announced, "The court stands in recess for one hour."

As I approached Attorney Reynolds he shook my hand and with a wink said, "Good job Abby." I knew immediately what his wink meant. It was a signal to me that although the prosecutor's objection to my comments about the stabbing incident was sustained, Attorney Reynolds felt that the incident would stay in the minds of each jury member and the judge.

***

Two weeks later, I received a call from Attorney Reynolds.

"Abby, I received word regarding the court trial that I wanted to share with you. Let me explain.

"After scouring the area that the gang member of The Savages had given me, my staff located a handgun which we believed may have belonged to Jacob Simmons. I informed the defense attorney of this and asked the judge for a recess of the trial while we had forensics analyze the gun and the ammunition found in the gun. The judge granted my request for a recess.

"The results of the forensics examination showed a match linking the gun with the bullet that murdered Jessie Darcey. Also, the fingerprints on the gun matched those of Jacob Simmons."

Hearing all this new information, Jacob, through his lawyers, changed his plea from not guilty to guilty. I have just found out that Jacob Simmons has been sentenced to twenty years in jail.

"Thank you, Attorney Reynolds," I responded. "While it can never bring my best friend back it is a relief that this case is finally closed."

***

After graduating from college, Jane began to work full time at the same bookstore that she had worked in since high school. After my graduation from Southern Connecticut, I began working full time at a small but very popular gift shop in Guilford.

Roger's job at an investment firm paid very well so for the time being he was the main breadwinner of our house. We both decided it was the right time for us to get married.

Having set our wedding date, Roger and I decided to have a very small intimate wedding, with invitations going out to a few of our friends. Our marriage was conducted in a chapel in nearby Westbrook, with Jane as my maid of honor.

Four-year-old Bobbie was so excited to be our little flower girl and took her assignment very seriously. I found a beautiful, white dress for her and a lovely flower crown for her to wear on the top of her head. Our friends who attended our wedding ceremony all remarked how adorable Bobbie looked as she marched down the aisle with such a serious expression on her face, carefully holding a bouquet of flowers in her hands.

Roger looked handsome in his tuxedo and had a huge smile on his face when he saw me in my wedding dress marching down the aisle.

After the ceremony, young Bobbie ran over to me to give me a hug. She was still wearing the flower crown but it was slightly tilted from running to me.

"Aunt Abby, did I do okay as the flower girl?" Bobbie always referred to me as *Aunt Abby* which pleased me greatly.

"Bobbie you were the best flower girl I have ever seen. You did a wonderful job. One day you will be the one getting married and you'll have your own flower girl."

This brought a big smile to Bobbie's face. I wished Jess was there to see her little girl, so beautiful, all dressed up and proud of her performance at the wedding.

Our reception was held at a small restaurant near the chapel. I was pleased with the service that the staff provided and satisfied with the meal that was served.

Towards the end of the reception, our photographer took photos of our wedding party and asked if she can take pictures of us with our friends outside on the restaurant grounds.

Once outside, I saw a beautiful water fountain and noticed Jane desperately trying not to laugh as she walked towards the fountain in her beautiful dress.

"Abby, are you thinking what I'm thinking?'

We both broke out into laughter recalling how Johnny D made a big "splash" that day after our high school junior prom. Roger smiled at us and we told him we would explain later.

The photographer said a photo in front of the fountain would make for a really nice picture. She asked if we could all form as a group in front of the fountain. As Roger moved next to me, I smiled and told him to watch his step. Seeing Roger's confused expression, Jane and I both cracked up again.

Both our wedding ceremony and reception were delightful and memorable occasions. It was fun to see all our wedding guests having such a good time.

***

"Funny you should ask," responded Jane when I called and asked her weeks later how things were going between her and Brian.

"Driving home from your wedding two weeks ago, Brian remarked that he really enjoyed both the ceremony and reception. He liked the intimacy of your wedding. I agreed.

"The next day, Brian surprised me when he proposed, asking me to be his wife. Of course, I said yes. He presented me with a beautiful engagement ring."

"Jane, I'm so thrilled and happy for you and Brian. The two of you make a wonderful couple. This is such wonderful news! I can't wait to tell Roger. And I'm so excited to get to see your ring and hear your wedding plans."

"Yes, when we get together I'll go into more detail. Right now, we're thinking next May would be a good time for us. As Brian mentioned, we've decided to have a small wedding like yours. Your wedding was so much fun and we hope ours would be as good as yours."

"Oh, I'm certain it will be Jane."

Jane was pleased to hear this and asked, "Abby, would you consider being my maid of honor?"

"I would be honored to be your maid of honor Jane. I know your wedding will certainly be wonderful. I can't wait! If you like, I can help you look for your wedding gown. I will also begin to look for a dress myself." Laughing, I said, "I know it's next year but it's never too early, you know."

"You are so right", Jane replied. "I would love it if you can help me choose my wedding gown."

Jane and I had a lot of fun going from one shop to another to find the perfect gown for Jane. Shopping was certainly one of our favorite hobbies. After numerous attempts, we came across a wedding gown that both Jane and I really liked. We both thought this was the right gown for her.

"Jane, you look beautiful in that gown. It's perfect! Brian is going to love seeing you wearing this at your wedding!"

Jane's wedding was a very joyous occasion. Roger said he really liked my dress that I picked out for the wedding, which made me happy. At the reception, I mentioned to Jane how wonderful it was that she married her high school sweetheart. I was so thrilled to see how happy Jane was and we had so much fun dancing and laughing throughout the wedding reception. We only wished that Jess was around to be part of this wonderful occasion.

***

As years passed, Bobbie began to ask me more and more questions about her mother and father. I didn't hold back and answered all of Bobbie's questions. I told Bobbie that her father is a good man who loved her mother very much. But he just couldn't handle being a parent at that time. I explained to Bobbie that her father had asked me to adopt her so he could pursue his education at Stanford University in California and that he gave me full consent to adopt her.

Bobbie told me that she had mixed feelings about meeting her biological father. At this time, she felt she was not ready but would inform me and Roger if she changed her mind. I told her that I completely understood.

Bobbie did ask me if I had heard from her father since he went to California. I shook my head.

"I haven't heard from Paul at all. At one point, I tried to reach out to him, but he probably felt he wasn't ready to talk to me. If or when I do hear from him, I will let you know and then you can tell me if you want to try yourself to reach out to him.

"If he does contact me, I want you to know it's completely your decision on whether or not to see him. I will respect whatever decision you make."

Bobbie was especially interested in hearing all about her mother's basketball heroics.

At one point, young Bobbie looked at me with a determined look on her face. Seeing the expression on Bobbie's face brought me back to the same look I saw from that nine-year-old girl I met at Webster Elementary School. In my heart, I knew what Bobbie was thinking.

It was not surprising to me when Bobbie proclaimed, "I'm going to learn how to play basketball just like my mom!"

When I mentioned to Jane what Bobbie said to me, Jane had a grin from ear to ear. We both wondered if Bobbie perhaps inherited Jessie's fierce determination and confidence.

***

Every week I would make a point of visiting Jessie's gravesite and plant flowers around her footstone, including snowdrops, the "flower of hope" and one of her favorites. On the fifth anniversary of her historic scoring record, I decided to visit Jess at her gravesite. Ironically, the weather was exactly the same as it was that memorable day years ago, very cold and snowy.

As I approached the cemetery I was surprised to find two other people who were leaving the cemetery, braving the inclement weather. Even though the snow was beginning to subside, I could not make out the two figures who were leaving, especially since they both wore heavy coats with hoods. I thought to myself that the two people must have also visited someone very special, given the heavy snowfall that was just beginning to let up.

As I have done every week, I stood in front of Jessie's headstone to say a prayer privately and give her an update on how her daughter had grown into a beautiful young woman.

I then knelt down on the cold hard ground to brush the snow off the bottom of the headstone. While brushing off the snow, I noticed several shiny objects that glistened as the sun made its appearance. Not knowing what the objects were, I picked up the items that were securely contained in two small plastic bags. I carefully opened the plastic bags and suddenly tears filled my eyes. The objects that caught my attention were the two small bracelets that were given to Gina and Debbie at the finale of their successful musical at Royalty Theatre. Also included in the plastic bags was a small note that read "To our idol, Jessie Darcey. We will love you forever. Gina and Debbie." Still kneeling on the ground I felt a warm feeling throughout my body. I smiled as I remembered how honored Jess felt as Gina and Debbie shadowed her all the time. I thought of how excited Jess was when she told me that the two girls ran up to her to proudly show the bracelets that the director had given to them that day.

As I looked up I saw the two figures ahead get into their car. I smiled as I thought of how Gina and Debbie, now teenagers, will never forget Jessie's kindness and thoughtfulness.

As crazy as it may seem, I felt that Jess somehow was aware of this beautiful gesture shown by her two fans who gave her such joy and love.

25

BRANFORD ELEMENTARY SCHOOL

In fourth grade, even at a very young age, Bobbie knew in her heart that she was capable of becoming an above average basketball player

When she was of age, Bobbie attended Branford Elementary School.

Just as Jessie did for me, I urged Bobbie to maintain good grades once she was old enough to understand. I stressed the importance of education in her life which would have significant results down the road when she would begin looking for jobs. I encouraged Bobbie to always stay at the top of her grade level throughout elementary school and eventually high school. Fortunately, Bobbie listened and promised me she would make it a priority goal.

Unlike Jess and myself, Bobbie was not an outgoing person, especially in elementary school. When Bobbie was in fourth grade, the topic of boys inevitably came up. Bobbie admitted to being very shy around boys. This made me smile as it brought me back to Jessie and my experiences with boys when we were her age. I assured Bobbie that it was perfectly normal to feel shy at her age when she is around boys. I explained that I was the same way. I shared with Bobbie how awkward we always felt around boys when we were young. I even brought up Jessie's experience with Johnny D and how shy we felt around him and his friends.

During our private moments, Bobbie continued to ask about her mother, especially stories about Jessie's heroics on the basketball court. She wanted to know, in detail, how her mother learned to excel in basketball. I could see in her eyes that same look that Jessie had at her age, a look that nothing was going to stop her from achieving her goal. It was then that I knew in my heart and mind that Bobbie wanted to follow in her mother's footsteps. All she needed was someone to teach her the skills needed to become a basketball star.

The area where we lived in Branford was much safer than the section of Bridgeport where Jess and I grew up. I had no hesitation in letting Bobbie walk to the nearby park with her friends once she reached middle grades in elementary school. It was at the park that Bobbie learned to become comfortable playing basketball against other kids her age and sometimes girls and boys older than her. Even at a very young age, Bobbie knew in her heart that she was capable of becoming an above average basketball player. But she knew that in order to accomplish this goal she would need some guidance and training from an experienced basketball player.

Once I knew how serious Bobbie was, I vowed that I would do everything I could to make Bobbie's dream come true. The first thing I did was to have Roger install a basketball hoop in the large driveway of our Branford house. Roger also purchased a brand new basketball at a nearby sports store. Bobbie's reaction to her very own basketball hoop and basketball was priceless. I recalled the many conversations I had with Jessie who was so appreciative of her dad's private drills on ball handling and foul shooting to make her a complete basketball player. I certainly knew that neither Roger nor I could be the ones to give her the kind of basketball training that Mike provided to Jessie. With this in mind, I made a call to the Boston College Athletics Department, knowing they would remember Jessie Darcey.

I asked the Athletic Director if he knew of a great basketball tutor in the Connecticut area. In particular, I asked about a tutor who would concentrate on teaching Bobbie the important techniques of ball handling, shooting and foul shooting. The Athletic Director said he knew just the right person who lived in nearby Guilford.

"Abby, there is a fellow by the name of Jack Davis who attends the Stamford branch of the University of Connecticut. He had signed with a professional National Basketball Association team but his career was immediately cut short due to a very serious, recurring knee injury. Besides being a good shooter, Jack was well-known for his outstanding ball handling. After his very brief stint with the NBA, Jack went back to school at UConn. I think Jack would be just the person you need and I'm sure he will agree to be Bobbie's tutor."

A few days later, I received confirmation from Jack that he would help out by teaching Bobbie some basketball skills. In speaking with Jane, she assured me that I contacted the right person. She said that she met several former UConn athletes at a party. They told her that Jack Davis left UConn and was well on his way to becoming an NBA basketball star prior to his career ending injury.

Two days later, I received a knock on my door. When I opened the door, I saw a very tall, handsome guy with a big smile on his face.

"Hi, I'm looking for Abby Girardi?"

"I'm Abby. Are you Jack Davis?"

"That's me," he said with a grin. "As we discussed on the phone, I'm here to give Bobbie some basketball lessons."

"Jack, that's Bobbie shooting some baskets in the driveway."

"Abby, I have to tell you. I followed Jessie's basketball career very closely and saw her play several times. I was really impressed. If Bobbie turns out half as good as Jessie she may very well become our next local basketball star. I guess I have my work cut out for me. I can't make any promises, but I assure you I will do everything I can to teach Bobbie some basketball techniques that I have learned over the years. Could you introduce me to Bobbie?"

"Of course." We both walked out to the driveway and interrupted Bobbie's shooting.

"Bobbie this is the man I was telling you about who can help you improve your basketball skills. His name is Jack Davis. I will leave the two of you alone as I know Jack would like to get started on your lessons."

"Hi Mr. Davis, glad to meet you" said Bobbie in her grown-up voice.

"Hi Bobbie. By the way, please call me Jack. Are you ready to begin your lessons today?"

"I sure am Mr. Davis, I mean Jack."

"Ok, let's get started."

Jack began teaching Bobbie the fundamentals of ball handling, learning to dribble with precision using both her right and left hands. He told Bobbie to be patient because these basketball drills will take some time to get right. At first, Bobbie found these basketball drills to be very difficult, as Jack had mentioned.

After their first lesson concluded, Jack told Bobbie he would be there the next day for their second lesson. When Bobbie came back into my house she looked discouraged.

"Aunt Abby, why can't I learn what Mr. Davis is teaching me?"

"Now Bobbie, I heard what Mr. Davis said about being patient. I know you can't wait to learn these drills but learning them properly is going to take some time. I want you to know that your mom, at first, had a lot of difficulty learning these same drills that your grandfather taught her. I know because I was there. But in time and with a lot of practice, your mom eventually learned these skills. So you just have to be patient and listen to everything Mr. Davis is saying. You will catch on, I promise you."

Jack's training also included a variety of shooting drills. Again, he impressed upon Bobbie that they would take some time to get right.

In time, Bobbie began to perfect these basketball techniques. She knew that this training was just what she needed. Bobbie was determined that she would follow in her mother's footsteps and eventually become a basketball star.

Jack's price for tutoring Bobbie was very, very reasonable, which I appreciated since I knew these sessions would take a long time for Bobbie to master.

On occasion, I would watch Bobbie's training from my kitchen window and it would bring tears to my eyes. I was immensely proud of Bobbie's confidence and determination to be the best player that she could possibly be. I couldn't help but think how proud Jessie would have been to see Bobbie's progress on the basketball court. For me, this was so reminiscent of how Mike Darcey must have felt watching his daughter Jessie during her basketball games.

While some of the state's elementary schools were beginning to form girls' basketball teams, Branford elementary and middle schools were not yet ready. So, when Bobbie was in seventh grade, she became a cheerleader for the boys' basketball team. This made me so happy as I thought about my own cheerleading experiences. I made it a point to attend all her games to watch her cheer on her team. Of course, I had no clue what was going on in the boys' basketball games, but it was fun just watching Bobbie cheering during the game and at halftime.

The lessons Jack had taught Bobbie were successful as her confidence in shooting grew steadily. After several years, Bobbie, like her mother, became proficient at shooting from all areas of the court. And, like Jessie, Bobbie became very good at the foul line.

After one of her training sessions, I heard a knock on my door. It was Jack. I asked him to come in for a cup of coffee. He accepted my offer and told me that he wanted to update me on Bobbie's progress.

After finishing his cup of coffee, Jack leaned back in his chair and said, "Bobbie has been an amazing student and has far exceeded my expectations. She has mastered all the training techniques I have taught her these past two years. Her shooting and dribbling skills are excellent. Now that she has entered eighth grade, I truly believe that she is ready to make the high school basketball team next year. She has become that good!

"Abby, to be honest, Bobbie no longer needs my training. There is nothing left for me to teach her. She has perfected all the basketball skills I have asked her to work on. So, if it okay with you, I think this will be her last lesson. I already told Bobbie that I would speak with you and tell you this."

"That's so great to hear Jack! Ok, let me go get your check for this lesson."

"No need Abby, this lesson is on the house. For me, my reward will be to see Bobbie on the high school court. I think she will amaze both her coach and the fans with her basketball skills. Thank you for having faith in me and it has been my privilege to provide all these lessons to Bobbie. Branford High School is about to experience something very special!"

During one of her visits, Jane joined Bobbie in our driveway as Bobbie practiced her shooting and playmaking. The first thing Jane noticed was a group of buckets on the ground towards the back of the driveway. Walking out to the driveway, I heard Jane roaring with laughter at the sight of the buckets.

"Well, what do we have here?" exclaimed an amused Jane.

"Jane, this was Aunt Abby's idea," responded Bobbie. "We put the buckets out in different places, and I use them to practice dribbling both lefthanded and righthanded. Jack also liked this idea. They have really helped me, honest! Don't you think this was a great idea Aunt Abby had?"

"Oh, I do, Bobbie. I really do," said Jane, looking at me with a wink, "I can't imagine how in the world your Aunt Abby came up with such a great idea!"

I chimed in, "Jane, this is my contribution to Bobbie's practice sessions. Bobbie says these buckets really have helped her with dribbling and maneuvering on the basketball court."

"Oh, I'm sure they do. I seem to remember another girl Bobbie's age who became an expert playmaker using buckets like these!"

With her eyes wide open, Bobbie asked, "Who would that be Jane?", asked Bobbie.

"That would be your mom, Bobbie," responded Jane. "Jessie became an outstanding dribbler with the help of your Aunt Abby here. In fact, your mom referred to Abby as her "bucket girl." Hearing this, all three of us broke out in laughter.

Later, Jane confided in me privately that Bobbie did not possess Jessie's playmaking skills. She continued by saying, "Of course, no one else has those kinds of skills. Jess was one of a kind. But what really impresses me is that Bobbie possesses the same confidence and competitive nature that Jessie had. That will certainly go a long way to help Bobbie become a very good basketball player. I can see that Bobbie has been working extra hard on all aspects of her game."

Soon, Bobbie's hard work would pay off.

26

BRANFORD HIGH SCHOOL

Bobbie glanced out the window of Eddie's restaurant and suddenly was overcome with a flood of emotions. In a nearly inaudible voice, Bobbie said, "I…I have to go, I'm so sorry.

Bobbie entered Branford High School with a bit of apprehension. For her, it seemed like such a major transition going from eighth grade to high school. The high school surroundings and being in the same school with juniors and seniors who seemed so much older and perhaps wiser caused her a great deal of anxiety. She found this daunting and, for her, it was difficult just getting through the first day.

When Bobbie returned home, I saw a worried look on her face. I asked her if she was okay and she assured me she was. But I knew something was bothering her. I asked Bobbie to sit down and to please share with me how her first day of high school went. Bobbie broke down in tears and opened up to me about her anxious feelings. She told me that before going to her second class she overheard two girls talking, saying how excited they were to finally enter high school. Bobbie said she wished she was able to feel that same excitement, but just couldn't. All she felt was overwhelming anxiety. She wondered if any other freshmen girls felt the same way as she or was she the only one.

Bobbie went on to say how difficult it was for her to fully comprehend what her teachers were telling their students when they were going over the school rules and what was expected of students in each class. She found it so difficult to concentrate. Bobbie knew she needed to relax and concentrate on what the teachers were saying, but she felt a bit traumatized by everything going on. She confided in me that so many things were running through her mind that first day of high school. Would she be able to maintain good grades as I encouraged her? Would she be able to make the high school basketball team? Would she be able to overcome her shyness and make friends? Bobbie turned to me with tears in her eyes.

"Aunt Abby, is it normal for me to feel this way?"

"Bobbie, your feelings are perfectly normal," I responded. "Even though, like your mom, I was basically an outgoing person, I had the same apprehension as you. What helped me quickly to adjust was the fact that I entered high school with my best friend, your mother. From the very first day of high school, Jessie would always make me laugh which took the edge off of any anxiety I might have had.

"Different people approach new beginnings in different ways. But I can guarantee you, all the students felt a certain degree of anxiety even though they appeared to be in total control. They may tell you or appear to be above any feeling of apprehension, but they're not. Don't let that fool you. This was only your first day. As time goes by, you will acclimate yourself to high school and your classes, I guarantee it. Just take it one day at a time. Soon, you will make friends both in school and outside of high school. Trust me."

"But Aunt Abby, you know how shy I am making friends, not to mention boyfriends and I…" her voice trailed off and she cupped her hands to her face and began to cry.

"Bobbie, please listen to me…you are a beautiful young girl with a wonderful personality. People gravitate to people like you. You'll see. Just be yourself and other people will want to be around you. My hope is that you will find that one person who will be your lifelong friend, just as your mom was to me. As far as basketball is concerned, Jack Davis told me that he is very impressed with your basketball knowledge and performance. I believe once the high school coaches see Bobbie Darcey in action they will be just as impressed."

With that, Bobbie gave me a big hug and thanked me for all my "valuable" advice. She promised me that she will give all of this some time.

About a week later, Bobbie got into a pleasant conversation with one of her classmates who sat next to her. Since they were both early for their biology class, the girl introduced herself and smiled.

"Hi, my name is Debbie Patterson. Can I ask you a question? Are you understanding these biology assignments? I'm already having a tough time with biology and I'm afraid I may never understand it. I'm doing okay in all my other subjects but I'm really afraid that I may fail this class."

"Glad to meet you, Debbie. My name is Bobbie Darcey. Actually, biology is one of my favorite subjects. Unlike my other classes, I seem to be able to follow these assignments fairly well. If I can be of assistance to you on these assignments, just let me know. I will be glad to help. Actually, it would even help me also."

"Do you mean it? That would be wonderful! Maybe we can get together and you can help me with some of the questions that I am struggling with?"

"That sounds great Debbie. Let's talk after this class and set up a time to work together on these assignments."

"Terrific! Thank you, Bobbie."

When she got home, Bobbie told me in glowing terms about her classmate Debbie Patterson. She had a smile from ear to ear as she informed me that they planned to get together each week for Bobbie to help Debbie with her biology homework and assignments. On top of everything else, Bobbie found out that Debbie also planned to try out for the Branford's freshman team. Bobbie told me all about her conversation with Debbie.

"Debbie moved to Branford with her family earlier this year from Nashville, Tennessee. They relocated because Debbie's dad was transferred by his job to the Branford area. Debbie told me that her middle school in Nashville actually had a girls' basketball team. The girls' team began when Debbie was in seventh grade. After a great deal of prodding by me, Debbie reluctantly told me that she was the star player on their seventh and eighth grade teams. She played guard and led the team in scoring and assists for both years. But she wasn't sure how much this meant to the Branford High coaches.

"As Debbie put it, 'I know I have to practice hard to show the Branford coaches that I have the ability to play on their freshman team. My guess is that they have no knowledge of what I did in my middle school and probably don't really care. We'll see, but I'm hopeful that I play good enough to make the team.'

"When I told Debbie that I was also going to try out for the Branford High basketball team, her response was, 'Bobbie wouldn't it be great if we both were selected as starting guards?' I told her that would be fantastic!"

Bobbie also found out that Debbie was a child star in Nashville for another reason—singing. When Debbie was young she performed onstage with her older sister at the famed Grand Ole Opry in Nashville. Hearing this, Bobbie told me that she begged a reluctant Debbie to tell her all about her singing background. Debbie finally agreed to tell Bobbie about her experiences singing on the Grand Ole Opry show.

"Okay," said Debbie, "it's not much of a story to tell. But anyway, here's how that came about.

"My mom died before I was born and my daddy did a wonderful job raising both me and my sister Patricia—who I call Trish. My daddy was a country singer who performed in local clubs in and around the Nashville area. He actually recorded several songs which were played on local country stations. Daddy's songs never made the top 100 songs on the country charts, but he was content performing at local restaurants and such.

"Daddy noticed that Trish and I harmonized nicely at a very young age. I guess we kinda picked up singing while listening to our dad. Even though Trish was only a year older than me, I looked up to her as I would my own mom.

"The Opry had try-outs near where we lived and daddy encouraged us to go. He was very supportive but never pushed us to perform. My dad had taught me a few chords on his guitar and I included guitar playing in our act—as best I could." Laughing, Debbie said, "It seemed like the guitar was bigger than I was.

"So Trish and I showed up at the tryouts, mainly to please our dad. We really enjoyed singing and performing in front of our family, but we never imagined achieving any kind of success. Anyway, to our surprise, we were asked to perform live at the Opry. I was only seven years old at the time and Trish was only eight. So being so young we didn't have any fear of appearing onstage, you know like stage fright or anything like that. We were called The Patterson Sisters and the name kind of stuck. Actually, we were asked back by the Opry to perform more tunes.

"Trish and I performed several songs our daddy taught us which were covers of tunes made famous by different rock and country stars. We even covered two songs made famous by Elvis called *When My Blue Moon Turns To Gold Again* and *Hound Dog*. For the song *Hound Dog*, I shook my hips like Elvis, with my guitar slung over my shoulder. The audience loved seeing this and we got a really nice reception from the audience. I guess we were kinda like a novelty act. Like all the other artists that performed, our songs were broadcast live from the Opry on the very popular Nashville radio channel.

"Trish and I never pursued a singing career after our experiences on the Opry shows. We did love being on that Nashville stage and often reminisce about our Opry performances. Every time I visit Trish at her house in Westbrook we inevitably begin singing together especially *When My Blue Moon Turns To Gold Again*, in our style. We love that song.

Bobbie asked, "Is your dad still around?

"No, he died years ago. Daddy was really proud of us both as singers and how he raised us. We both miss him very much."

"I would love to hear both of you singing together. Any chance you can get Trish to come over to your place so I can hear you both singing?"

"Sure, as long as it's a private thing. We quit singing in public years ago." Laughing, Debbie said, "And don't expect me to do my Elvis impersonation!"

"Oh shoot Deb," Bobbie kiddingly replied, "I was really looking forward to that!"

When I heard Bobbie talking about Debbie on such wonderful terms, I kept my fingers crossed that this girl that Bobbie just met would eventually become a very good friend. As I sat in the darkened room of my den, I closed my eyes and thought of how I met that spirited nine-year-old girl who would change my life forever. I hoped the same for my daughter Bobbie.

***

In her first few basketball practices, Bobbie struggled since this was her first experience playing on an organized team. During her third practice session, the coach split the team in two in order to play a scrimmage game against each other. Bobbie found it difficult to free herself from her defender to get off a clear shot at the basket. When she got home, she told me how frustrated she was about her inability to get off a clear shot at the hoop. This was one situation that didn't come up during her training sessions with Jack Davis when Bobbie was in elementary school. I advised her to give it some time since, in my opinion, it seemed very early in the process. But I did tell her that if she couldn't work it out herself during her practice sessions to let me know.

At home, Bobbie tried various ways to "shake off" her defender to free herself up for a shot at the basket. One of the ways was to ask me, of all people, to defend her while she practiced her shots. She told me to stand in front of her pretending to be her defender and asked me to try to steal the basketball away from her. I reminded her that I didn't know anything about basketball but would give it my best shot. Bobbie practiced moving around me to free herself up for a clear shot, asking me all along to try to steal the ball. Thinking back on my role as the "bucket girl" during Jessie's home practices, I smiled and whispered to myself, *"Oh boy, here we go again!"*. Not knowing what I was doing I did my best to try to steal the ball from Bobbie and not allow her to dribble by me. After fifteen minutes of the drill, Bobbie thanked me but I knew it wasn't quite what Bobbie had in mind.

"You know what?" I called out, "Let me find out if Jane is available to help you with this. Jane was an exceptional basketball player and I'm sure she can give you some pointers."

I phoned Jane and she told me she would be thrilled to help Bobbie out in any way. The next day Jane stopped by. After talking with me for a few minutes, Jane turned her attention to Bobbie.

"Bobbie, before we get started, I want to let you in on a few basketball tips that Jessie taught me which may be helpful to you. The first thing your mom taught me was the value of 'court vision'. Jess impressed upon me the value of knowing where all her teammates were on the court at all times.

"Just as important, your mom taught me the value of knowing where all the defenders were located, especially the defender right in front of me. Jessie taught me the art of 'visualization'. She learned this method from her dad, your grandfather. With practice, Jessie learned how to visualize her every move on the court. In particular, she told me how she would free herself on the court by 'tricking' her defenders."

"What does tricking her defenders mean?" asked Bobbie.

"Let me try to explain. Jessie perfected the skill of 'faking out' her defenders to think she was moving one way, only to dribble the ball the opposite way. As a basketball player, your mom was one in a million. In her case, she learned the technique of faking out not just one defender but two or three players that defended her.

"Initially, Jessie learned the skill of maneuvering around her defenders from her father. This did not come easy to Jessie at first. But after many hours of practice, she eventually managed to master this simple but important technique. Using this skill in official games, Jessie was able to easily outmaneuver as many as three defenders with her very deceptive moves and her dribbling abilities. In my mind, your mom perfected this skill after receiving a very intensive four hour training session from a guy by the name of Ed Carlson. Ed is better known by the name 'Downtown'."

Laughing, Bobbie asked, "Why was he called 'Downtown'? Seems like a silly name to me."

"Your mom and I will tell you all about 'Downtown' on another day.

"Suffice it to say, as great a basketball player as your mom was, she learned a very valuable lesson from 'Downtown' during her private practice sessions with him. The lesson that Jessie learned that day was this: No matter what the odds, no matter what the obstacles, you have to truly believe you will find a way to make that shot. As Ed, or rather 'Downtown', impressed upon Jessie, 'It's not enough to think you are going to make that shot. You have to *know* you're going to make the shot'. This is especially true in pressure situations in which you need to make a difficult shot.

"Let me explain. There was this one important game when it appeared certain that we were about to go down to defeat. There were only five seconds left in the game, and we were losing by one point. Everyone was certain that our unbeaten record was about to be broken. Everyone, but Jessie. The thought of losing was a tough pill to swallow because, up to that point, we were so proud that we went through the season without a loss.

"The ref signaled for me to take the ball out at the outside line at half court. I could, in no way, envision anyone making this half-court desperation shot in this pressure situation with only five seconds to go. And that included Jessie who was the best player that I have ever seen. In my mind, not even Jessie would be able to pull off this miracle. I say this because three defenders stood in front of Jess ready to prevent her from shooting.

"Before play began again, I asked Jess, 'Do you think you can make this half-court shot?'. Your mom's response startled me. With a calm expression on her face she said to me in a matter of fact way, 'Jane, I *know* I'm going to make this shot.' Even after she said that to me I was convinced that there was no way on earth that she would be able to make this miracle shot with only five seconds left in the game. And with three opponents defending her? No way!

"In any event, I passed the ball to Jess, ready to head back to the lockers once the buzzer signaled the end of the game and the scoreboard showed our defeat. Jess received the ball and immediately faked out all three defenders with her deceptive move and then made that extremely difficult half-court shot. As her teammate standing within feet of Jessie when she took that shot, I just couldn't believe what I saw. Once again, Jess proved me wrong."

An astonished Bobbie exclaimed, "Holy Cow Jane! That is so incredible!"

"Yep, and your mom always gave credit to 'Downtown' who instilled in her the confidence she needed to shake off those three defenders and, within a few seconds, make that unbelievable shot at the buzzer. As gifted a basketball player as Jessie was, she needed the confidence that 'Downtown' impressed upon her in order to fake out those three defenders in just a few seconds so she could free herself up to make that shot.

"As I mentioned, Jess was one in a million. I share this example knowing that neither you nor I or anyone else could accomplish what Jess did to win that game. What I want to convey to you is the lesson that Jess learned that, hopefully, I can pass down to you. The lesson is to truly believe you can outmaneuver your defenders in any situation, in order to free yourself up for a clear shot. As 'Downtown' impressed upon Jessie, it's not enough to think you can do this, you must have faith in your abilities and *know* that you can do it. Have total confidence in your basketball skills, not in a boastful way, but in a self-assured way.

"So, in your case, the way I see you overcoming the obstacle that you face is for you to fool that one opponent standing between you and the basket. In order to get a good shot off, you have to make the defender truly believe that you are about to move in one direction before moving in the exact opposite. That is the key to this deceptive move. It may sound easy, but you would be surprised at how many players do not carry out this deceptive move properly.

"For example, once you get the ball and the defender is within inches, you would fake to your left and have the defender believe you are going in that direction. In the split second that the defender moves to your left, you make a quick move to your right and that will free you up, since the defender normally would not be able to recover and adjust that quickly. But again, you must make that fake move *believable*, otherwise the defender would not be fooled.

"For Jessie, court vision not only enabled her to get off a clear shot but also it enabled her to clearly see when one of her teammates was unguarded under the hoop. When she saw that, Jess would quickly shake off her defenders and pass the ball to the unguarded teammate for an easy layup. This was one of the reasons why Jessie's assist totals were so high.

"So, let's now practice this technique and maybe it will help you to overcome the obstacle you were referring to."

When they first began to practice this technique, Jane stole the ball away from Bobbie every time. Jane decided to make every effort to steal the ball or block her shots and not to make it easy for Bobbie. She did this to make Bobbie work harder on "faking Jane out" when Bobbie had the ball.

A frustrated Bobbie exclaimed, "Jane, no wonder you won all those defensive player MVPs, I can't seem to get around you!"

"Never mind about the MVPs, just keep practicing what I told you and you'll get the knack of it. But remember, you have to make me believe you are about to move in one direction while quickly moving in the opposite direction."

After an hour of practicing this, Bobbie began to figure this out and was able to free herself from Jane's attempt to steal the ball. Soon, Bobbie began to feel comfortable using this simple but important technique that Jane learned from Jessie years ago.

"That's the idea, Bobbie. Now you got it!"

"Yep, now I understand how this is done."

Bobbie told Jane she couldn't wait to try this out during her scrimmages.

"One in a million", Bobbie exclaimed out loud, "Yep that's what made my mom so special and why I am so proud to be her daughter!"

After thanking Jane for taking the time to work this out with her and for all the advice Jane gave her, Bobbie said she was looking forward to her team's next practice. With a short break from her practice schedule, Bobbie used the time to visualize and mentally adopt the skills that Jane learned from her mom. She began to think of the valuable lesson that Jessie received from the player known as "Downtown" and how Jessie learned to truly believe and *know* that she can make that incredible shot. Bobbie suddenly realized that this same mental attitude applied here. It was not enough to think that she can outmaneuver her opponents— she must truly believe and *know* that she can do this on a regular basis. Carefully pondering all of this, Bobbie thought to herself, *"That's it! Now I understand mom!"*

***

During her next scrimmage two days later, Bobbie used the technique that Jane taught her and found it much easier to free herself from her defender. She kept reminding herself that her defender had to believe her "fake" to properly carry out this deceptive move.

Bobbie began to make her shots on a regular basis. Seeing Bobbie scoring at will from all areas of the court made the coaches sit up and take notice. They also made note of the fact that Bobbie's foul shooting was extraordinary. During these scrimmages, the coaches didn't keep a record of scoring percentages but knew that Bobbie's scoring average was very high both at the foul line as well as her regular shots at various areas of the court.

Bobbie easily made the freshmen team and was informed that she would be one of the starting guards. Debbie Patterson also impressed the coaches, not so much for her scoring ability but more for her leadership skills and how she controlled the pace of the game. Debbie was informed that she was selected to join Bobbie as the team's other starting guard.

Seeing how Bobbie and Debbie complimented each other on the court, Head Coach Mary Plunkett decided to make Debbie the "point guard" and Bobbie the "shooting guard." As the head coach explained, Debbie's role as a point guard was to direct the action on the court, set up plays for the offense, and orchestrate the team's play strategies. She was not expected to shoot a lot. On the other hand, Bobbie, as the shooting guard, was expected to do just that—shoot—preferably from all areas of the basketball court.

Besides knowing full well that she did not have that innate basketball ability that her mom had, Bobbie still felt she was now ready to excel as a high school basketball player.

Debbie and Bobbie worked on perfecting their basketball techniques both during and after practices. Bobbie spoke very highly of Debbie and told me that they had formed a close friendship.

Bobbie far exceeded her coaches' expectations, as she led the freshmen team in scoring, including an outstanding 85% free throw average.

In the second game of the season, Bobbie scored 42 points, with 12 assists, and she shot 100% at the free throw line. Ever since that second game, Branford High fans flocked to all of her games. Each home game was a sell-out. In addition, Branford's varsity coaches began to attend the freshmen games to observe Bobbie's performance on the basketball court.

Like her mom, Bobbie received the Freshmen MVP award. A very excited Jane Kenny called Bobbie to congratulate her on this hard earned achievement.

***

Academically, sophomore year presented some challenges for Bobbie. Despite studying very hard there were a few courses that she struggled with to barely get a passing grade. Bobbie spoke with her guidance counselor about this. Her counselor suggested that she find one of her classmates with high grades who would be willing to study with her. Bobbie knew just the right person.

Despite all of her clowning around in school, Debbie maintained an A average in most of her studies. Bobbie asked Debbie if she would agree to be her study buddy to help her improve on the courses she was struggling with. In return, Bobbie promised to teach Debbie some basketball techniques that she learned over the years. Debbie told her she would absolutely help her study and give her some study hints along the way. "Besides", Debbie said, "you helped me out a lot with my biology homework. Those lessons really paid off for me. And, it will be fun hanging out even more often."

Thanks to Debbie's daily "tutoring" sessions, Bobbie and Abby noticed a marked improvement in all of Bobbie's courses.

***

Bobbie's early struggles with some of her school courses did not have an impact on her performance on the basketball court. Jane and I began to see how much Bobbie and Debbie complimented each other both on and off the court.

In her interviews with reporters, Coach Christie Sutton made a point of praising her entire team, noting that they were destined to become an even more stronger and cohesive group the following year. She especially raved about Bobbie and Debbie and the chemistry that developed between the two.

Led by Bobbie's outstanding shooting and Debbie's brilliant display of leadership on the court, the Branford sophomore team compiled a record of 17-3.

***

Junior year meant the high school semi-formal. Although it was still months away, Bobbie was worried that she would not be asked to go to the formal. Debbie was already going steady with a guy by the name of Stan Peters. On the other hand, Bobbie had only casual dates, and she was sure none of them would ask her to the prom. In honesty, she secretly wished that they wouldn't ask her since she was not really attracted to any of them. Hearing Bobbie's concern, Debbie said she would contact her friend Cindy Allison who attended Bridgeport High School. A while back Cindy had told Debbie that there was a senior at Bridgeport High by the name of Doug Anders who attended some of Branford's boys' and girls' basketball games. Doug's friend attended Branford High and invited him to some of the games. Cindy mentioned that Doug showed a great deal of interest in Bobbie while watching her during Branford's basketball games.

Smiling, Debbie said, "Bobbie, let me do a little bit more research on this guy. It would be a shame for an attractive girl like you to stay at home without a date for the formal."

Bobbie secretly was amused by Debbie's "research" but that did not stop Debbie from pursuing this.

Doug Anders was a star outfielder for Bridgeport High's baseball team. He was a tall, handsome teenager with a ruddy complexion. Debbie found out that, like Bobbie, Doug was also on the shy side. With this in mind, Debbie and her friend Cindy Allison schemed to get Bobbie and Doug together to see if there was any chemistry between the two. The two of them arranged to separately invite both Bobbie and Doug to meet them at Eddie's burger joint after Doug's baseball practice session. They felt Eddie's was a logical place since it was so close to Bridgeport High and Doug would often go there after practice. They figured he would not suspect the matchmaking scheme that Debbie and Cindy were conjuring up.

Debbie picked up Bobbie at my house and told her they were meeting Cindy at Eddie's in Bridgeport As they left to go out the door, a smiling Debbie looked back at me and winked. So I knew something was up but I didn't want to intrude in whatever "master plan" Debbie was cooking up.

Bobbie had never gone to Eddie's but heard that was a place where a lot of high school kids in the Bridgeport area would meet. When Bobbie and Debbie showed up at Eddie's, Cindy and Doug were already sitting at a table. Once she got to their table, Bobbie was introduced to Doug. As she shook Doug's hand, Bobbie shyly said, "Nice to meet you."

Once Debbie and Bobbie sat down at their table, the waitress walked over with their menus and introduced herself. "Hi, I'm Phyllis Sullivan and I'll be your waitress. Would you like some time to look at your menus?" Cindy replied, "Yes, we just got here so we'll need a little time." The waitress replied saying, "Sure, take as much time as you'd like, just signal me when you're ready to order."

Just then, an older man walked over to their table with a huge smile on his face.

"Please excuse me for the interruption. My name is Smitty and I'm the owner of this place. I'm told that Jessie Darcey's daughter Bobbie is here?"

Bobbie raised her hand slightly and said, "Hi, I'm Bobbie Darcey. And these are my friends Debbie, Cindy and Doug.

"Nice to meet you all. Oh, my goodness," said Smitty looking at Bobbie, "You look so much like Jessie. Hey EJ," he yelled across the restaurant, "look who's here! EJ walked over and introduced himself saying, "My name is Eddie, but please call me EJ. You're so right Smitty, she does look a whole lot like her mom. Smitty and I both thought your mom was the greatest, not only in basketball but also just a wonderful, kind person. Jessie actually got me my job as assistant coach for the boys' basketball team. She believed in me when I didn't even believe in myself." Smitty chimed in, "Yeh, that sure was our girl, Jessie, she was so kind and generous. She and her friends were always hanging out here, joking and laughing all the time. EJ and I sure do miss Jessie. We certainly do. Ok, I'll stop babbling and go back to the kitchen. Order all that you want. All your meals are on the house. Please give our love to Abby and tell her and Jane to stop by to say hello." With that, Smitty and EJ left to go back to the kitchen.

Once Smitty and EJ left, the waitress came over to the table saying "I hope those two guys didn't talk your ears off!" Turning to Bobbie she smiled and said, "I just want to add to what the guys just said. I played alongside Jessie as the starting forward. It was such a thrill and honor to play alongside Jessie. To this day, I have never seen anyone—male or female—who has come close to Jessie's basketball skills. She inspired me and taught me so much. I too miss her a great deal. When you see Abby and Jane, could you tell her that Phyllis Riley says hi? Riley was my maiden name. Ok, did you want to order, or do you need more time?"

Looking at the three of us, Debbie said, "I think we're ready to order now."

While waiting for their order to be delivered, Doug and Bobbie got into a conversation about sports and seemed to hit it off very well. Debbie looked at Cindy and they both smiled thinking that their matchmaking scheme was a big success.

As their menus were delivered to the table, Bobbie happened to glance out the window and saw the sign for "Baby Land." Just then a flood of emotions overcame Bobbie remembering her conversation with Aunt Abby, that her mom was shot in that very parking lot.

Without warning, Bobbie got up from her seat and said, "I…I have to go, I'm so sorry."

Debbie jumped up and followed a tearful Bobbie out the door.

"Bobbie, are you alright?"

Bobbie broke down in tears and, wiping her eyes with her head lowered, pointed to the far end of the parking lot.

"Debbie, that's where my mom was killed. I didn't realize it until I saw the sign for that baby shop. I just needed some air."

Debbie gave her a quick hug and said had she known she would have arranged to meet for lunch at another location.

"No, it's okay," replied Bobbie as she regained her composure. "It just startled me for a moment. You know what, Aunt Abby once told me that Eddie's was my mom's favorite hangout. So why don't you and I go back in and I will apologize to Cindy and Doug."

"Bobbie are you sure because we can go somewhere else for—"

"Yes, I'm sure Deb," said Bobbie interrupting. "Doug seems like a nice guy and I'd like to get to know him. That is, if he doesn't think I'm crazy!"

This caused both of them to laugh as they both walked back into Eddie's. When they got back to their table, Doug stood up and asked if everything was okay. Bobbie apologized and proceeded to tell Doug and Cindy why she left.

"Okay, let's eat," Bobbie said, "I'm starved."

During lunch, Bobbie and Doug got into a discussion about Doug's baseball team and eventually to things they both had in common. As it turned out they shared a lot of things which they both liked…both sports and non-sports activities.

Debbie smiled at Cindy when they saw that Bobbie moved her chair closer to Doug and they talked and laughed quite a bit almost oblivious to the fact that there were two other people at the table. After spending a long time in the restaurant, the four of them got up to leave.

As they were leaving, Bobbie touched Doug on the sleeve, and her face became flushed.

"Doug, Branford High's semi-formal is coming up. And I'm…I'm wondering…if you haven't been invited yet…would you want to go to the formal with me?"

"Sure, I would love to go with you," Doug said without hesitation.

Debbie and Cindy's matchmaking paid off as Bobbie and Doug began dating on a regular basis. With the semi-formal approaching, dress shopping became a high priority.

After several days of shopping, Cindy and Debbie helped pick out the perfect dress for Bobbie. They both remarked how beautiful Bobbie looked in the dress. Bobbie was so pleased that she would be attending the semi-formal with her two very good friends and their dates. It turned out to be a very fun occasion and Bobbie thanked both Debbie and Cindy for introducing her to Doug.

Jane and Brian stopped by to pay us a visit on the day of Bobbie's semi-formal. While Brian and Roger were fixated on some sporting event on TV, Jane and I spent the evening reminiscing. We both shared our fond high school memories. We thought back at our own school formals and all the fun we had at those dances. Some of our memories brought us tears of joy. Our conversation suddenly took on a more serious note as we thought about Jessie and how much she had impacted our lives and continues to do so. We also thought of that tragic day when Jess was murdered during that senseless gang fight.

"Jane," I asked, "do you think the hurt will ever subside?"

"I don't believe it will ever go away. But I've always felt that good always wins over evil. So, at the same time, we feel this hurt, we should never forget the many, many people that our beloved Jess inspired, including her beautiful daughter!

"How true that is Jane. We have been so blessed to have Jess in our lives. I thank God every day for that!"

THE "YIPS"

This seemed so foreign to Bobbie since she felt that she can make that shot blindfolded.

The year 1987 saw the emergence of the "3-point shot" in basketball.

Bobbie, now a junior year at Branford High, knew she would have to practice very hard shooting from that range on the court. So, during practice, Bobbie devoted a lot of time shooting 3-pointers until she and the coaches felt she was comfortable shooting at that distance. It was a shot that none of her teammates could make with any consistency. Bobbie's coaches told her that even most of the boys her age were struggling with the 3-point shot.

Bobbie knew that the 3-point shot could be a valuable scoring weapon for her. She was already effective at scoring from long distances on the court. So she taught herself to step back another foot or two and learn to shoot from that distance. By doing so, her shots would then count for three points as opposed to the previous two points. This would increase her scoring substantially.

Bobbie's fierce determination and competitiveness began to pay off. Within very little time, Bobbie did take full advantage of this new basketball technique and quickly became an expert 3-point shooter, with an incredible 50% average at the 3-point range. In one game towards the end of her junior high basketball season that year, Bobbie scored an impressive 61 points with 10 assists. Fans and critics alike began to draw comparisons between Bobbie and her mom. For the first time, people began to think that maybe Jessie's single game record was attainable after all. And, maybe Jessie's daughter was just the one to break that amazing record.

***

Bobbie said she often thought of how many more points her mom would have had in her basketball career if she had access to the 3-point shot. I told Bobbie that Jane and I also thought the same thing. We knew how proficient Jess was at shooting from long distances so her total points would have increased immeasurably. And sometimes we would get a bit giddy thinking that a 90 or more point game that special night would most likely have been achievable for Jessie if the 3-point shot had been available. The new 3-point shot was one advantage in basketball for Bobbie that her mother never had. It became a very important weapon in Bobbie's basketball arsenal.

***

During Bobbie's many discussions with me about her mom's basketball successes, the one thing that Bobbie could not understand was Jessie's difficulty scoring on easy layups. This notion seemed so foreign to Bobbie since she felt that she can make layups blindfolded.

"Aunt Abby, I cannot for the life of me understand why this was such a problem for my mom. From what you and Jane have said she seemed to score at will in all other areas of the basketball court. Why was she not able to score on easy layups?"

"Bobbie, that is a question I cannot answer. I know your grandfather and even Jessie herself were perplexed by that.

"Jessie's dad even had her practice shooting layups for hours as part of her training sessions in her driveway at home. But that is one shot that she simply could not make, as unusual as that may be.

"That's unbelievable, there must be a reason for that!"

"There may have been. But, I think Jessie felt that as long as it didn't affect her scoring average she would just live with it. I'll tell you what. Jane is coming over to the house tomorrow and let's ask her about this. Since she was your mom's basketball teammate, she might be able to shed some light on this.

Two days later, Jane came over to my house for a visit.

"Jane, Bobbie would like to ask you a question about Jess. She would also like to share some information which you might find interesting. I know I find it fascinating myself. But I was never an athlete so maybe it would make more sense to you."

"Jane," Bobbie asked, "when you were in high school, did they have sports doctors who treated athletes in your school?"

"Not to my knowledge. At least not for our basketball team. When Jess and I attended high school, all we had really was a school nurse, but that's about it. Maybe other schools had sports doctors, I'm not sure. Why do you ask?"

"Do you remember that my mom had difficulty scoring on easy layups?"

"Yes, I could never understand why that was, especially because she was able to easily score from every other area on the court. I know that she and her dad were aware of this. In fact, her dad included layups as part of his basketball training schedule he set up at home.

"Every one of those training techniques that Mike had Jess work on really paid off for Jessie—Well, every one except shooting layups. In our games, every time Jess got really close to the basket she would shy away from taking a layup and chose to shoot a short jumper instead. We all didn't think much of it since we figured that she would have scored the basket one way or another."

"Jane, I did a great deal of research on this subject. I believe that my mom's inability to make easy layups is a condition known in the sports world as the 'yips'."

"The yips?"

"Yes, it's a condition that affects some athletes. Apparently, this condition has baffled doctors for years.

"Here, I'll read you a portion of this article."

In sports, the "yips" are a sudden and unexplained loss of ability to execute certain skills in experienced athletes. It affects certain muscles that have long been used repeatedly to perform a task, and suddenly cannot perform that task anymore. Yips can cause a great deal of anxiety in athletes. Some athletes can adjust to this condition by changing the way they perform the affected task. For example, a right-handed golfer might try putting left-handed. Or basketball players may adjust by shooting with their left hand.

"I find this condition fascinating as it relates to my mom's fear of shooting easy layups."

Jane thought for a moment and then said, "Bobbie, I think you're right on target with your research of…wait…what did you call this condition?"

"The yips"

"Right…the yips. After all these years this explains why Jess had such a fear of shooting layups. As I mentioned, Jess was aware of this problem but refused to let it interfere with her scoring ability. Bobbie, your mom was in an elite class of basketball players, actually athletes for that matter. Many fans and critics considered Jessie to be the best female high school basketball player in the country. And, possibly, the greatest female high school basketball player in sports history, when you factor in her scoring and ball handling abilities. Jess was gifted enough and talented enough to make last second adjustments on the court. By doing this, Jess would turn a potential problem into something that worked to her advantage. I saw her do that so many times. So, if she did have a case of the yips, which apparently she had, Jess just made a quick adjustment and shot a short jumper instead of a layup.

In sports, she never treated anything as an obstacle—she just dealt with the situation and made an adjustment. Very few athletes had the ability to properly adjust to those kinds of obstacles, especially in those days. But Jessie was one of a kind. She —"

I interrupted Jane for a second.

"Jane, do you remember the time Smitty was clowning around and demonstrated how he would always throw the ball widely to first base? We all laughed except for Jess who had this serious look on her face. She must have realized that Smitty had the same problem and fear as she had. But the difference was that Smitty was unable to make an adjustment like Jess did. Smitty was actually released because of his condition. But Jess just dealt head-on with her fear and was talented enough to not let it affect her scoring in any way."

"You're right Abby," said Jane, "I do remember that day at Eddie's and Smitty explaining why he was released from baseball. He told me privately that the media used the word 'choke' when they referred to his flaw. But, from what Bobbie researched, it wasn't a matter of 'choking' since there were other factors involved. I felt bad when Smitty told me this, but that's the way the reporters saw it, especially in those days. Smitty just couldn't make the adjustment to overcome that condition. Only gifted athletes like Jess are able to constantly make those last second adjustments so that they worked to her advantage."

Jane turned to Bobbie and said, "What you uncovered is amazing to me. This is just one more example of why I respected Jess so much and how I was in awe of her God-given talents on the courts. Bobbie, I cannot tell you how much I was inspired and influenced by your mom."

Jane then changed the subject and the three of us discussed other matters at the kitchen table while I poured them each a cup of tea.

After Jane left, Bobbie told me that she was grateful that the yips was one condition that she didn't inherit from her mom, since easy layups were never a problem for her—at least not up to that point.

28

BOBBIE'S SENIOR YEAR HEROICS

The "buzz" in the stands grew louder and louder. Fans and reporters began to believe that Bobbie may be just the person to break Jessie's long standing single game scoring record.

At the beginning of the basketball season in Bobbie's senior year, Coach Sutton selected her as the team captain, a decision that received unanimous approval by the rest of her teammates. Bobbie's scoring average continued to climb dramatically, and so did her 3-point average. She also was phenomenal at the foul line. Bobbie had two games where her single game scoring totaled over 60 points, hovering near Jessie's record.

All of this led many fans and reporters to believe that Bobbie may be just the person to break Jessie's long standing single game scoring record. Bobbie took all of this talk in stride. The one thing that made Bobbie so proud and thankful to her mom was her ability to master a sport that she truly loved. There was no doubt in Bobbie's mind that she inherited this gift from her mother.

Bobbie loved playing basketball and foremost in her mind was to be the best teammate possible for her team. She received encouragement from her coach and teammates alike to continue her scoring prowess, since they all felt that this was one of the major keys to their victories. This encouragement was important to Bobbie. She always prided herself on being a selfless team player and the thought of achieving an individual goal at the risk of losing a game was so foreign to her way of thinking. The ultimate goal of each and every team member—including Bobbie—was to win the basketball state championship.

However, Bobbie privately had another goal that she wished to pursue. As much as basketball meant to her, Bobbie always thought there was more to life than playing sports. Like the mother she never knew, Bobbie felt in her heart that a career outside of basketball may be even more rewarding to her once her high school years were completed.

Bobbie asked my opinion on whether or not she should pursue a career as a sports doctor. I agreed and strongly encouraged her to follow that career path. Bobbie told me that one of the reasons that she wanted to get into this occupation was to try to impress upon athletes the confidence that is necessary to excel in a particular sport. She also wanted to emphasize the importance of being a true teammate, especially if the athlete wanted to reach the next level in a sport. Bobbie hoped to have the opportunity to work with athletes who developed a case of the "yips" and help them overcome, if possible, this sports phenomenon. She especially wanted to instill in these athletes a love for the sport they are participating in, the same kind of love and passion that both she and her mom had for the game of basketball. For now, Bobbie kept her ambition of becoming a sports doctor to herself, with the exception of asking my advice. For the time being, Bobbie wanted to remain completely focused on her remaining games and, hopefully, winning the state championship.

Academically, Bobbie maintained an excellent grade point average, with courses like biology and chemistry being her favorites. Once she became a high school senior, Bobbie began to place universities with excellent pre-med credentials at the top of her wish list.

***

On a snowy night in February, Branford High was set to meet their rival, Madison High School. Like Branford, Madison had an unbeaten record. During her pre-game pep talk, Coach Sutton made a point of emphasizing to her players that Madison was a powerhouse team. In order to beat Madison, Coach Sutton told her players that they needed to all bring their "A-Game" to this contest. The game was played at Branford High but the coach made certain that this was not necessarily a big advantage against a team like Madison High.

Despite the inclement weather, the game was sold out. Like her mother, Bobbie Darcey had become a local legend, and fans in the Connecticut area came out in droves to see their local hero and to see how she would match up against such a formidable foe.

As the game began, Bobbie did not disappoint her fans, immediately scoring three 3-pointers in a row. As the game progressed, the "buzz" in the stands grew louder and louder. Nearly all of Bobbie's shots were falling in and her point total surged. In the fourth and final quarter, Branford had a sizable lead. It soon became apparent that a Branford win was inevitable. What kept all of the fans on the edge of their seats was the fact that Bobbie was edging closer and closer to Jessie's single game scoring record.

With 1 minute to go, Branford called a timeout and Coach Sutton called the team into a huddle. She noticed that Bobbie did not seem flustered about the possibility of setting the state record. As the team got out of the huddle, the coach took Bobbie to the side to make sure Bobbie was aware that she was closing in on the school record.

"Bobbie, how do you feel? What do you think?"

"What do I think? I think I'm going to break the record tonight. Everything is falling in for me." Bobbie said this in a confident but not boastful manner. The coach nodded her head and had a proud smile from ear to ear.

Once they walked out of the huddle and onto the court, the fans erupted, chanting "Bobbie, Bobbie, Bobbie." They were about to witness local history and the cameras were all focused on Bobbie. Looking up, Bobbie saw the display on the scoreboard "Bobbie Darcey has scored 70 points and is within 2 points of breaking the single game scoring record set by her mother Jessie Darcey years ago." Once the crowd saw the scoreboard display, the sound from the stands was deafening.

Madison took the ball down the court as the scoreboard clock began to wind down. Branford needed to get the ball back if Bobbie was to break the record.

And then it happened.

Branford's fleet footing guard Debbie Patterson stole the ball and dribbled just beyond half-court. At the pleading of Coach Sutton, Debbie called timeout and the coach called the team into the huddle. Bobbie couldn't help but look up at the scoreboard. The time remaining was 12 seconds.

Everyone in the gym knew what was on the line. Get the ball to Bobbie somewhere near the basketball hoop. Then it would be up to her to make the shot and make this a magical night for everyone involved, especially for Bobbie. While in the huddle, Coach Sutton drew on her small whiteboard a play they had practiced many times. This play was designed for Bobbie and if executed properly, Bobbie would have an easy shot at the basket. But Bobbie heard none of the discussion in the huddle. Tears began to well up in her eyes, thinking about the mother she never knew but felt so close to, especially at this moment. Bobbie knew what she must do and what she knew her mother would want. At that moment, she remembered what I told her that were Mr. Darcey's words of encouragement to Jess in situations like this, *"If you play your game, no one can stop you. But the main thing is to relax and be in total control."*

Bobbie took a deep breath and walked to her place on the court. Just before the buzzer sounded, one of the defenders gave her a broad smile and said, "Congratulations on a great game!" Bobbie felt uplifted by this generous comment.

And then the buzzer sounded to begin play. The designed play was executed perfectly. Bobbie got the ball with 4 seconds left but a defender jumped in her way. Bobbie expertly dribbled around her for an easy layup with one second left on the game clock. As Bobbie had said it was a shot that she could make blindfolded. The ball circled the hoop—but, unexpectedly, the ball dropped to the court. Bobbie missed the shot!

There was an audible gasp from the fans in the stands. They seemed to be in total disbelief. How could that possibly happen, especially since it was such an easy shot? After missing the shot, Bobbie immediately dropped to her knees with both hands holding the top of her head. The tears began to flow. Bobbie needed help from Debbie and another teammate to get up. Once on her feet, Bobbie began to walk to the locker room with her head lowered. Members of both her team and her opponent's team surrounded Bobbie to congratulate her on her point total and her gallant effort to break the state scoring record. Likewise, all the fans stood and applauded Bobbie on her amazing game. But it seemed that Bobbie was unaware of all of this as she appeared to be numb as she walked off the court.

The local media, for the most part, was very kind to Bobbie in reporting her 70-point game, avoiding the word "choke." Reporters were mainly in disbelief that Bobbie would miss such an easy layup, blaming it on the fact that she may have simply misplayed the shot. One article in the local newspaper explained in detail how the shot was missed.

Bobbie Darcey's Missed Shot

A replay of Bobbie Darcey's now famous "missed shot" reveals that Bobbie took her time but merely misplayed her layup against the backboard which led to the ball spinning around the hoop and eventually dropping to the floor. Technically speaking, the ball hit the backboard just inches away from the correct location needed to enable the ball to land in the basket.

There is no reason whatsoever to believe that Bobbie choked or rushed her shot, it was just merely the placement of the ball against the backboard. It was as simple as that. As other players will testify, sometimes it's the easiest shots that can undo a fine performance. It can be a missed foul shot or a missed easy layup. No matter, it was a valiant effort and we are all very proud of Bobbie.

And so, Jessie Darcey's 71-point record performance that was set years ago still stands. Bobbie has nothing to be ashamed of. We applaud Bobbie Darcey for her outstanding performance.

Before she reached the locker room, Bobbie was besieged by a bunch of reporters. They all wanted a statement about her missed layup. Instead of a statement about the missed shot, a despondent Bobbie merely responded, "The main thing is that we won the game against a very good team. My main focus now is for our team to win the state championship." With that, Bobbie politely excused herself and said she wanted to meet with her team in the locker room.

29

CONNECTICUT STATE CHAMPIONSHIP GAME

Team captain Darcey, implored her teammates to step up their game and not to look to her to carry the scoring.

Branford and Madison High schools would meet up once again. This time it was for the state championship. Madison High had the home court advantage for this important game.

Branford maintained an unbeaten record while Madison's only blemish was the drubbing they took earlier at the hands of Branford High. However, the Madison girls had played much better since that game and easily swept through all their other opponents. So, this championship game was shaping up to be a classic, with Branford considered only a slight favorite.

During the day, there was a torrential downpour leaving puddles in the street and the sidewalks wet even after the rain subsided. As she rushed to the gym, Bobbie twisted her ankle stepping into a puddle. She walked it off and her ankle felt better as she walked to her locker room. Bobbie informed Coach Sutton that she twisted her ankle but felt that it shouldn't affect her play as her ankle was feeling better. The coach asked Bobbie to keep her updated on her ankle throughout the game. She also made sure that Bobbie's ankle was wrapped up securely.

The state championship game that year lived up to its billing. At halftime, the score was tied. The Madison girls paid particular attention to Bobbie Darcey, defending her extremely close, especially preventing Bobbie from freeing herself up to take a 3-point shot. Bobbie's ankle began to flare up making her lateral movement a bit more difficult. This made it easier for her defenders to guard her. During the regular season Bobbie's 3-point average was phenomenal, shooting 3-pointers at an incredible 60% clip. But Bobbie knew that if her ankle continued to flare up it wouldn't be a great scoring night for her.

As it was, Bobbie was not the outstanding ball handler that her mom was so Madison needed only to put no more than their two top defenders against Bobbie at all times (unlike the two or three defenders that her mom regularly faced in her games). Bobbie's twisted ankle began to pose more of a problem than Bobbie expected. She found her defenders to be more aggressive and the overall defense to be more effective than in their previous encounters. The fine defensive play coupled with Bobbie's ankle problem resulted in a low halftime point total for Bobbie.

In the locker room at halftime, Bobbie whispered to her coach that her ankle was really beginning to flare up. She told the coach that she could still play but her injury was affecting her lateral movement, making it tough for her to get off a clear shot. She didn't want anyone else to know this especially her opponents who she was hoping would still put two defenders on her. Bobbie asked Coach Sutton if she could address her teammates while still in the locker room. The coach said that would be a good idea. Team captain Darcey then addressed the entire team and implored all her teammates to step up their game and not to look to her to carry the scoring. Bobbie emphasized the importance of every member of the team to become the effective team player they were all capable of.

"You can do this, I know it,", Bobbie pleaded. "My shots are just not falling in so you need to look to each other for the open shots. To beat this team you must all step up your game and be precise in your passing, shooting, and on defense. They decided to put two players on me, so that means one of you will be open at all times. So, let's take advantage of that. I'm very proud of all of you and I know you can do this!"

As she spoke, Bobbie saw that each of her players and her coach were listening intently. Once Bobbie finished her locker room speech, the entire team applauded and ran out to the court.

Bobbie's locker room pep talk paid off. The Branford High players began taking matters into their own hands. They did this by pinpoint passing, pressure defense and always looking for the open player. As Bobbie had mentioned there was always one of their teammates open since their opponents put two players on Bobbie at all times, and her teammates took advantage of this. Heeding Bobbie's inspirational halftime speech, the players made every effort to try not to depend on Bobbie for scoring, leaving that up to all the other players. The result was a balanced scoring attack coupled with pressure defense which seemed to rattle their opponents.

In a real nail-biter, Branford won the game 73—72. Bobbie was so thrilled and proud of how all their players stepped up knowing that she was still hampered by her ankle injury. With that win, Branford became State Champions!

In particular, Monica Mendoza and Debbie Patterson played the best game of their career and were the catalysts for the team throughout the entire second half of the game. For all their hard work, Monica and Debbie were co-recipients of the team's MVP award. Bobbie couldn't be more pleased and was so proud of the two of them as well as the entire team.

Amazingly, Bobbie was not much of a factor, scoring a total of only 11 points. But her teammates all pointed to Bobbie's halftime pep talk as the real reason for their success. When interviewed after the game, Branford players made note of Bobbie Dacey's inspirational halftime speech and her unselfishness as the real reason why they won.

Before leaving the locker room, Coach Sutton walked over to Bobbie who was now limping noticeably and said with a smile, "You know Bobbie, I've seen you have so many remarkable moments throughout your high school career. But, in my opinion, this was your finest moment. I know you were far less than 100% but somehow you managed to inspire our entire team to do something incredible and win this championship. I want to tell you that I am so proud of you!". Bobbie responded shyly, "Thank You coach and congratulations to you also."

***

Bobbie graduated high school with honors and accepted a partial non-sports related scholarship to the prestigious Harvard University medical program, pursuing a pre-med degree. She decided to concentrate on her studies and forego sports on a formal level at the college.

Bobbie was on her way to fulfilling her goal of becoming a sports medicine doctor.

30

"SANDY SAVANNAH"

At Harvard, Bobbie maintained an outstanding grade point average and was one of the top students in her freshman class.

At the same time, she managed to have an on-going social life. Bobbie became a close friend with her classmate Sandra Delaney. Sandra was a cute, personable young lady with long brown hair that she would sometimes put up in a bun. She always seemed to have a smile on her face. Sandra hailed from Savannah, Georgia. Bobbie nicknamed her "Sandy Savannah." She would often kid Sandra about her heavy but delightful Georgia accent. For example, when she and Sandra would attend one of Harvard's formal events, Bobbie would imitate Sandra's cute southern drawl saying, "Well look at you all gussied up!" In return, Sandra would impersonate Bobbie's Connecticut accent, much to Bobbie's amusement, saying "Hey Bobbie, let's go to the sandwich shop and get a *grinder* for lunch."

Besides being reliable "study buddies", Bobbie and Sandra shared many fun experiences both in and out of college. They both thought of each other as forever friends.

Bobbie also stayed in close touch with several of her former classmates at Branford High School, including Debbie Patterson, Cindy Allison and Monica Mendoza.

On one occasion, Monica invited Bobbie to a party she was hosting at her home in Bridgeport. Bobbie accepted the invitation and asked if she could bring along her friend Sandra. Monica told her she definitely could invite Sandra. At Monica's party, Sandra met Greg Sanders who lived in nearby Fairfield. Greg was a few years older than Sandra, having graduated from Fairfield University with a B.A. in Sociology. He put his major to good use when he found employment with a large non-profit agency in Bridgeport.

Sandra and Greg hit it off immediately. Before the party ended, Greg asked Sandra for a date and Sandra accepted. On the way home,

Bobbie told Sandra that it was so cool that she would be dating a guy from Fairfield since she spent a lot of time in Fairfield when she lived in Branford. Bobbie explained to Sandra that several of her former teammates were from Fairfield and she would often hang out at their homes after games.

During one of Harvard's formal dinner events, Sandra introduced Bobbie to her brother Dean. She mentioned that Dean also attended Harvard and was a year ahead of them. Bobbie felt an instant attraction to Dean, only to be disappointed when Dean mentioned that his girlfriend was not able to join him because of a business conflict. Sandra couldn't help but notice the attention that Dean and Bobbie gave to each other at the dinner. She was tempted to mention this to Bobbie but decided to hold off. Days later, Sandra called Bobbie and asked Bobbie if she would like to go with her to an art museum. After Bobbie said she would like to go, Sandra asked if it was okay for her to bring a friend with her to the museum. Bobbie told her that would be great.

Bobbie arrived at the museum early. When Sandra showed up a bit later she was accompanied by a familiar face. It was her brother Dean. When Sandra re-introduced Dean, Bobbie felt a bit awkward, hoping that Dean didn't pick up on Bobbie's feelings when they first met. At one point while touring the museum, Sandra said she realized that she needed to put more coins in the parking meter and would be right back. This left Bobbie and Dean alone in the museum with Bobbie once again feeling awkward. Looking at one of the paintings in the museum, Bobbie noticed Dean walking over to her.

"Bobbie, I hope this doesn't sound too forward of me, but are you seeing anyone at this time?"

"If you mean like a steady boyfriend, no just casual dates. But why do you ask?"

"Well, the girl I was dating for a short time is moving to California with her firm. We both decided to part as friends. So, what I guess I'm asking is, would you like to have dinner or something with me sometime?"

With a surprised look on her face, Bobbie replied, "Sure, that sounds like a wonderful idea."

The two were interrupted when Sandra returned saying, "Sorry about that. I was afraid I would get a parking ticket if I didn't add more money in the meter. Did I miss anything?"

Bobbie and Dean smiled at each other and Bobbie said, "We decided to wait for you to come back before continuing to look at anything else here."

Thirty minutes later, Dean said, "Well, if you will excuse me I have to get going. Looking directly at Bobbie, Dean said with a smile, "I will see you both soon."

Once Dean left, Bobbie turned to Sandra with a big knowing smile on her face.

"You little sneak! I know what you did with your bogus excuse about putting more coins in the parking meter!"

"Well, did it work?"

Bobbie lightly punched her friend in the arm and said with a Georgia accent, "Yes ma'am! And that's what I love about you!"

31

HARVARD GRADUATION

Bobbie was on her way to achieving her goal of becoming a sports medicine physician.

J ane and I, along with our husbands, attended Bobbie's graduation from Harvard. We were so proud of Bobbie, especially when it was announced that she graduated with high honors from this prestigious institution. We were pleased to meet her good friend Sandra and also Bobbie and Sandra's boyfriends. Jane and I both agreed that Bobbie had grown into an amazing woman and we couldn't be more proud of her!

Bobbie subsequently was accepted into Fairfield University's pre-med graduate program, receiving a full scholarship. She was on her way to achieving her goal of becoming a sports medicine physician.

When she heard that Bobbie would be returning to Connecticut, Jane hosted a party for Bobbie as both a welcome home and a congratulatory celebration. Jane invited some of Bobbie's friends from Harvard University and Branford High School including Sandra Delaney, Greg Sanders, Debbie Patterson, Monica Mendoza, and Cindy Allison, as well as Bobbie's boyfriend Dean. At one point during the party, Jane gave a very touching and delightful toast to Bobbie. This made Bobbie blush but I know she appreciated the party and all of our congratulations and well wishes.

Bobbie eventually purchased a small house in Madison, Connecticut, with help from Roger and me. I told her that Roger and I would be quite happy to help her out financially until she had settled in, which Bobbie greatly appreciated. I could tell it was a great relief for Bobbie to know this.

Once she settled in at Fairfield University, Bobbie began working part-time in the administration office at the school. The job didn't pay very much but at least Bobbie felt she was contributing a little toward her expenses while Roger and I helped her out.

Now living in Madison, Bobbie would occasionally run into one or two of her high school opponents from Madison High School who inevitably would ask her about her infamous missed layup. Bobbie's response was the same as it was years earlier—that winning the game was the most important thing. Plus, she would now delicately add, "And, as you know, we went on to win the state basketball title, which I'm very proud of."

***

Bobbie's boyfriend Dean Delaney was a very good athlete. At Harvard, he made the baseball squad in his freshman year. He became an above-average pitcher for the college's baseball team. After graduating from Harvard, Dean found a nice job at a pharmaceutical company in Westport, Connecticut.

Dean was also an avid golf fan. He became very close friends with a former schoolmate by the name of Jimmy Nelsen, who was a few years older than Dean. Jimmy was a gifted golfer and began his major golfing career in style, winning one amateur championship after another. He eventually joined the PGA ranks and won his first three PGA events. They were not major golf contests, but people and golf critics began to take notice. He was hailed as the new phenom with a very promising career. Dean attended as many golf tournaments as possible to cheer Jimmy on.

Jimmy was on the verge of winning his fourth straight championship, needing only a two foot putt to win. Uncharacteristically, Jimmy's easy putt rolled right by the hole and landed on the edge of the green. It took him three more putts to finish, causing him to lose the championship. Noting that this was just an aberration, Dean encouraged Jimmy to look forward to his next tournament and not dwell on how he lost this match. Jimmy agreed and told Dean that he must have just misread the putt. He was excited to get back on track during his next match.

Dean noticed that Jimmy began having the same problem in his subsequent matches. For whatever reason, he seemed to be unable to make the easiest of putts, even ones that normally were one foot "tap ins." He became overly self-conscious of his inability to make these short putts, especially in pressure situations.

Because of this unexplained condition, Jimmy's golf game really suffered, and his anxiety grew even worse. After losing his next few matches, Jimmy became increasingly discouraged and depressed. He became even more disheartened when several golf critics wrote articles in several golf publications with statements such as "Jimmy Nelsen choked again under pressure" and "Jimmy Nelsen can't seem to handle the pressure that's inherent in professional golf." The media no longer referred to him as a phenom and the coverage of his golf game began to dry up. After losing another one of his matches Jimmy tried to explain to Dean what was occurring.

Checking the PGA schedule for Jimmy's next match, Dean saw that Jimmy would be participating in the Hartford Golf Invitational Tournament in a few days. Knowing this, Dean called Jimmy and asked Jimmy if he and his girlfriend Judy would like to join Bobbie and him for dinner sometime before his match. Jimmy thought it was a great idea and said it would be a great opportunity for Bobbie to meet Judy. During their phone conversation, Dean explained that Bobbie was working towards becoming a doctor of sports medicine and was near completion of her residency. He asked Jimmy if he would feel comfortable describing his putting dilemma to Bobbie.

"Maybe Bobbie can somehow help you with your situation or know of a doctor who specializes in what you're going through on the course. But if you're not comfortable with———"

Jimmy interrupted him saying, "Listen, I'm in favor of anything or anybody who can help me get to the bottom of this and get me back to normal. To be honest, if this continues I may have to quit the PGA. Right now, this is no fun. And it seems only to be getting worse. I have no idea why this is occurring. I would have no problem discussing this with you and Bobbie."

Dean made a reservation for the four of them to have dinner at a popular restaurant in Madison. Bobbie found Jimmy and Judy very easy to talk to and thought they made a very nice couple. After finishing their dinners, the four of them ordered dessert. While waiting for dessert, Dean turned the group's attention to Bobbie.

"Bobbie, I mentioned to Jimmy that you're well on your way to fulfilling your dream of becoming a sports medicine doctor."

"Yes," remarked Jimmy, "that's remarkable. I know how proud Dean is of you."

Bobbie glanced over at Dean with a smile, thinking that perhaps there was more that Dean wanted to bring up. And she was right.

"Bobbie," said Dean, "I hope you don't mind, but I mentioned to Jimmy that you may be able to give him some advice dealing with a problem he has been having on the golf course."

Laughing, Bobbie remarked, "Well, I really don't know a whole lot about golf. But I'm guessing it has something to do with the medical side of the game?"

"Well," replied Jimmy, "I'm not sure what it is which is why I'd like to ask for your advice."

"Sure," said Bobbie. "But I want to remind you that I'm still in medical residency and can only give you my personal advice and not speak for any physicians."

"Yes, I understand."

"Okay, tell me all about this and when it began."

"I'm not sure, but Dean may have told you that I'm a golfer on the PGA tour.

"Yes, he has and Dean is very proud of you, as I am."

"It's so great to have such a good friend like Dean and, of course, receive all the wonderful support I receive from my girlfriend Judy here. I know I have put Judy through a lot lately, being so discouraged about what was going on with my golf game." Judy smiled and reached over to hold Jimmy's hand. "Let me explain what my problem has been lately.

"Up until now I was very satisfied and comfortable with all facets of my golf game, including my long game, short game, and putting. I got off to a great start on the tour, winning my first three tournaments. But then something came up out of the blue which has greatly affected my golf game."

Bobbie then asked, "So it just came up unexpectedly?"

"Yes, and I have no idea how or why it started.

"Okay, please continue."

"During my fourth PGA match, I began having difficulty making my putts. What concerned me was that I even began missing very short putts. While this did bother me, I thought it was an aberration and that I would get back to my very good putting game in the next match. But that didn't happen. The next match was even worse. I missed even one and two foot putts. These were putts that I could have made in my sleep! And this problem of mine continued in my next couple of matches.

"All of this made me very anxious and depressed. I—"

Bobbie interrupted and asked, "During the course of the golf match, at what point do you start thinking about your putting? And can you describe how you feel when you are about to putt?"

"Lately, my anxiety begins once I step foot on the green waiting my turn to putt. My heart starts beating fast, my hands begin to sweat and I no longer can visualize making my putts, even the very easy putts. I just don't know what's going on. This never occurred in all my years of playing golf. I began playing when I was very little and even as a youngster I was known to play thirty six or more holes each day. I always had confidence in my putting ability and always maintained a positive approach to all facets of my game. In fact, my putting game was my best and most important component of my golf game. It's the reason why I won many matches. But now"…his voice began to trail off.

"Jimmy," said Bobbie, "I think I may know your problem"

"You do, what is it?"

"The yips", responded Bobbie.

"The what?"

"Well, before I try to explain what the yips are and why I personally believe this may be your problem, I want you to remind you that I'm not a doctor as yet. I'm still in residency so I don't want to say with certainty exactly what your condition is. But what you're describing was a condition that my mom had when she played basketball at Bridgeport High School. I—"

Jimmy interrupted, asking, "Wait…are you Jessie Darcey's daughter?"

"Yes, I'm her daughter. Mom died before I was born but I'm proud of the legacy that she's left me."

"Wow, that's terrific Bobbie. I just didn't make the connection. As a former Connecticut resident and basketball fan, I followed Jessie's career very closely. Like so many others, I was in awe of Jessie's basketball skills. I agree with all the sports critics that your mom was the greatest female high school basketball player in sports history. And also, congratulations on your fabulous career. You certainly would have made your mom proud!"

"Thank you so much, Jimmy. But let's get back to your situation. As I was saying, my mom had the same problem as you have. In her case, it was her inability to make very easy layups in her basketball games. Even with all the extra training sessions she had with her father—my granddad— she just could not seem to make those easy shots.

"Jane Kenny was her teammate and close friend. From what Jane has told me, my mom would get very anxious at the thought of making layups. She even came up with excuses to not have to shoot layups during warm ups prior to her game. During the game, she would move away from the basket and shoot a short jumper instead of trying a layup. Because she was such a prolific scorer no one noticed this flaw. The only people who were aware of her condition were Jane, my mom, and her dad. My mom never figured out what caused this flaw. As I mentioned she came up with innovative ways to work around taking a layup and she managed to score almost at will in other areas of the court even knowing she had this flaw.

"I purposely wanted to share my mom's experience to demonstrate to you that you are not alone with your condition. My research has shown that athletes—even some well-known athletes— developed this condition in sports such as golf, basketball, and baseball." Bobbie noticed that Jimmy, still holding Judy's hand, was listening intently to what she was saying.

"To get back to your personal dilemma, here is what I think *may* be causing you to miss all those putts. Please understand that this is not a diagnosis, it's just my personal opinion.

"As I mentioned I believe you may be suffering from a condition known in the sports world as the "yips." The technical term for this condition is focal dystonia, or dystonia. In sports, this condition is merely referred to as the "yips", a phrase coined by the 1920s golfer Tommy Armour.

"For a long time, the general consensus was that the yips were caused by stress, which kind of makes sense on the surface. However, it is now thought that dystonia is a neurological condition affecting specific muscles that have been used repeatedly to perform a task, and suddenly the person cannot perform that task anymore.

"The 'yips' are a sudden and unexplained loss of ability to perform certain skills, especially in experienced athletes. In your case, this condition may be affecting specific repetitive movements of muscles that you use when putting —namely, your wrist, fingers, and hands.

"Jimmy, I want to make clear that these are my own personal thoughts and not a diagnosis of your condition. I tell you all of this because they seem to match the one basketball flaw that my mom had. I may be totally wrong which is why I highly recommend that you consult an expert for a proper diagnosis. If you have no one else in mind, I would highly recommend seeing Dr. Rodriguez who specializes in sports medicine. He works out of Yale-New Haven Hospital but has his own office on Whalley Avenue in New Haven.

Judy spoke up saying, "Bobbie thank you for taking your time to explain what Jimmy may be dealing with. We realize that this is not a diagnosis on your part but it's a wonderful first step." Looking at Jimmy who nodded in agreement, Judy went on to say, "We will make an appointment with Dr. Rodriguez and hopefully he will be of help to Jimmy with his golf problem. What a relief that will be for Jimmy." Smiling, Jimmy added, "And for Judy who has been my rock through all of this."

Leaving the restaurant, Dean said to Bobbie, "I hope I didn't put you on the spot during dinner. But Jimmy is such a great guy and a very talented golfer. I know he appreciates your advice and will consult with the doctor you recommended.

In a kidding fashion, Dean said, "I know I don't have a case of the yips in golf. I just miss those short putts because I'm a lousy golfer!" This made both of them laugh as they got into Dean's car

32

PAUL MARI'S VISIT

Paul then glanced over at Bobbie and said, "Oh my God Bobbie, you look just like your mother!"

After not hearing from Paul Mari for years, I received a package in the mail with the return address of P. Mari, Stanford, CA. I sat down at my kitchen table and opened the package. Inside the package was an envelope. Once I looked inside the envelope tears began running down my face.

In a whispered voice I said to myself, *"Oh my God."* I closed my eyes and immediately felt Jessie's presence in the room, stronger than ever.

Days later, Bobbie visited me and stayed for dinner. When we sat down after dinner, I turned to Bobbie and told her I wanted to share something with her.

"I want you to know that I received a letter from your father a few days ago." With that, I handed the letter to Bobbie, who read the letter out loud.

Dear Abigail,

I hope this letter finds you and Bobbie well.

My courses were a bit challenging, but I managed to earn my graduate degree at Stanford. The graduate degree helped me obtain a very good, high paying job here in California. I know this sounds (and is) very selfish on my part, but I also know that, in my heart, I am just not ready for fatherhood.

I followed Bobbie's amazing basketball accomplishments as best as I could. I subscribed to the online version of the New Haven newspaper and also there was a news segment about Bobbie on local TV here in California. I am so thrilled and proud of Bobbie. And I know Jessie would have been even more proud!

Abigail, I know that I made the right decision to have you adopt Bobbie, and, knowing you, I am certain that she is in very good hands.

I'm not sure if Bobbie knows anything about me and can't blame her if she doesn't want to know. I'm sure you handled all of that in the right way. I am very comfortable in having Bobbie know everything about me if that is the wish of both Bobbie and you.

I can't blame Bobbie (or you) if she thinks giving her up was a selfish thing for me to do. There is a good part of me that would agree with that. It was solely my decision to further my education to help my chances of landing a good job. But I also believe, for Bobbie's sake and for her future endeavors, you are the best person to provide her the proper guidance along the way that she truly needs—especially when things get a bit tough, which they inevitably do at times.

Enclosed is a beautiful necklace which was sent to me from the hospital where Jessie was admitted to after that horrible shooting incident. It arrived shortly after Jess passed away. I just recently found it when I was going through some of my own belongings. I had put most of my stuff in a box but forgot all about it. When I found the box I decided it was the right time to go through some of these items.

When I saw the envelope containing the jewelry and the note I called the hospital. I reached the nurse who treated Jess. She told me that she mailed it to me because she had no idea who to send it to. In their records, it showed my name, my relationship to Jessie, and my Bridgeport address. My former landlord in Bridgeport forwarded the envelope to me. Thankfully, he kept that envelope in his lost and found (I think you know how organized he was with things like that).

The nurse told me the whole story behind the jewelry and I hope you will share with Bobbie what she told me. The nurse explained to me that Jessie's dad picked up the jewelry on his way to watch Jessie play in that state championship game. He said that he had paid for the item a couple of days before and then picked it up on that day. By looking inside the locket, I think you can guess why he needed it a couple of days before he picked up the jewelry.

Mr. Darcey also told the nurse that he bought the jewelry because he was so proud of Jessie's accomplishments both in sports and how she grew into such a wonderful person. He said he wanted to surprise Jess either before or after the game. So typical of Mr. Darcey who loved Jessie with all his heart!

Mr. Darcey said he put the item in his jacket pocket but right after that, he was hit by another car when it crossed over the white line. He was rushed to the hospital and, as you know, was not able to go to Jessie's game that night. He informed Jessie about his gift and Jess picked up the necklace at the hospital's front desk.

I am hopeful that you show this jewelry to Bobbie. But I will leave that up to you.

Abigail, I want you to know how much I treasure our friendship and hope someday you will find it in your heart to forgive me. I think of how Jessie always looked up to me and how much she loved me. I truly loved Jessie and couldn't wait to marry her. As devastating as her tragic and senseless death was, I am grateful for one thing—that Jessie died believing that I was a strong and confident person who would take care of our child for the rest of our lives. That thought has stayed with me and has kept me going all this time.

I think about Jess every day and losing her like that certainly was the most difficult thing I have ever or will ever encounter. Jessie will always be the one true love of my life!

I pray that someday my daughter will want to get to know me. I am hopeful that I can someday meet Bobbie if she agrees. If Bobbie prefers not to meet me, I truly understand. As I said before, I am so proud of Bobbie, especially how she has turned out to be a beautiful person (inside and out)—just like her mother!

Abigail, thank you for reading all of this and if you would like to contact me I would love to hear from you. My phone number and my California address are enclosed on a separate paper. Please feel free to contact me at any time. I would love to hear from you. If you prefer not to contact me, I understand. What is comforting to me is knowing that you will always be there for Bobbie.

With all my love for you and Bobbie,

Paul

Once Bobbie finished reading Paul's letter, I gave her the piece of jewelry that Jessie's father had purchased. It was a beautiful necklace with a locket.

"Bobbie this is something you should have and I know you will treasure it." When she opened the locket, Bobbie put her right hand to her cheek and burst into tears.

"Oh my God, these are photos of my grandfather and grandmother. I'm speechless. And to think my granddad was going to surprise my mom at the game with this wonderful gift. I have goosebumps throughout my body just thinking how thoughtful that was. You're right, this is so meaningful to me and it brings me even closer to both of them."

With a huge smile, Bobbie put the necklace and locket on her neck.

"Bobbie, the other thing I want you to know is that right before the shooting your mom showed me that locket and told me she would treasure her father's gift forever. Bobbie, she was wearing that necklace and locket when she was killed that day."

Hearing that her mom was wearing the necklace on the day she died, a tearful Bobbie touched the necklace that she put on. "That makes it even so much more special to me.

"Aunt Abby, would it be alright if I thought about meeting with my father and get back to you on that?"

"Of course, sweetheart, take all the time you feel is needed. I know that this has been a very emotional experience receiving this letter from your father that seemed to come out of the blue. I want you to know that this is your decision and Roger and I will completely support you, no matter what you decide."

A few days later, Bobbie informed me that she would really like to meet her father. I told her that I would contact Paul and let him know. I told Bobbie that once I reached Paul I would invite him to my house and, if it was okay with her, I would make dinner for the four of us—Paul,

Bobbie, Roger, and myself. Bobbie thought that was a great idea, especially since it would be more informal than meeting him in a restaurant or some other place.

I thought to myself that since he owns his own plane and has been flying a great deal it would be fairly easy for him to visit our house in Connecticut.

I did manage to reach Paul and he agreed to fly to Connecticut and finally meet Bobbie at my house. He said the idea of having dinner at my home was perfect.

A few days later, Bobbie visited us in Branford. She said she was a bit nervous at the prospect of meeting her father. I told her that it was normal for her to be nervous given the fact that she never met her father.

Paul soon arrived at our house. When I opened the door I gave him a big hug.

"Abigail, it is so wonderful to see you after all this time. You haven't changed a bit!"

"Neither have you, Paul"

After shaking Roger's hand and introducing himself, Paul then glanced over at Bobbie who was shyly standing in back of me.

"Oh my God Bobbie, you look just like your mother!"

Bobbie, feeling a bit awkward and shy, gave Paul a quick hug. When she did that, I could see that Paul began to tear up. It was a very emotional meeting for both of them.

Much to my surprise—and I believe Bobbie's also—our dinner conversation went smoothly with very few awkward moments. After our desert was finished, Paul looked at us and I could tell he wanted to say something.

"You know, California is not that far away. I would love for you to visit me sometime when you have the opportunity. I promise I will clear off my schedule for as much time as you would like to spend out there. I can even fly you to different parts of the West Coast. I am an experienced pilot now, so you should have no worries about that."

"I would love to visit you in California," Bobbie said without hesitation. "I hope that Aunt Abby will be able to join me."

"Of course I will Bobbie. I would love to see Paul out in California."

With that, Paul got up and gave us both a big hug. As I escorted him to his car, Paul said, "Abigail, I cannot thank you enough for taking such good care of Bobbie. I know now for sure that I made the right decision to have you adopt her. Bobbie has turned out to be such a wonderful person thanks to you. I am very proud of you. I will see you both soon when you come out to California." Paul then got into his car and drove away, waving as he left. Bobbie waved from the doorstep.

***

Since graduating from college, a while back, Jane and I kept in touch on a daily basis, either by phone or in-person. On one of her visits, Jane asked if I would join her in taking acting lessons after work. She told me her intention was to join a group of local actors and actresses to perform occasionally at small music theatres in the area. She said that this was not a big ensemble of performers, but it would be a good start for us. I told Jane that this sounded like fun and I would love to join her in taking those classes. We both felt that this would be a good way to gradually get involved in community theatre, which was always of interest to us. We believed that our singing had improved but taking acting classes would definitely help us since musical plays involved acting skills as well as singing.

Jane and I thought this was so ironic since we knew that owning a musical theatre was a dream of Jessie's. We both had established our own businesses unrelated to the music field. I had left the music store a while ago and purchased a gift shop in nearby Guilford. Jane left the bookstore where she had worked since high school and purchased a small bookstore called *The Right Book*. However, our hearts were in the field of musical theatre.

33

RECOGNITION

Knowing Jessie as well as I did, I was sure that this gesture by the theatre would have meant more to her than any of the athletic recognitions, including the National Hall of Fame.

As years passed, I became an advocate for my best friend Jess to receive the true recognition she so deserved. I was able to convince organizations to consider Jessie for a variety of awards and inductions.

It began when Bridgeport High School renamed its brand new gymnasium and basketball court the Jessie Darcey Gymnasium. Invited to Bridgeport High School's tribute to Jessie in the refurbished gymnasium were Bobbie, Dean, Jane, Brian, Roger, and myself. Bobbie asked her friend Sandra to join our group and to make sure she brings Greg with her.

With the assistance of former Bridgeport coaches, I also nominated Jessie for a special national award. Our nomination was accepted and Jessie Darcey was inducted into the prestigious *National High School Hall of Fame.* Bobbie and I attended the induction ceremony which was held in Indiana.

One of the guest speakers at the ceremony was basketball star Bobby Steed. As Bobbie got up to leave at the end of the ceremony, she felt a tap on her shoulder. Bobbie turned around and it was Bobby Steed. Smiling, he told Bobbie that he wanted to meet her and congratulate her on all the success that she had as a basketball player. He also mentioned that he attended one of her mom's basketball games and he was so impressed that he suggested that the Boston College administrators consider recruiting Jessie. Bobbie shook his hand, saying it was an honor to meet him, and thanked Bobby for his kindness and thoughtfulness.

Soon after, the Connecticut High School Commission renamed the award presented each year to Connecticut's high school basketball top scorer—male or female—as "The Jessie Darcey Basketball Award."

Perhaps the one recognition that Jessie would have been the most proud of was the unexpected tribute to Jessie given by the Royalty Theatre in Bridgeport. The theatre acknowledged Jessie's love of musical theatre and her unselfish dedication to the Royalty Theatre despite her busy schedule. They even decided to rename the gallery portion of the theatre as the "Jessie Darcey Gallery Room."

Knowing Jessie as well as I did, I was sure that this gesture by the theatre would have meant more to Jessie than any of the athletic recognitions, including the National Hall of Fame.

I felt comfort in knowing that my best friend Jessie touched the lives of so many athletes during the short time that she lived. And seeing how Jessie had such an effect on others outside of sports pleased me even more, knowing that was always Jessie's wish.

34

TRAGEDY

I could hear in Jane's voice that she had been crying and she said to me in a panic-stricken voice,
"Abby, turn on the TV right away"

On a beautiful, sunny morning I was tending to my outside flower garden

when I received a frantic call from Jane Kenny. I could hear in Jane's voice that she had been crying, and she said to me in a panic-stricken voice, "Abby, turn on the TV right away. There has been a serious crash." Hearing this, I ran into my house, not knowing what Jane was referring to and fearing the worst.

After a commercial break, the news anchor described a tragic event that just occurred.

"Paul Mari, former Bridgeport resident and CEO of the prestigious Mari Corporation, was killed this morning in a private airplane crash in Los Angeles.

We are told that Mari informed the LA traffic control tower that he needed to make an emergency landing at the Los Angeles Airport. However, the Cessna airplane that he was flying crashed in a large uninhabited field near the airport. Mari was the sole occupant of the plane. The crash is now under investigation. We hope to have an update on our 11:00 p.m. newscast tonight. Please stay tuned."

Shocked and in disbelief, I couldn't help but think how wonderful it was that Bobbie was so happy to finally see her dad when she met Paul at my house. Roger and I tried our best to break the news to Bobbie as gently as we could. However, once she heard the news Bobbie cried very hard and was in a momentary state of shock.

Paul's obituary was extremely impressive. It stated that Paul was the CEO of a very prominent high-tech firm which did a great deal of business overseas. It mentioned that Paul was single and his next of kin was not mentioned. No services would be held and he would be cremated as was his wish. Friends and family were encouraged to donate to their local charities.

35

THE LEGACY MUSIC THEATRE

"You know Abby, it just seems that things have gone full circle."

About a month later, I received a letter from the law firm of Smith and

Robertson requesting the presence of Bobbie and myself at the reading of Paul's will. The letter stated that, for our convenience, the reading would take place in New Haven. At first, Bobbie wasn't sure if she wanted to attend but reluctantly agreed to join me to meet with Paul's lawyers.

As it turned out, Paul died a multi-millionaire, amassing a very large sum of money in the stock market. As he was about to read the will, Attorney Robertson stated that he got to know Paul very well and remarked what a wonderful person Paul was.

During the reading of the will, Attorney Robertson stated that it was Paul's wish that all his fortune be left to Bobbie and myself. Paul's wish was clearly stipulated in his will.

Needless to say, all of this caught Bobbie—and me—by surprise. Bobbie was completely stunned to hear that this man who she happily met for the first time was not only very wealthy but had left her a great deal of money. Her inheritance from her father was enough for her to be financially independent. I could tell that Bobbie had a difficult time processing all of this—as did I. When she broke down in tears, I got up and gave Bobbie a hug. I tried to fight back tears as I thought of Paul's untimely death. Despite everything that happened, Paul was first and foremost a close friend and the fiancé of my very best friend. So wealthy or not, I already missed Paul very much. It was indeed a bittersweet moment for the two of us.

It took a while but reality finally set in for Bobbie. She began to plan on how she would make the best use of her inheritance. Bobbie took my advice and hired a financial planner who would help her wisely invest much of her money.

I decided to use my inheritance in a way that I felt would honor Jessie and preserve her legacy. Knowing how much Jess loved the theatre, I thought I would use my funds to purchase a small musical theatre. It would be a tribute to Jessie and also to Paul since I remembered that their favorite dates were attending musicals at local theatres. But first I wanted to explain to Bobbie what I had in mind and get her approval. When I mentioned my idea to Bobbie, she not only gave her approval but insisted on contributing to the funding of the theatre. She told me it was a wonderful way to pay tribute to her mom.

A few weeks later, Jane and I met for lunch at Eddie's. When we saw Smitty we gave him a big hug. He looked about the same with the exception of a little graying at the temples. Smitty seemed excited to see both of us.

"Well, look at you two beautiful women!", exclaimed Smitty in his familiar gruff voice. "Man, it's been a while since I saw both of you. How have you been? Abby, how's Bobbie doing? I am so proud of how she turned out to be such a wonderful young lady. So smart and so talented, just like her mom."

"Bobbie's doing well, Smitty. Thanks for asking. And you look like you're in good shape.

Jane chimed in and jokingly asked, "Hey Smitty, any thoughts of trying out for the minor leagues again?"

An amused Smitty replied, "Well, you never know Jane. I still got my good knuckleball, you know! Hey, how 'bout I get you two ladies a burger special with fries?"

EJ stopped by our table and sat down saying, "Well look at you two ladies! Haven't seen you two in a while. So what's new?"

"Hi EJ," I said happily, "So nice to see you also. We decided to stop by and see both of you. And, of course, enjoy one of Smitty's fabulous burgers!"

"Of course," chuckled EJ, "you can't come in without having his world famous burgers!

"Hey, guess what girls? I recently got married! Joanie and I flew to Vegas and had a Justice of the Peace marry us out there. And I talked the old man in the kitchen—Smitty—into being my best man! Joanie's sister Margie was her maid of honor. Margie is also divorced. I have to tell you that Smitty and Margie hit it off very well and they began dating. So we turned our visit into a nice little vacation. We had a great time and had so much fun that we didn't even feel like gambling!"

Hearing this, Jane and I congratulated EJ and told him we were so happy for him and his new wife. I told him, "EJ, your new wife is so lucky to have a wonderful guy like you as her husband." Jane chimed in, "This is so exciting! I wish both of you all the best."

"Thank you, girls. Well, you know what they say—'third time is a charm!' Joanie is such a lovely person—inside and out. I think you will agree when you see her."

"Oh without a doubt EJ," I said.

"Actually, girls, she's kind of a saint putting up with me. But I think this time things will work out since I'm older, sober, and a bit more reasonable now.

"Okay, I got to get back to my job or else Smitty will chew me out. Don't be strangers you two!"

Smitty returned a short while later holding two plates.

As he put the plates down at our table, Smitty proudly said, "Okay ladies, these are on the house!"

"Why thank you, Smitty, that's very nice of you," said Jane in an appreciative voice. Smiling, I said to Smitty, "Hey, you forgot to tell us that EJ is a married man now!"

"Oh yeh, I forgot. Isn't that cool? Joanie is a saint being married to EJ."

"Those were EJ's exact words," I said.

I then added, "And what's this we're hearing about you and Margie?"

"Oh yeh. Margie and I are getting along really well. I guess it's never too late to begin dating again. I'm looking forward to having you meet Margie. Such a sweet, wonderful person!"

"We can't wait to meet Margie and Joanie," Jane said. "Our congratulations to all four of you!"

"Ok," responded Smitty. "I have to go back to the kitchen. Hope to see both of you beautiful girls soon."

Looking down at her burger special meal, Jane turned to me and remarked, "Same old Smitty and same old hamburgers." We both laughed but it was reassuring to us that—aside from the great news about their marriage and dating—nothing seemed to change at Eddie's Best Burgers.

After updating each other on what was going on in our lives, I shared with Jane my decision to purchase a musical theatre. Jane was absolutely thrilled and told me that she would very much like to contribute towards the funding of the theatre as a tribute to Jess. Jane did say that she didn't have a great deal of resources, but she would contribute as much as she could. She also said that she was willing to help in any way possible, whether it was marketing, lining up productions and performers, or whatever. Hearing this, I told Jane that if she was able to contribute whatever she could plus help out on the administrative side, I would make her a co-owner of the theatre. A surprised Jane shook my hand and exclaimed, "It's a Deal!" She said she was flattered by my offer to become a co-owner of the theatre.

Jane reminded me of a conversation that Jess and I had on the day of the shooting regarding Jessie's goal to one day become an owner of a musical theatre. I was reminded of Jessie's idea to call the venue The Legacy Theatre. I had forgotten all about that part of our conversation that day. And so, Jane and I decided to call our theatre The Jessie Darcey Legacy Theatre.

"You know Abby, it just seems that things have gone full circle. Owning her own musical theatre was Jessie's dream, and now we have the opportunity to make that dream a reality!"

Jane was excited when I suggested that she and I perform a few original songs as a duo in one of the performances at the theatre. Jokingly, Jane said, "I don't think *Frankie My Love* would fit in with any performances at the theatre, do you?" Laughing, I completely agreed.

I whispered to Jane if she thought it would be okay to tell Smitty about our plan to purchase a music theatre. Jane smiled and said she thought Smitty would love to hear our plan.

As Smitty walked by after serving other customers, I stopped him and said, "Hey Smitty, Jane and I wanted you to know that we're planning to purchase our very own music theatre. What do you think?"

"Really? How amazing is that?. Way to go girls! Hey, if you ever have a need for a washed up baseball pitcher in one of your productions, I'm your man!"

"We'll certainly keep you in mind," I replied. "We plan on calling our theatre The Jessie Darcey Legacy Theatre."

What I said must have taken Smitty off guard because he got all choked up.

"I…I think that is so wonderful girls. I sure do miss Jess. I can just picture her sitting right here next to the two of you. Don't think I'll ever get over what happened to her. I…I know you both feel the same way."

Standing there in front of us I could see tears in his eyes. His lips began to quiver and I could sense his awkwardness.

"I…I have to get back to the kitchen but I'll be back before you leave."

Jane and I knew he didn't want to cry in front of us. We both agreed that Smitty was a great guy and a true friend.

As we were about to walk out of the restaurant, our waitress ran over to us and said to me, " Smitty asked me to give this to you." The waitress handed me an 8 x 10" glossy black and white photo and said that Smitty asked that I be sure to show this to Bobbie.

Once I looked at the photo, I immediately called out to Jane, "Oh my God Jane, you have to see this!" It was a team photo showing the entire girls' Bridgeport High basketball team with the inscription "State Champions." We both began to giggle, seeing all the familiar faces in the photo.

"There you are Jane, right in the front row"

"Yep, and there's Jess in the middle holding the game's basketball. How I miss that wonderful smile. I remember all of these amazing girls. I lost touch with most of them. I often wonder what they were all up to after graduation. This brings back so many memories for me. I do remember sitting for this photo but I somehow lost my copy. Look how young we all look!"

"Yes, so young and happy, " I said. "Now look on the back. Every player signed the back of this photo."

"Wow, this is so cool! Now I remember signing along with everyone else."

"I will be sure to have a copy made of this photo to give to you, and also Smitty and EJ."

"That would be great Abby, and don't forget to show Bobbie. This is a real keepsake!"

"I sure will. I know Bobbie will love seeing this. How nice of Smitty to give us this photo. We'll have to thank him the next time we're in here." Jane nodded her head in agreement.

***

Within a short period of time, Jane sold her bookstore at a fair price to focus on our new venture. She said she knew of a group of seasoned actors and actresses for us to consider and would begin lining up potential casts of performers. Jane also said she would get to work on creating several original scripts for our productions. She mentioned that she already had several ideas for musical productions at our theatre and wanted to run them by me for my approval. Jane also said she would be happy to be in charge of marketing if it was okay with me. I happily agreed.

After scouring up and down the Connecticut shoreline for a potential theatre location, we came across an old, abandoned, small building in the historic town of Essex. The building was in much need of repair but Jane and I both thought the location was ideal for what we had in mind.

The next day we met with the realtor who informed us that the building was once a popular vaudeville theatre and was home to a number of famous celebrities including appearances made by a young comedy team known as Bud Abbott and Lou Costello. It later became known as *The Shakespearean Theatre*, with regular performances of plays by Shakespeare and other important playwrights. It had a 130-seating capacity and balconies on both sides of the theatre. The lobby was a good size and had a beautiful chandelier in need of repair, which we hoped to restore. There was also a large parking lot in the back which was a plus since parking was at a premium in that small town. We were pleased to be informed that the asking price was well below what we anticipated.

So now we had the building which, after major renovations, would house The Jessie Darcey Legacy Theatre in memory of our dear friend. As Jane said, it did seem as though things had gone full circle.

In time, the run down building had been turned into a beautiful showcase. As promised, Jane lived up to her end of the deal and lined up a full season of wonderful productions complete with very talented seasoned performers. We hired a guy from New York City—Dan Dugan— who produced several off-Broadway shows. Dan agreed to work with us on our productions. He and Jane worked very well together.

To our surprise, Debbie Patterson and her sister Trish agreed to perform a few numbers as part of the theatre's gala opening. Bobbie had somehow managed to talk Deb and her sister into temporarily coming out of retirement just for our theatre. The Patterson Sisters received a standing ovation after performing a beautiful rendition of *When My Blue Moon Turns To Gold Again*. Their harmonies were impeccable and beautiful.

Also at the gala opening, Jane and I worked up the courage to sing a few ballads. Our first song was a cover of *All I Have To Do Is Dream* by the Everly Brothers. After going back and forth we decided, for old times' sake, to perform our original B-Side tune *Frankie, My Love*. We were satisfied with our harmonies, and it appeared that the audience liked our performance.

I was so pleased when many of the shows that Jane, Dan, and I produced were sold-out productions. Our theatre eventually became a very popular venue for many theatregoers.

As patrons entered the theatre's lobby, they were greeted by a large portrait of Jess, donated by a local business. A beautiful, smiling Jessie Darcey was shown holding a basketball tucked in her right arm and the inscription at the bottom of the portrait reads "In loving memory of Jessie Darcey - an outstanding athlete, teammate, and friend to all."

Every day I walk into that theatre I feel Jessie's presence and it gives me such comfort.

After one of the performances of a musical directed by Jane, I was approached by a man who asked if I was Abby Girardi.

"Yes, I am. And you are?"

"My name is Dr. DiNicola. I know you are—excuse me, you were—very good friends with Jessie Darcey. I was in California for the start of my pre-med classes when I heard about Jessie's death, so I wasn't able to attend her services. You may not remember me but when I was in high school, Jessie actually saved my life by administering CPR after I choked on my lunch at Eddie's burger place. I —"

"Wait…is your first name William?" I asked as I interrupted him.

"Yes, William DiNicola.

"Abby, I want you to know that Jessie's unselfish action, saving my life that day, inspired me to get into pre-med and become a doctor. After that incident at Eddie's, I always meant to thank Jessie but for whatever reason, I never did, which I regret. I wish she was around today for me to thank her in person. I just wanted to let you know that I have never forgotten what Jessie did that day.

"I know I don't have to tell you, but you had an amazing friend! Congratulations on this beautiful theatre and I wish you much success. It sure is a nice tribute to Jessie!"

As Dr. DiNicola walked away, I looked up to the sky and said to myself, *"Well, Jess, you've done it again! You continue to amaze me at how many lives you've touched in such a short period of time.*

"I miss you so much Jess!"

JESSIE'S THANK YOU NOTE

Months later, during one of her calls, Bobbie said that she had some

good news to share with Jane and myself. Despite my prodding, Bobbie refused to tell me what the good news was, saying she would like to tell both Jane and me at the same time. Bobbie asked that we both call her back once Jane got to my house. So I asked Jane to come over to my house and we would call Bobbie from there. I mentioned to Jane that Bobbie wanted to share some good news with us both but she wanted to wait until we both were together to tell us about this news.

"Okay," said Jane, "I'll be right over. The suspense is killing me."

"Me too," I replied.

Once Jane got to my house, I made her a cup of coffee and we then proceeded to call Bobbie with my phone on speaker.

In a very excited voice, Bobbie exclaimed, "Aunt Abby, Jane, I wanted you to be the first to know that I am now a full-fledged doctor.

"After I completed my medical residency at Yale New Haven Hospital I became a board-certified doctor. However, I chose to pursue a medical fellowship so I could gain expertise in my field. It took me twelve years in total but it's all worth it. I wanted to wait until I finished my fellowship to tell you both that I am officially a doctor of medicine!"

Hearing Bobbie's news, Jane and I were jubilant. With tears of joy, we both congratulated Bobbie on her monumental achievement.

"My goodness Bobbie," I shouted into the phone, "Jane and I are so excited for you. We knew you were so busy working to become a doctor but we didn't realize how close you were. So this is such a wonderful surprise! We both know how hard you worked and how dedicated you were to achieve your goal to become a doctor."

Jane chimed in, "My dear Bobbie, this is such wonderful news and we will definitely celebrate your amazing accomplishment."

I then added, "My oh my, I am overwhelmed with pride knowing that our Bobbie is now Doctor Roberta Darcey! Jane and I love you so much and we can't wait to see you so that you can tell us all about this!"

"Thank you, Aunt Abby," replied Bobbie. "I want to thank you both for all your encouragement, support, and love. You helped make my dream a reality and I love you both! I will see you soon."

***

Days later, Bobbie visited me at my house. After giving her a big hug,

I motioned to Bobbie to have a seat at the kitchen table. Pouring her a cup of coffee, I said, "Okay I want to hear all about your future plans as Dr. Darcey. By the way," I said, "is it still ok to call you Bobbie?" We both laughed at my request.

I listened with such pride as Bobbie filled me in on what her future plans were. I saw so much of Jessie in her. Like Jess, Bobbie grew up to be a very attractive and personable young lady.

As Bobbie spoke, my eyes teared up as I heard the excitement in her voice and saw that wonderful smile of hers. I thought of what a special gift I was given to be able to raise Bobbie after losing my closest friend on that tragic and fateful day.

After a while, Bobbie decided to change subjects and she asked for an update on how things were going with me, Jane, and our musical theatre. I told her that Jane stops over my house frequently and we share such wonderful memories. I also mentioned that things were going very well with our theatre and was pleased to say that the theatre had become a very popular venue in the local area.

Bobbie asked me if Jane and I ever discussed the Bridgeport High School team that her mom and Jane played on.

"Well, now that you mention it, I would like to show you something that Smitty gave me." I got up from the table and returned with the Bridgeport High basketball team photo that Smitty gave me.

"Oh my goodness Aunt Abby," an excited Bobbie said, not lifting her head while she looked intently at all the players on the team. Turning to me she asked, "That has to be my mom holding the basketball, right?"

"Yes, it is Bobbie. And there's Jane in the front row. That's Phyllis Riley in the back row who you said you met at Eddie's."

"Yep, she now goes by the name Phyllis Sullivan. She's such a nice person."

"I agree. Bobbie, this is the original photo and I would like you to have it. I had a copy made for Jane, Smitty, EJ, and myself."

Turning the photo around Bobbie said excitedly, "Aunt Abby, look! All the players signed the back of this photo! There's my mom's signature!"

"I know, this is such a special memento!

"Thank you, Aunt Abby, I can't wait to put this photo up in my new office! I'm so proud of my mom and I'll cherish this photo forever."

***

After dinner, Bobbie asked if we could sit in my living room since she wanted to share something else with me. When we sat down, I noticed that Bobbie had a serious look on her face. Her look told me she wanted to share something very important with me.

"Aunt Abby, I have a confession to make. I have been holding on to a bit of a secret ever since my senior year in high school. I have never told anyone this up until now, but I wanted to share something with you.

Nervously, Bobbie said, "Aunt Abby, I…I missed that layup shot on purpose at the end of that game. Unlike my mom, shooting layups was something that came naturally to me. As I have said before, I could have probably made layups blindfolded.

"The papers were right when they said I took my time to make that shot. What they didn't realize was that I knew the exact spot on the backboard to shoot so that the ball would NOT go into the basket. Funny thing is that I actually practiced missing that shot for hours when I was by myself in the gym.

"My one link with my mom was her scoring record and I decided in the last few seconds of that game that I would like to see her record live on, even if it was only for a few more years. Amazing that it hasn't been broken in a very long time, but I realize that someone will come along and break that record one day. I just didn't want to be the person to do it. After I missed the shot I dropped to my knees in sheer exhaustion—both physical and mental exhaustion. I didn't regret my decision at the time and don't regret it to this day. This was my mom's record and I wanted it to remain her record.

"When I think about her accomplishments I feel a sense of pride, even though she passed away without me ever getting to know her. But her scoring record is the one thing I feel is a connection between the two of us. I know how competitive she was and perhaps if the tables were turned she would make sure she scored that record breaking point. I'm not sure, but I know that I just couldn't get myself to break her record.

"Aunt Abby, do you think my mom would have been disappointed in me for not breaking that scoring record?"

Hearing this, I felt that a full explanation was needed.

"Bobbie I knew your mom ever since we were nine-year-old kids in fourth grade. At the time, my home life was a mess and I hated school.

Even at nine years old I knew I was headed down the wrong path. Your mom taught me the value of a good education and was my inspiration from the first day I met her. She continues to inspire me to this very day. So, I got to know your mom very, very well.

"As far as sports are concerned, Jess considered herself a good teammate first, more so than a great athlete. She learned the value of teamwork from her dad. But she told me many times that sports was not a main priority of hers.

"While she was proud of her accomplishments in sports, Jess always felt that there was much more to life than playing basketball. She very much wanted to settle down and have a normal family life just like her mom and dad — your grandparents. I believe she was on her way to achieving that goal when she was taken from us.

"Bobbie, your mom would have been proud of you whether you broke that scoring record or not. I know your mom was proud of her record, but, in all honesty, she wasn't as excited about that record as many of her fans were.

"Your mother was very intelligent. As I mentioned, she realized at a young age that there was more to life than sports."

I then got up and went to the top drawer of my dining room hutch and pulled out an envelope.

"Bobbie, I think this will answer your question. After your mom set the state scoring record, I mailed her a note saying how proud I was of her and so thankful that we remained best friends ever since fourth grade at Webster Elementary School. I told her that I thought what she did on the basketball court became her legacy.

A few days later I received this thank you note in the mail."

Bobbie opened the thank you card with Jessie's note and read her mom's message out loud.

Hi Abby Gabby,

Thank you for your kind words. You never cease to amaze me on how thoughtful you are. You mentioned the term 'legacy'. As my best friend, I think you will understand what I am about to say.

Setting basketball records is fine, but I would like my legacy to stand for something else. I haven't quite figured that out yet, but I would like people to see me for something other than a good basketball player.

I would love to settle down sometime and start a family. I know I would be a good mother and look forward to raising a child who would be successful in life and not just sports. To me, that would be my own personal legacy.

Abby, my "bucket girl", you are, and always will be, my best friend.

I am REALLY looking forward to all the fun experiences you and I will continue to share!

With Love, Jessie

After Bobbie finished reading the note, she took a deep breath, dropped her hands to her legs, and then slowly looked at her mom's note again. She appeared to be overcome with emotion. It took her several minutes to look up as she sat there staring at her mother's thank you card and note.

"Bobbie, please take comfort in knowing that immediately before the shooting, your mom told me that she was the happiest she had ever been in her life. My goodness, Bobbie, she was so happy, you can see the joy on her face! Being pregnant had brought her such joy and happiness.

She told me at that moment that she was looking forward to sharing so many wonderful adventures with her child and was determined to raise her daughter to be a success in life. And, knowing your many achievements and how you achieved your goal of becoming a sports doctor, she would have been so proud of you.

"Bobbie, if your mom was here with us right now she would smile and say—for her, that basketball record was not her legacy.

"She would say her true legacy is *you*."

***

And so, despite everything that had occurred and all the years that have passed, the legend of Jessie Darcey lives on.

260

ABOUT THE AUTHOR

Tony Renzoni is the author of the well-received books:

- *"Connecticut Rock 'n' Roll: A History"*;

- *"Connecticut Softball Legend Joan Joyce"*;

- *"Connecticut Bootlegger Queen Nellie Green"*;

- *"Historic Connecticut Music Venues: From the Coliseum to the Shaboo"*;

- *"Connecticut's Girls of Summer: The Brakettes and The Falcons"*;

- *"Joan Joyce: The Wonder Girl"*;

- *"Rock 'n' Roll Radio: Magic Moments and Unforgettable Disc Jockeys"*;

- *"The Legend of Jessie Darcey"*

Tony had a thirty-eight-year career with the federal government. As district manager in Connecticut's Fairfield County, he oversaw the operations of four field offices, serving over 100,000 beneficiaries. He wrote over one thousand weekly columns that were published in the Connecticut Post newspaper and on the paper's website. Tony was a recipient of more than forty awards, including his agency's highest honor award.

Renzoni serves as a consultant for the hit Joan Joyce Musical, which is based on his book Connecticut Softball Legend Joan Joyce.

A lifelong resident of Connecticut, Tony is a graduate of Sacred Heart High School in Waterbury and Sacred Heart University in Fairfield, CT

Front and Back cover photos — author's collection
Author Photo Credit — Mary Ellen Blacker